P9-DDK-853

With the crime rate on the rise in every major country in the world it is obvious that prisons, at best, incarcerate but do not rehabilitate. In *Prisons Inside-Out,* Benedict S. Alper, an internationally known authority on penal reform, presents an analysis of the problems of prisons and inmates and offers realistic, workable solutions to many of the situations which exist in prisons. Drawing on experiments in the United States, Europe and Japan, he analyzes in detail the recent proliferation of alternatives to traditional institutions and traditional programs within them.

Increasing public realization of the failures of the present system, coupled with the rising public outrage at crime in the streets, prompts Alper to examine the system of criminal justice from the court process itself to diversion from court action. He looks at the increasing emphasis on community action to deal with offenders who for various reasons are diverted from the court—at the parole system in the United States, often based on no more than how crowded a particular prison is at the time the parole board meets—at the soaring per capita costs of incarceration as compared to community based programs. He also compares current methods of dealing with mental disease and retardation and sees the possibility of applying the same methods to offenders. He points out that historically communities dealt with both prisoners and those suffering from mental disorders and sees this as an effective way of rehabilitating prisoners.

Prisons Inside-Out brings together valuable information from both American and international sources. A highly readable book it will be of vital importance to people actively involved in developing a penal system that is both beneficial to the community and rehabilitative for the offender.

torture, maiming, and execution of prisoners in Japan during the Hansei period, 1600–1858. The scroll is reproduced on the cover with the kind permission of the Museum.

Prisons Inside-Out
Alternatives in Correctional Reform

Prisons Inside-Out

Alternatives in
Correctional Reform

Benedict S. Alper
Boston College

Foreword by
Milton Rector
National Council on Crime
and Delinquency

Foreword by
Atsushi Nagashima
Correction Bureau of Japan

Ballinger Publishing Company ● **Cambridge, Mass.**
A Subsidiary of J.B. Lippincott Company

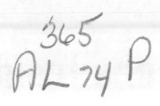

Copyright © 1974 by Ballinger Publishing Company. All rights reserved. No part of this publication may be reproduced, stored in a retrieval system, or transmitted in any form or by any means, electronic mechanical photocopy, recording or otherwise, without the prior written consent of the publisher.

International Standard Book Number: 0-88410-200-9 (Hb)
0-88410-211-4 (Pbk)

Library of Congress Catalog Card Number: 74-2268

Printed in the United States of America

Library of Congress Cataloging in Publication Data
Alper, Benedict Solomon, 1905–
     Prisons inside-out.
     Based on a series of lectures delivered at the United Nations Asia and Far East Institute for the Prevention of Crime and Treatment of Offenders during the spring of 1973.
     1. Corrections—Addresses, essays, lectures. 2. Rehabilitation of criminals—Addresses, essays, lectures. 3. Correctional institutions—Addresses, essays, lectures. I. Ajia Kyokutō Hanzai Bōshi Kenshū-jo. II. Title.
HV8665.A47   364.6   74-2268
ISBN 0-88410-200-9 (Hb)
     0-88410-211-4 (Pbk)

Dedicated to the United Nations
Asia and Far East Institute for
the Prevention of Crime and
Treatment of Offenders

166057

Contents

Foreword

Anyone who stands before some of the awesome prisons of the world—San Quentin, Maidstone, Regina Coeli—is immediately struck by the sense of permanence in these institutions. Their solidity and grimness appear to say to all who see them: "We shall endure because we protect." Nothing could be further from the truth. They do not protect and it is likely that they shall not endure.

The grim bastilles of the world are living on borrowed time. They shall fall sooner or later because they reflect only one stage in the evolution of correctional history. And the more one learns about them, the more one feels that they have already been with us too long.

It is important to know with certainty that the prison whose massive construction, iron bars, and high walls bespeak eternity is in reality not an institution for all time. Given man's long history of crime, prison is a rather modern concept and now it has had its day.

If one looks back at the punishment meted out to the offender— branding, flogging, dismemberment, maiming, and death through a variety of unpleasant forms—imprisonment indeed represented a step forward at that stage of civilization's development. Beccaria, the Italian reformer who argued for prison in place of capital punishment, was very much a product of the eighteenth-century Enlightenment. His philosophy of imprisonment, which significantly influenced the penology of much of Europe and the United States, was forward looking. It was right for its day.

Of course, prisons have changed—not everywhere, but surely in many places. There is a world of difference between Greenhaven (whose walls not only rise 30 feet into the air, but reportedly go 30 feet into the ground) and such an institution as the Leesburgh prison in New Jersey which doesn't look like a prison at all. Leesburgh, in the United States, Fleury, in France, and Rebibbia, in Italy, are breathtakingly modern, antiseptically clean institutions, and no doubt a source of satisfaction to their architects.

But they are *prisons*. And as correctional institutions, or rehabilitating facilities, or rebuilders of the men and women who enter them, they are, in the main, failures. The offenders who leave them are rarely reformed into upright citizens. And those who are released and who become law-abiding may do so despite their experience in prison and not because of it.

People who feel reassured by the high walls of the prison, its sentries, control towers and its remoteness from population centers are naive. Most prisoners leave their institutions at some point. In the United States, 95 percent are released after an average imprisonment of 24 to 32 months. Other countries have much shorter prison terms. So the protection offered by the prison during the incarceration of the offender is surely a short-term insurance policy and a dubious one at that.

If there is any rationale for a prison today, it is as a place to keep the offender so dangerous or assaultive that release would prove a significant hazard for the community. And even here, one is prompted to question whether prison is the proper setting for dangerous individuals, if the long-term goal is to fathom the reons for and ways of remedying their state of dangerousness.

There are those who see the prison as a laboratory, a place where modern knowledge may be applied to the correction of deviancy. For those who wish to use scientific technology in reforming the imprisoned offender, we offer only cautious encouragement. That path is fraught with dangers.

We are only a generation or so away from the greatest perversion of research by misguided, perhaps evil, doctors who sought to extend the horizons of science at the expense of their captives. We do not impugn the motivation of today's penologists who seek rehabilitation through drugs, psychosurgery, sensory deprivation or imposed psychiatric disciplines. We simply do not believe there is a compelling ethical basis for utilizing some of these modalities.

There comes to mind the remark of the poet, Rilke, who was asked why he would not accept psychiatric help. He replied that he feared that in casting out his devils, he would cast out his angels, too. We cannot impose on the imprisoned offender an involuntary medical discipline which may possibly remove an antisocial disposition, but leave him a conditioned puppet whose freedom to make good or evil choices has been severely restricted.

That there are alternatives to imprisonment has long been known. What is new is the evidence of scientifically controlled experiments. It shows that alternatives which deal with the offender in the community are better than incarceration, lower in cost, and more in keeping with an enlightened and humane society.

The important thing to keep in mind as we read about these alternatives is that we are only now on the threshold of developing community programs for the offender. New ones will be developed and will supplant those which function now with limited effectiveness.

This is as it should be. Dealing with the offender is an age-old problem. It is an evolutionary matter. It is a search for the protection of society, the redemption of the criminal, and ultimately, for justice tempered with wisdom and mercy.

Milton G. Rector
President
National Council on Crime and Delinquency

Foreword

The author's intent to review the history and extent of international cooperation in crime prevention and corrections was already sown in his mind when I met him first at the meetings of the United Nations Consultative Group of Experts in Geneva in 1968. After that he delivered two lectures on this subject at UNAFEI in August of 1970 before the Fourth United Nations Crime Congress met in Kyoto.

His concern that more and more citizens in the community be involved in all stages of the criminal justice process led to his further study on the alternatives in correctional institutions and penal reform: programs dealing with offenders in the community, voluntary probation officer system, and discretionary prosecution practices employed in Japan, in particular.

Later, when I became the Director of UNAFEI, I invited Professor Alper to come to the Institute to deliver lectures on alternatives to traditional institutions and their programs. Two years later, when he lectured before the participants from Asian and Far Eastern countries at the Thirty-third International Training Course at UNAFEI, he had gathered much material from the United States, Europe and from Asian countries. I met him last in June 1973 at the Ministry of Justice before he left Japan, after completing his series of lectures at UNAFEI. Much of this unique book, with international flavor, is based on those lectures.

I feel that the contents of this book need no further comment from me. However, I cannot resist the impulse to touch on a personal matter. Benedict Alper is my old friend and teacher in criminology. He co-authored *Halfway Houses* with Oliver J. Keller, Jr., also my old friend, from whom I also learned much while studying at the Center for Studies in Criminal Justice at the University of Chicago Law School under the kind guidance of Professor Norval Morris, who was the first Director of UNAFEI. These three friends are my real teachers, and Japanese corrections, I hope, will continue to develop because of their influence.

I wish to express my sincere thanks to the author for his kind offer to dedicate this book and donate the proceeds of any royalties to our UNAFEI Special Fund. This book and this kind of continuing support will contribute much to the betterment of relations and to the increase of knowledge in the field of crime prevention and control between the United States and Asia.

Atsushi Nagashima
Director General
Correction Bureau
Ministry of Justice of Japan

Preface

A series of lectures delivered at the United Nations Asia and Far East Institute on Prevention of Crime and Treatment of Offenders is the basis of this book. Located in a village some miles west of Tokyo, the Institute was organized originally under joint United Nations and Japanese auspices. Today it is administered by the Ministry of Justice of Japan, in close cooperation with the United Nations. It is the only training institute of its kind in the world, and in the ten years since it was established, has had—during the 33 courses and close to 700 students—persons professionally concerned with every aspect of the criminal justice systems in their home countries. These range from the Philippines round to Iran.

It was my pleasure, during the spring of 1973 in the course of these lectures, to meet with the participants from these countries, all of whom reported increased crime rates, and, like the United States were groping for solutions. I attempted to share with them an understanding of what could be done to scale down the severity of and the dependence on institutionalization, a steadily growing trend in recent years, as the problem of crime itself has grown.

Many of the countries represented around the hollow square where we met and talked are described—though they do not thus describe themselves—as underdeveloped or developing. That is, they are not yet as urbanized or industrialized as is most of Western society. But as they come increasingly onto the world stage, as they struggle out from old colonial forms of control into independence—and in some places, some larger measure of economic well-being—they begin to be bedevilled by the same social ills as contemporary Western society: a questioning of some of the old values, such as tribal customs and the control of the family; the striving of the young for a larger measure of independence, with resulting increased involvement of the young in criminal activity, and a larger ingredient of violence in much of their antisocial behavior.

In some Southeast Asian countries, stealing of water buffalo may still go on. But there is now the new offense of bicycle stealing, even of auto theft, unknown when motor cars did not exist in quantity. With autos come traffic offenses, drunken driving, and the related offenses which crowd U.S. courts—and now theirs, too. In Japan, for example, violations of road traffic laws in the course of a year totalled 1,330,000, while the ordinary crimes against the person and against property are in the range of only 420,000. The rise in the homicide rate—manslaughter by automobile, some of it criminal when committed negligently or recklessly or under the influence of alcohol— is perhaps Japan's most serious social defense problem today.

The significance of this is twofold. The participants from Asia and the Far East represented twelve different countries, all of which had once had traditional ways of dealing with offenders. It was important to realize that as crime sprang from their distinctive social and economic structures, so their ways of dealing with it in the past had derived from their traditional mores and values, some of them—as in Hindu or Moslem societies, from religious teachings, law and practices.

Together we explored the proposition that simply because their societies were seized by an influx of criminal activity—as was the West—that they did not have to turn to the same Western sources for solutions. Inherent in their mode of life, from their past, were ways that still had value and pertinence for today. These should not be abandoned, to be replaced, for example, by large and expensive penal institutions or complex juvenile courts. How could they rear their criminal justice system on their own indigenous foundations? If, in the United States, prisons were being abandoned in some places and offenders returned to their communities, why should the developing nations have to repeat these same steps, which might well lead, in the end, to the levelling of walled institutions when their rates of failure came to equal our own?

The factor of expense is crucial for the economy of small and struggling countries. They simply cannot afford to drain manpower and materials into construction of stone piles with barred cages when they are in dire need of economic betterment and social services.

For our part, there was an opportunity provided to learn from these Asian and Far East countries how they were dealing with their erring young and with the challenge of crime generally. It may be some small consolation for us to learn that we are not alone in confronting that challenge, nor in our search for effective ways of coping with it.

The pages that follow will set out the materials taken up in this series of lectures and the ensuing discussions. Japanese sources will be quoted from, for the Japanese faculty and resource staff were most generous in sharing their experience. Additional materials are drawn from thirty countries and from over half of our own states. Here so much is happening in the court-correctional area—and so rapidly—that it is almost impossible to keep up with it all. A large part of this material is ephemeral, appearing in newspapers and magazines, in reports of commissions and research agencies, and in brochures of bold new private ventures. The time seemed to be auspicious, therefore, to record some of the evidences of the new breakthroughs.

This book presents material covering the important aspects of the court-correctional continuum—jails, criminal courts and peno-correctional institutions, what is happening to them, both inside and out. The juvenile and adult offender are included. The emphasis is placed heavily on alternatives, for that is where most of the action is taking place. No claim is made of exhaustiveness; it is hoped that what is put forward will be found sufficiently representative, both here and abroad, to have merited inclusion.

The emphasis will be on programs for dealing with offenders in the community and on community resources at all stages of the criminal justice process. For the benefit of those interested in inquiries or visits to the places herein described, their names are included in the notes, and where known, so are addresses.

Acknowledgments

As an expression of gratitude by the author for the kind hospitality extended to him and his wife during their delightful stay in Japan, this book is dedicated to UNAFEI. Thanks go also to the Japan Ministry of Justice, which extended the invitation to appear at the Institute and provided for the taping and transcription of the lectures. A special note of appreciation for their counsel and encouragement is extended to Zen Tokoi, Director of the Institute, and to his Deputy, Minoru Shikita. The Ms. Tomoko Ito and Mitsue Kawamoto capably and generously lent their special talents in recording, transcription and translation.

Thanks go to Susan Anderson and Sue Anne Marshall, graduate students in sociology at Boston College, who were indefatigable in helping to search out materials and summarize them for inclusion; and to Evelyn Friedman for checking references. To my expert and helpful colleagues, Lorraine Bone, Alice Close and Shirly Urban, a deep debt of gratitude is extended for their tireless retyping of the manuscript and invaluable editorial help.

Sid Seamans has, once again, imparted his keen editorial sense in the preparation of the manuscript for publication, and I thank him for that.

To Atsushi Nagashima and Milton Rector, old friends, appreciation is here expressed for their introductory remarks, as for their other kindnesses.

The proceeds of any royalties earned by this book will go to a special UNAFEI fund, to be used by the Institute in any way it may deem appropriate, for interchange between the Institute and the United States of information and research and of scholars and practitioners, in the hope that this may lead to heightened cooperation and further sharing of knowledge between our two countries.

Benedict S. Alper
Chestnut Hill, Mass.

January 1974

Chapter One

Changing Concepts of Criminal Policy

International concern and action in the prevention of crime and treatment of offenders began in 1825, long before persons in the fields of health, of labor problems, of the weather, or of international postal control gathered in international meetings to discuss matters of common professional interest. The deliberations and resolutions of criminologists and penologists are recorded in more than eighty international conferences held between then and 1970.[1] In the fall of 1972, the Secretary of the United Nations appeared before the General Assembly, and in an unprecedented message urged increased efforts on a worldwide scale to cope with the volume of crime, which had mounted in almost every nation. The unprecedented rash of international events—of kidnappings, assassinations and terrorism, of larceny of securities and art treasures, of skyjacking—was one area under review. He stressed the economic seriousness of the problem in his statement that social defense costs ran as high as 26 percent of public expenditures in some countries.[2]

Other criminal phenomena, national in origin yet universal in extent, are but the extension of a trend that clearly began at the end of World War II: greater criminal activity of young people and women, a high degree of anonymous or "faceless" crime, and a large concomitant element of violence.

The rate of crime in the United States between 1960 and 1970 rose fourteen times faster than the rate of population increase. "Over one million juvenile delinquency cases, excluding traffic offenses, were handled by juvenile courts in the United States. Between 1960 and 1970, the number of juvenile delinquency cases more than doubled (106 percent increase), as compared to the 28 percent increase in the number of children age 10 through 17. . . . Between 1965 and 1970, girls' delinquency cases increased by 78 percent, whereas boys' cases increased by 44 percent."[3]

The tremendous proportions of the penal problem can be seen in the number of persons affected by criminal court sentences—almost 6 million of them—in the families of persons placed on probation, committed to prisons, or released on parole during the course of a single year. On any one day, federal, state, and local penal institutions hold close to half a million inmates.[4]

At the same time, the entire criminal court-correction process is today under critical review on many fronts. More innovative ideas are being advanced and applied in this field than at any time since the 1780s, when the then radical idea of the penitentiary was first launched and private prison societies flourished in many states. More organizational effort and more individual concern and activity is being manifested in the area of prison reform than this country has seen since 100 years ago, when the notion of the reformatory was the subject of heated debate, both here and abroad.

Of all reported crimes, less than 25 percent are today cleared by the police.[5] The deterrent effect of arrest is seriously weakened if, as Cesare Beccaria stated more than 200 years ago, sureness of apprehension is the best deterrent of criminal acts.[6] All too often the solution is sought in the "beefing up" of police hardware or in computerization of data on private citizens, without regard for civil liberties and the right of privacy.

In order to free the police to deal effectively with truly serious crimes, a wide variety of offenses now must be stricken from the criminal calendar. Many of these offenses derive from religious sources—in times when religion played a more predominant role. As religious influences have waned, such acts are being dropped from the statute books.

This is not true in all jurisdictions, of course. As this is being written, for example, *Time* magazine reports that the Georgia Supreme Court has confirmed the one-year jail sentence of a man found guilty of having asked an eleven-year-old girl who had stopped by his car, "Have you ever been laid?"[7] The law he had violated had been passed as recently as 1968, forbidding "obscene and vulgar or profane language in the presence of a person under the age of 14." At a time when two of the most popular films being shown to audiences all over the country treat, respectively, of anal copulation and fellatio, the anomaly would indicate far from universal agreement as to what constitutes decent or even lawful conduct.

Detention before trial represents a staggering load of persons who must either post bail or go to jail; an experience—especially for those who have never been there before—which can be a degrading advanced course in higher criminal education. Our criminal justice system, based on the presumption of innocence, has the responsibility to assure the dignity of detained persons. Provision of opportunities for them to utilize their waiting time advantageously takes on added significance in that at least one-half of all detained suspects are released—one way or another—after their court appearance.

Those who are sentenced to imprisonment find themselves confined to places with a high rate of acknowledged failure. It has taken us two centuries to realize that penitentiaries do not make penitents, reformatories do not reform, correctional institutions do not correct.

Classifying prisoners into minimum, medium, and maximum security all too often depends upon the number of cells available for each category. If one-third can provide maximum custody, one-third of the prison population will be found to require it. Without maximum security, prisoners could be classified only as medium or minimum. As the severity of degrees of security is scaled down, less turmoil and less disciplinary problems may result. As the categories of security are redefined, so will the prison population, and with that, a recasting of attitudes will take place.

Herbert Spencer wisely observed "the universal truth that the instrumentalities by which the subordination of others is effected, themselves subordinate the victor, the master or the ruler."[8] The keeper and the kept, like the captor and the captive, are fastened to the chain which binds them both; "the master is not alone the master, but the slave as well," as Rousseau once said.

The riot at Attica Prison in September 1971 was only the most fatefully extreme of a long series of prison disturbances that have rocked American penitentiaries and reformatories since the end of World War II. The demand of the victims of Attica to be treated like men was not simply a dramatic plea for better conditions.[9] No mere tinkering with prison regulations can satisfactorily answer that demand or others like it.

The need now is to confront that demand in its essentials: to take a fresh look at our underlying concepts, to try to fashion a rational system of criminal justice which will be consistent as well as effective. Reliance upon the community for the treatment and rehabilitation of offenders—juvenile and adult—comes to be seen as more effective than the fixed institution, which serves only to warehouse offenders until they are ultimately discharged back into these same communities.

Men behind bars have never before had any effective constituency on the outside to fight for betterment of their conditions. Politically—at least until recently—prisoners have been the least powerful members of our society. Parents of school children, or of the retarded, families of psychotics, veterans, the physically handicapped, the aged—all have lobbies and organizations to campaign in their behalf, while hardly anyone has stood up before our legislatures to demand an end to brutality in prisons.

That is, until recently. In the past few years the prison world has become politicized to an unprecedented degree. Young people jailed for opposition to the Vietnam War or for involvement with narcotics, adults caught up in the courts and prisons as the result of political activities, as well as blacks who see the prison as an extension of the larger ghettos where they are condemned to pass their lives, have stirred the conscience of America. They are demanding an end to places that dehumanize hundreds of thousands of men and women each year, which drearily report high rates of failure, at a cost of tens of millions to build and thousands every year for each person confined.

As a result, the concept of diverting away from the criminal justice system as many persons as can possibly be handled by other means is today much to the fore. Some of the impetus for this movement derives from critiques of the inadequacy of the criminal justice system. It may also arise—if only in part—from a sense of desperation.

For in an earlier stage of our own development, the community was the place where social problems were dealt with. It is clear that at the time of President Andrew Jackson, coincidental with the rise of industry and the beginnings of urbanization, people with problems began to be shunted into institutions. This movement seems now to have reached its peak and begun to diminish, as we seek again for alternatives within the communities themselves.

No one can at this point assess the direction or the end of these new measures. So deep is the dissatisfaction with the present court-correctional system at every point, so admittedly ineffective its handling of crowded jails, clogged court, and bad prisons, that we may well be standing today on the threshold of a real breakthrough in our dealing with offenders, leading ultimately to more effective delinquency prevention and a drop in our abnormally high crime rate.

Diversion has been increasingly applied to the juvenile court since the 1967 Supreme Court decision *in re Gault.* [9] Nonjudicial ways of dealing with juvenile offenders have precedents in the Scandinavian countries, the Panchayat Courts of India, and the Peoples' Courts of the socialist countries. All of these embody the concept of community dealing with misconduct. Such diversion may take the form of referral to social and clinical agencies, with suspension of a finding of delinquency if the youngster responds satisfactorily to such programs. Much of what is called delinquency today was once called mischief. It is interesting to speculate on what would have happened had there been a juvenile court in Hannibal, Missouri when Tom Sawyer and Huckleberry Finn were boys.

Diversionary programs are also being gradually introduced into the adult court for selected offenders. This move to divert is found at every step in the criminal process.[10] In jurisdictions where laws against public drunkenness have been repealed, the police now pick up those who would formerly have been arrested and sent to jail, only to return to the street by a "revolving door" process. Drunkards may now voluntarily commit themselves to the same institutions where they were formerly sentenced, thus diverting themselves.

Such changes in procedure reflect and affect changes in attitude—public, legislative, and judicial—thus taking the heat out of the criminal process. There will always be a certain number of people who will commit certain acts because these are forbidden. The more of such laws that are stricken from the books, the less laws they will be tempted to disobey. This has particular significance for the young, who traditionally take delight in doing what is forbidden. Diversion applied to juvenile institutions in one state resulted in the transfer of almost 1000 juveniles to the community, back with their parents, enrollment in private boarding schools, placement with foster parents or in group homes or residential centers, or on college campuses.

Today we are deinstitutionalizing the mentally disturbed and retarded; we no longer lock up the orphan, exile the poor, or send the aged to workhouses.[11] Communities have the responsibility for such persons in need of care, including the criminal and the delinquent. By returning these responsibilities to the community, and the means for dealing with them, society will cope more effectively with them, at the same time helping to reduce the sense of powerlessness which marks our fragmented society.

NOTES

1. Benedict S. Alper and Jerry F. Boren, *Crime: International Agenda* (Lexington, Massachusetts: D.C. Heath, 1971), especially Chapter 2.
2. "Crime Prevention and Control," Note by the Secretary General, New York, United Nations, 19 October 1972. Document No. A/8844.
3. *Juvenile Court Statistics, 1970* (Washington: Department of Health, Education, and Welfare, January 7, 1972), p. 2.
4. "The National Profile of Correction," *Crime and Delinquency* (January 1967), pp. 229–60.
5. *Crime in the United States* (Boston: Beacon Press, 1965), pp. 93–94, Table 8.
6. Cesare Beccaria, *An Essay on Crimes and Punishments* (Albany; W.C. Little Company, 1872).
7. *Time*, May 21, 1973.
8. Herbert Spencer, *Fact and Comments* (New York: D. Appleton & Co., 1902), p. 159.
9. *Attica: The Official Report of the New York State Special Commission on Attica* (New York: Bantam Books, 1972), p. 223.
10. 387 U.S. 1, 18L. Ed. 2d 527 (1967)
11. David J. Rothman, *The Discovery of the Asylum* (Boston: Little, Brown, 1971).

Chapter Two

Antecedents of Alternatives

Before proceeding to a consideration of the various ways in which alternatives to present methods are being introduced into the criminal justice system, it is well to take a look at some of the precedents which existed in early times. For, as no idea ever dies, so no idea is ever truly new—it simply comes round again in a new form, depending upon the circumstances that bring the old notion once more to the fore.

Society has been dealing with offenders since the dawn of time, and there is literally no totally new approach that cannot be found to have existed in another time and another place. Much of what is thought of as penal progress is, in fact, only a new emphasis, the pendulum frequently being a better gauge of where we stand than other ways of measurement of penal reform.

A study made at the University of Southern California, based on the experience of Los Angeles County, concluded that unless drastic changes are made in the system, and a truly consistent procedure developed among all of its components, "criminal justice will soon be inundated and will ultimately collapse."[1]

For one thing, the criminal justice system is not, as we are wont to think of it, an integrated, consistent set of agencies or processes for apprehending offenders, ascertaining guilt or innocence, and dispensing justice in the form of an appropriate sentence. We tend to think of it as flowing in some order in which each succeeding step proceeds from, as it is influenced by, what went before. There is another perspective which sees succeeding steps as retroactively affecting preceding stages. For example, the clearance rate of offenses set by the police not only determines who will come into court, it may actually determine prospectively who will commit offenses. If the police are known to be efficient in making arrests, that fact will undoubtedly discourage people from committing certain offenses. Similarly, the actions of the court against persons who are arrested and brought before it directly affect the role the police play, as in cases of prostitution. If the court dismisses women arrested on this charge, if they do not deal with them on a consistently severe basis, the police will be discouraged from making arrests for soliciting, because they become, understandably, loath to participate in the system which only lets the arrested woman out again.

Similarly, the correctional process can often influence court action. For example, at the present time, Japanese prisons operate at about 80 percent of capacity.[2] So there is room to incarcerate all the convicted persons the judges think require imprisonment. But if their institutions were full—as happens in some places in the United States from time to time—the rate of discharge from them would be determined by the rate of sentencing. The rate of sentencing by the courts could also be determined by the rate of release from the institutions. For example, a judge in the juvenile court in Minneapolis refused to commit any more juveniles to the state reform schools because they were seriously overcrowded. In this instance, the institution determined the court action. The judge appealed on the radio for families in the area to open their doors for foster home placement of children who were in need of care.[3]

Finally, parole can influence the prison. If a parole board has a policy of not releasing men who have committed certain offenses, or of requiring certain conditions prior to release, of taking a soft line or a hard line in response to public opinion, the institution is directly affected. One of the basic reasons for many of the riots in our prisons lies at the door of parole boards, which may not be releasing people rapidly enough or are being unreasonable in their requirements for parole. Parole-board actions thus retroactively influence conditions within the institution itself, and play a decisive role in setting the tone of many prisons, quite apart from whatever a warden may be trying to do to make his programs effective.

Thus the criminal justice system is not a logical and consistent continuum from arrest through correction; rather, there is a to-and-fro relationship among its various components and, not infrequently, antagonism between them. Because it is not a wholly rational and consistent process, it presents a challenge to those who would improve its effectiveness. Because of these contradictions, there is room to experiment and to innovate.

The idea of shorter, more intensive sentences is not new. The "short, sharp shock" program adopted in England a few years ago is an apt parallel. Most men who do not resume criminal activity after release from prison agree that if the institution had benefited them at all, it had done so within the first few years. There is a great deal to ponder in the twin facts that the United States has the longest sentences—and one of the highest crime rates—in the world. The time has come for total examination by all countries of their traditional attitudes toward prisons. It is of more than passing historical interest that the Walnut Street Jail in Philadelphia was established in 1784 at the same time the first prison society in the world was organized. The Pennsylvania Prison Society,

under Quaker auspices, is now in its 186th year. It was followed by the establishment of prison societies in New York, Massachusetts, Delaware, France, England,
and Russia.[4] There are few other new social institutions which, like the
penitentiary, are accompanied by the establishment of agencies that call into
question their basic assumptions and the programs introduced into them.
Questions about those basic assumptions continue to this day.

ANTECEDENTS OF THE INSTITUTION

One tends to think offhand that prisons have always existed. That is true, but
not as places of punishment. Up to 200 years ago, such institutions were used
only for temporary detention of persons awaiting trial, or for political prisoners.
The Bastille held political prisoners under *lettres de cachet*.[5] The prison of
Chillon, in Switzerland, celebrated by Byron, chained political prisoners in its
gloomy cellar.[6] The Tower of London was a well-known "keep" for those
whom the king wanted out of the way—temporarily or until he could do away
with them for good.

Otherwise, persons were not held in institutions as punishment.
That is a relatively new idea. Before people were locked into penitentiaries,
they were killed—or exiled—or physically harmed. Of the first two human beings
born on this earth—according to the Biblical version of creation—one killed the
other just as the world was starting. And the murderer, Cain, was exiled—
banished by God from his home and made to spend his life wandering the world.
The Greeks used banishment, as in the tale of Oedipus; so did the Romans. It
was a favored practice during the Middle Ages, and in our own century, the
Russians and the French used Siberia and Devil's Island, respectively, as places
of exile for convicts. Britain transported its convicts on ships and sent them far
away—to the American colonies and Australia.

Persons found guilty were tortured with a wide variety of most
ingenious methods and devices. If they were thieves, they had a hand cut off;
some were branded on the forehead, had their tongues cut out if they were liars,
or blinded, whipped, or put in stocks for certain other offenses. Today's
institutions—the penitentiary, with its tradition of solitary confinement, hard
labor and repentance, and the reformatory—which were originally intended to
replace those early forms of punishment, were each considered in their day
as enlightened, forward steps. Yet instead of superseding the physical forms of
punishment which were used before the penitentiary, these are now, in a sense,
incorporated into our prisons. In other words, the penitentiary has simply
replaced these former types of treatment or punishment, and has also included
them in other, newer ways, into the penal system plus the added factor of
confinement. This statement, upon examination, will be seen not to exaggerate.
For example, the death penalty is still used, only today it is often preceded by
long periods of confinement while the condemned man awaits death. So we

have not wholly replaced death as a penalty. Nor have we rid ourselves of exile as a form of punishment. For banishment on a wholesale scale occurs when sentenced offenders are sent to institutions located far from their homes—making it difficult for them to communicate with their families by visits, and making them feel that they have been cut off by long distances. This, for human beings, is a form of punishment in and of itself. Most of our penitentiaries are placed out in the country as if they were for lepers or for people with contagious diseases. As if isolation did not in itself constitute punishment, most penitentiaries, even in rural settings, are surrounded by high walls which make it impossible for anyone to jump them, or even to look out to the greenery, the horizon, or the setting sun. A prison journal recently reported the story of a man released from jail who wrote a letter to the woman in the house next to the jail, thanking her for the joy he received from looking out each day at the wash hung out on her balcony.

Exile at the same time satisfies society: if offenders are removed from their midst, the problem is in some curious way also removed. If everybody who is emotionally disturbed or retarded or criminal or sick is sent out into the country, the problem ceases to exist because it has been flushed away out of sight and it no longer confronts you. Philip Slater describes this aptly as "the Toilet Assumption."[7] Persons found guilty of certain minor offenses are spared a jail sentence on condition that they leave town. Non-citizens, after serving a portion of their sentence, are often returned, at government expense, to their native country. So penitentiaries still combine, together with confinement, one of the forms of sentence which they were supposed to replace—exile.

Physical punishment is also still practiced in our institutions. People are put in solitary confinement, they are placed on reduced diets, they are deprived of communication with others, all of which are forms of punishment additional to the imposition of confinement.

But at least, one might say, we no longer brand people or shame them in public by ducking them in water or forcing them to sit in stocks. We don't put a "T" on the hand of the thief or an "A" on the forehead of the adulteress.[8] True. But in other ways we still brand our prisoners, only today there is a new word for it. It is called labeling,[9] and many persons go through life, having once served a prison sentence, as if they had a "P" for prisoner or "C" for convict burnt in their foreheads. They are deprived of many of their civil liberties and many of their freedoms because they were once prisoners. The "P" or "C" is in the dossiers in official places, accessible to employers, government offices, and credit agencies.

Maiming—the cutting off of a hand or the removal of an eye or a leg—may no longer be done officially, but there are places in the world which report hundreds of instances of self-mutilation, where prisoners maim themselves or commit suicide.[10] They do so out of a feeling of despair or of worthlessness, or in order to bring themselves to public attention, or in order to receive medical services which they might not otherwise get if they did not have to be sent to the hospital, or be otherwise removed from the regular prison population.

All of these forms of punishment added together total to a realization that one of the reasons why imprisonment as a form of treatment has failed is because it still bears within it most of the elements of punishment which preceded it and which it was intended to supplant.

The recent Supreme Court decision has probably slowed down, if it has not put a complete stop to, the application of the death penalty. [11] But, instead of capital punishment, we have something almost its equivalent in the sense that civil disabilities—such as restrictions on voting, on getting licenses, on practicing certain trades or professions, on holding government jobs, or running for office, getting married, or changing one's residence—very often accompany an ex-con to the end of his days. [12]

If we view imprisonment as one of the more inconsistent elements in the criminal justice system, it is because we have not fully resolved in our own philosophy and attitudes what the purpose of imprisonment is. We still argue whether it exists for restraint, for deterrence, for penitence, for expiation, for reformation, for rehabilitation, for correction, for reintegration. Until we resolve that basic problem on some kind of a rational and consistent basis, and as long as imprisonment bears within itself the elements of punishment which it was intended to replace, the institutions will continue to fail in a very large percentage of cases, varying from the 25 to 30 percent which is reported in Japan, [13] up to 50, 70, or 80 percent which is the accepted rate in many jurisdictions in the United States. [14]

A recent newspaper story illustrates the thesis that in the field of punishment, as in many other areas of human activity, "plus ça change, plus c'est la même chose"—the more things change, the more they are the same. When overseas transportation of prisoners by England and France stopped (in the American colonies at the time of our Revolution; in France with Devil's Island after World War II), it did not entirely disappear as a form of punishment. The British continued to use ships, old and unseaworthy hulks, tied up at the harbors and river mouths to house convicts who came ashore only to work on the fortifications. [15]

In New York City in 1965, an aircraft carrier tied up at the federal Navy Yard, was about to be taken out of service. It was proposed that it be adapted as a prison. The City Commissioner of Corrections rejected the proposal, not because this was an ancient and inhumane form of punishment, but because there were so many exits in the ship, so many torpedo tubes and so many vents for air conditioning that the carrier would constitute one enormous escape hatch for prisoners, and so the idea was shelved. As recently as the spring of 1973, the Sheriff of Suffolk County urged that a discarded aircraft carrier in Boston

Harbor be utilized for jail detention, but he withdrew the idea after a storm of protest.

The process of transporting convicted criminals overseas may well have inspired the later development of the open prison. Certain elements, especially as developed by England, appear to have been adopted by the open institutional systems in the Philippines in the twentieth century, particularly in the huge penal colonies of Davo and Iwaghig.

"The English transportation of criminals to Australia began an extraordinary social experience, the attempt to reconcile penal policy with a colonial purpose. The general principles under which the system operated were a communal system of labor, a system of assignment of convicts to private settlers, and a system of absolute or conditional pardons. By an unconditional pardon, the term of the sentence was remitted and, with some exceptions, the ex-prisoner was entitled to leave the settlement immediately. The conditional pardon contained a declaration by the Governor that the unexpired portion of the convict's sentence was remitted on condition that he continue to reside within the territory during the term of his original sentence.

"Further, as a matter of necessity, but also to encourage good conduct, well-behaved convicts were rewarded. Some were appointed to positions of responsibility or profit (overseers, policemen, etc.), others were granted 'tickets of leave' which freed them from normal convict labor obligations and permitted them to work for themselves in a prescribed district, although liable to report to the police regularly and to have their tickets withdrawn for any offense. At the expiration of their sentence, they were given grants of thirty acres of land to cultivate for their own livelihood with extra acreage for wives and children. In addition to the land, the prospective settler was given a year's supply of provisions for himself and his family, and seed and stock to commence his farm. He was assigned a servant supported by Government for an eighteen-month period." [16]

The open institution also has roots in the system of prison labor called "open" (*a l'aperto*), which was introduced in Europe in the latter half of the nineteenth century, following upon the work of Montesinos in Spain [17] and Maconochie in Australia. In this system, clearly a transition between the classical prison and the open institution, the prisoner worked under guard outside the prison walls during the day, and returned to custody within them at night.

The penal settlement at Norfolk Island under Alexander Maconochie pioneered in open corrections. [18] He believed that reform of the criminal could be assisted by encouraging him to pass through ordered stages of decreasing deprivations leading to the final stage which approximated conditions of freedom and unencumbered living. Order and control in the institutions were maintained through the self-discipline of the inmates; the inmate group was made responsible for the conduct of its members. The conception of the reformatory had its origins in the innovative experiments of this progressive penal reformer.

It was during this period that Sir Walter Crofton developed the so-called "Irish System," which provided a graduated transition for offenders from confinement under maximum security conditions to release under supervision in the community. The program called for three distinct stages of treatment: (1) punishment in solitude for two years; (2) congregate labor under a marking system that regulated privileges and determined the date of discharge; and (3) conditional release under a "ticket-of-leave."[19]

EARLY COMMUNITY DEALING

Historical precedents also exist as antecedents to the way we presently deal with the social problems of other groups of deviants: the mentally diseased, the mentally retarded, the aged, the orphaned, and the poor.[20] In early society, in many undeveloped countries, and in many countries now highly developed, persons with these conditions did, of course exist. There have always been the insane, the feeble-minded, the dependent, the young, the old and the poor. Most simply put, such persons were dealt with in the community. English literature tells of the village idiot, so called, the person who is "not all there," who in yesterday's terms was called feeble-minded, whom we describe today as mentally retarded. In early, particularly agricultural society, while survival is possible even for those who cannot read or write, such persons can be endured and accommodated. They may not have played a major contributory role in the social or economic life of the community, but they were not regarded as so deviant that they had to be put away. The same is true of many of the people who used to be called lunatics. They could adjust in a society which was less highly organized than today, where fewer demands were placed upon them. Children without parents were adopted by or placed with other families. Many of these children were in fact indentured servants and apprentices and were no doubt exploited to one degree or another, but they were, nevertheless, dealt with as persons inside the society, not as rejects or exiled from it.

Those who were vagrant, unemployed, or old were taken care of in the community in so-called work-houses. In their earliest years, our hospitals took in sick people when they were about to die; less ill patients were taken care of and nursed at home by the family. The criminal went abroad in the society after he had been branded or tortured or put into stocks—if he was not killed—and once more took a place in the community. With the coming of the Industrial Revolution, these problem groups became institutionalized, many of them for long periods of time, some of them permanently, until they died. We have reached a point in our society today where we have perhaps overinstitutionalized such individuals and we are beginning now to witness a reversion to earlier ways of dealing with them—in the community.

THE ANCIENT VILLAGE OF GEEL [21]

To the Low Countries, Switzerland, and England goes credit for being the first to settle persons with mental disturbances in homes, usually in small, rural neighborhoods. The ancient Flemish town of Geel, in Belgium, is the best-known of these community programs, having begun, to judge by the earliest extant record, in the thirteenth century. Legend has it that in the eighth century, an Irish princess, attempting to escape her father's incestuous designs upon her following the death of his wife, fled to Belgium. Here, in the town of Geel, she was overtaken by her demented father, who decapitated her. The town became a shrine to the memory of her sainthood, and in the course of time some of the pilgrims who came to pray remained to become residents in the town, making their home with the village people. In 1852 the government of Belgium took over the maintenance and supervision of the colony, and provided an infirmary for the care of the sick, as well as for the initial reception of patients who came to settle in the town.

In this century, the number of mental patients housed in the village has reached almost 4,000, at times, in a total population of 20,000 persons. The main occupation of the villagers is agriculture. Patients who make their homes with them engage—to the limits of their ability—in work on the farms, as well as in the shops and stores of the community. So ancient is the tradition of extending care to persons who would otherwise be hospitalized in the chronic custodial wards of mental hospitals, that some families have boarded the same patient over more than one generation. More than one-half of the patients—men, women and children, mostly from Belgium, but including citizens from other countries—are mentally retarded, while a third are classified as schizophrenic. Families that can pay for the support of their relatives are required to do so; the state bears the cost for all others. Most of the patients are chronic cases which can never be cured, and therefore require constant care and understanding. They spend their lives as normally as their infirmities permit, most of their time with normal people. In addition to working, their activities include cycling, walking, attending dances and movies, or sitting in the cafes. They eat at the tables and sleep in the homes of their hosts. The townspeople are so accustomed, over the centuries, to living with mentally deficient and disturbed individuals, that they have developed a special sensitiveness and skill in dealing with them. Today, with the encroachment of industry and the growing involvement of the people of Geel in factory rather than farm work, the future of this extraordinary community is in some doubt.

A conclusion to be drawn from its unique history is that one of the penalties we pay for urbanization and industrialization is a heightened tempo of life. The same conditions which create criminals and mentally disturbed people seem to be the very same as deprive us of the capability to deal with them. For one thing, the level of expectation of performance is so much higher today, that merely to survive requires a higher level of intelligence and a greater degree of emotional stability than ever before. As a result, more and more people below that level are dropping out—or being dropped—and becoming dependent on others, where in a more simply organized community they could not only survive, but also be productive. Part of the surplus value of the labor of all goes to support those who have difficulty in adjusting to the demands of today's technical society. In the same sense, then, that much of mental retardation and psychosis is created by the complexity of our society, so is the criminal.

"The problems of the aged are not problems of crime, and do not appear so dysfunctional to society, yet the aged are similarly alienated from the culture, except perhaps in the villages and certain other communities. It seems highly probable that societies which integrate aged persons into their culture have few problems with juvenile delinquency. Chinese minorities are well known for both their care of the aged and their low delinquency rates. It seems that societies which reject deviants reject them in terms of a number of dimensions. If they can integrate deviants of one form, they tend to be able to integrate deviants of another form."[22]

There is an added argument that if we have done so at an earlier stage in our development, we can do so again. In this context, as communities turn to themselves for the solutions to local problems, so can they be expected to find the ways and the facilities to handle those members of the community who are troublesome, but the root of whose problems may well lie in the neighborhoods where they reside.

In the field of mental health, clinics which started as in-city, out-patient facilities have added diagnostic and short-term residence facilities. Persons who may not need commitment to, or have been discharged from, a mental hospital, and who require a short period of care in a neighborhood facility, can come voluntarily and benefit from a relatively short term of care.[23]

As a result of such community efforts as these, the commitment to and the number of patients in mental hospitals shows a steady rate of decline. New York State mental hospitals, for example, "held 93,000 patients in 1955; their number dropped . . . in 1970 to 64, 239. A similar decline has occurred in correctional institutions. In 1940, 131.7 prisoners per 100,000 of the population served time in federal or state penitentiaries; in 1965, the number fell to 109.6 per 100,000, and this without a concomitant drop in the number of crimes committed or criminals convicted. Dramatic changes have also affected the young. The orphan asylum has almost disappeared, and the juvenile correction center has also declined in use. As for the poor, the almshouse or traditional poorhouse is no longer a specter in their lives."[24]

Voluntary individuals and organizations in Japan, in a little-known historical precedent, established in the 1880s halfway houses for the care of discharged prisoners.[25] The consistent drop in the Japanese crime rate in the past decade is perhaps better known: from 1961 to 1971 the number of "major penal code suspects" fell from 131,044 (11.7 per 1,000 of the population aged 14–19) to 102,335 (10.1 per 1,000) for juveniles; from 278,810 (4.9 per 1,000 population over age 20) to 227,096 (3.2 per 1,000) for adults.[26] Coincident with this reversal of a trend in crime rates in Japan, which is almost unprecedented in other industrialized nations, stands a formidable datum: that in the fifteen years between 1956 and 1971, the percentage of juvenile offenders committed to institutions was halved, from 17.1 to 8.9 percent. For adults the comparative percentages are 72.4 and 57.1 percent.[27]

Today's reversion to earlier ways of dealing with the eternal problem of crime comes about as a result of a wide variety of contemporary reasons. One of these relates to the size of the crime problem and its enormous costs. In France and in the United States, 5 percent of the gross national product, it is estimated, is diverted from productive uses by the cost of crime.

A questionnaire sent to 25 member nations in a United Nations survey reported that the cost of crime ranged from a median of 3 percent in the big budgets of rich and developed countries to 9 percent of the small budgets of poor and developing countries.[28] One of their problems is the accumulation of surplus funds for investment in capital productive capacity. If 10 percent is taken away for problems of crime, it cannot be invested in future production, thus causing a very serious economic drain on the economy of such countries. Therefore, anything that can be done in the way of finding alternatives to the expensive cost of coping with crime is to the special advantage of countries which are newly come to independence.

In the United States at the present time, to build one cell for one man in a prison of maximum security costs around $30,000, and that is for just the walls, bars, essential equipment and facilities: a bed in a secure setting. The interest on the cost of this one bed at 7 percent is over $2,000 a year just for the cell, without including costs of food, clothing, staff and program. What could be done for one offender with $2,000 a year in the community? If a probation officer were to supervise only ten men and were to be paid $20,000 a year, that would be the equivalent of the interest on a bond issue floated to construct 10 cells to serve those 10 men. With a caseload of only 10 to supervise, a competent probation officer could initiate and carry through an intensive, carefully developed plan of community care on an individualized basis.

Costs of confining juveniles in institutions are soaring even beyond those for prison care, leading many states to examine community alternatives under the pressure of rising budgets and tax rates. In one New England state, the 1970 per capita cost for the school for delinquent boys was $14,000, with $16,000 projected for 1973. The costs for the girls school, with only 30 girls in care, came to $21,000 per capita for the year 1972.[29]

But the factor of cost is not the only reason for urging greater reliance on community alternatives to traditional modes of confinement. There are humanitarian reasons of prime importance, as well. Nor is it necessary to go abroad in search of bold new ideas for replacing old primitive ways, for newer and more understanding programs, which are, at worst, no less effective.

In the state of Maine, there is a reformatory for women, built in the 1870s.[30] An extraordinary woman became the superintendent of that institution ten years ago. The first thing she did was remove the walls of the institution. She next replaced the striped uniforms of the women with individual dresses. Then she abolished the rule of silence, a practice which goes back to the earliest days of the penitentiary. The idea then was to lock a prisoner in a small room, forbid him to talk with anybody else because he might become infected, leave him only with the Bible, and he would surely repent his sins, he would himself drive out the devil, and he would as a result become a person of good character and thereafter law-abiding. The reason for the rule had long since been forgotten, but that regulation forbidding talking by women still prevailed—except for one hour on Sundays.

After these initial drastic changes had been introduced without disrupting the institution or resulting in the escape of the female inmates, two houses on the grounds formerly used for staff areas were then turned into halfway houses. The staff were encouraged to live in the nearby town because one problem besetting all institutions is that the custodial personnel themselves become institutionalized at the same time the prisoners do.

When we think of prisons, we think only of their effect on the inmates; we do not usually think of their effect on the people who run them, just as schools have an effect on the teachers who teach in them. If an institution is run brutally, it brutalizes the keepers as well as the inmates. The reverse of that is also true—if people are dealt with under conditions of freedom, the keepers are also freer and more open in their dealings. The Maine Reformatory for Women now has two halfway houses on its grounds, one for inmates who attend school in the nearby town, the other for those who go out every day to work. Both are coeducational, with young men and young women sharing the same programs and many of the same facilities.

Ten years ago, for the first time, more convicted offenders in federal courts were placed on probation or otherwise allowed to live in the community than were committed to institutions.[31] Since then, the trend continues in the same direction, so today there are more and more convicted persons in the community, and less and less of them in prisons. It can be said that as the volume of crime increases, more of those apprehended and found guilty are being returned to the community without first passing through an institution. Without implying any causal connection between these two data, it is well to keep in mind a statistic earlier quoted—four-fifths of the serious crimes committed are by persons who have previously served time in penal institutions.

Nor is this trend limited to the United States. In Sweden for example, noninstitutional offenders under sentence who were under supervision in the community increased from 13,500 in 1960 to 23,000 cases at the beginning of 1967, an annual average increase each year of more than 1,000 cases. During the sixties, sentences of imprisonment were used less frequently for many offenses that previously would have been punished by imprisonment.[32] As a result, many of the offenders not in institutions are reported to have a higher degree of criminality and include the more serious and more socially handicapped individuals. Understandably those offenders who are placed elsewhere now require more treatment resources and are more difficult to rehabilitate.

That this is a continuing commitment on the part of the Swedish government may be seen from their projected trend in criminality between 1970 and 1976, which indicates a rise in those six years from 500,000 to 600,000 crimes known to the police, an annual average increase of 3 percent. The institutional population is nevertheless expected to remain constant, while the noninstitutional sentenced population is expected to increase by 1,000 in each of the six years.[33] It is anticipated that as more of the "tough" offenders are placed in the community, the more difficult the problems of dealing with them are going to be. At the same time, many more resources are available in the community to render specialized services than usually obtain in the institution. It also means within the institutions a much higher residuum of serious and very troublesome offenders. It has already been pointed out that the savings derived from placing offenders in non-institutional facilities, and making it possible for them to support themselves, can be spent now on more intensive therapeutic and other services for those who absolutely must be removed from society.

OVERRELIANCE ON THE INSTITUTION

Just as there is, in most jurisdictions, an overreliance on the law for the solution of many social problems, so is there a resort to overinstitutionalization for the solution of individual problems. In a study conducted a few years ago in Ohio, it was concluded that over one-half—55 percent—of the children committed to the state training schools were, in fact, not in need of institutional care.[34] It is not possible to infer from this the exact percentage of those children unnecessarily committed to institutions who will later wind up in adult institutions for offenders. But we do know that the earlier the age at which young people are incarcerated, the greater is the probability of recidivism.

This is but one of the reasons why today there is a reversal away from institutionalization, and a search for other forms of dealing with the lawbreaker. There is a further factor that accounts for this turning back to the community: a realization that the community has a responsibility for dealing with problems which in the last analysis are created in it. Crime in any community does not result from the application of some exterior force. It arises from the community because those who live there—for a variety of reasons, many of them beyond its control—have not been dealt with properly.

In stressing the role of the community, it is valuable to keep in mind that the alternative to dealing with the offender under conditions of relative freedom is dealing with him in confinement. It is a truism, as George Bernard Shaw has said, that you cannot expect to train people for freedom in conditions of captivity; that is like expecting to turn a tiger into a Quaker by putting him in a cage.[35] There is the additional fact that very few persons committed to prison do in fact spend their whole lives there; almost all of them are ultimately released back into the community. Shaw goes on to say that to be perfectly consistent, society would kill off the truly dangerous offenders, and then lock up everybody else for life. The problem would be solved. This approach is not without difficulties and its costs, but it is at least consistent. Instead of that, ultimately we release all but a few of the people in prison back into free society, after having treated them during their stay as if they were without any capacity to live in that society. If you do not wish to lock people up forever in institutions, you might very well consider locking them up until they were 29 or 30 years old, until the factor of "maturation" has set in, after which the offender no longer represents so serious a threat to society. The close of the third decade of life generally represents the peak of physical prowess among males not in prison, but among those who lead criminal careers, perhaps because of the pace at which they live, the onset of the process of deterioration, or maturation, seems to set in earlier.[36]

So if close to 100 percent of offenders are going to be returned ultimately to society, their resocialization cannot be done in isolation, because the two terms—isolation and socialization—are in opposition. Isolation means being apart from others; socializing means being together with others. And just as crime would not exist if each of us, like Robinson Crusoe, lived alone, so the process of socialization must take place in association. It was not until his man Friday came into his life that the possibility of crime arose. The same factor that makes possible the commission of crime suggests a way of dealing with it: only when people associate together can the process of socialization take place.

Criminologists and penologists are increasingly concerned with the physical effect of imprisonment on prisoners, quite apart from this process of socialization. When the eyes are limited in their focus, in their vista, to at most ten or twenty feet, actual physical deterioration of the eye takes place. When some prisoners are almost never exposed to direct light, or to the sun, the same result takes place. When men do not converse or hear the voices of others over a long period of time, the auditory apparatus begins to deteriorate. If that is true with regard to the physical senses of seeing and hearing, how much greater must be the deterioration of the social sense in persons thus isolated for long periods of time?

In a prison as well organized and well administered as any to be found anywhere, I once visited the death cells where men were confined who would have been executed but for the recent Supreme Court decision on capital punishment. There I saw two men, each locked in adjacent cells. They were playing a game of checkers, each lying on the floor inside his barred cell, one arm stretched outside the bars playing checkers on the corridor floor with his neighbor. They never saw each other, and were doomed to live that way for the rest of their lives. They are taken out separately for exercise. Otherwise, they never leave that cell, day in, year in and out. What is to happen to their eyes, to their ears—what happens to the social sense of people who are treated in that fashion?

Admittedly, these are men convicted of heinous crimes who were perhaps going to be detained for their entire lives. Yet their conditions were little different, except in a matter of degree, from the conditions experienced by people who were going to serve a limited sentence. If methods more humane than confinement are available for dealing with human beings, then they should be chosen as against the inhumane if our society deserves to be described as civilized. If the aim of medicine is the elimination of pain and the provision of positive good physical health and longevity, then in the field of crime control we are justified in advocating more humane and less painful ways of dealing with offenders.

If we reduce the inhumanity of the conditions under which prisoners live, we make less inhumane those charged with keeping them in custody. Persons with a college degree and a professional attitude are not easily accepted by the custodial staff in correctional institutions, especially adult security institutions, because they are viewed as "soft" and unsophisticated, because those with whom they work have been on those jobs so long that they have become brutalized. And in order to survive that kind of an atmosphere, a person in correctional service has to make himself hard, otherwise he will be rejected by the culture of the guards. When attitudes have become so fixed, when the brutalizing process has gone on so long, the situation has to be completely altered—or abolished—before the attitude of the guard himself can be changed.

One of the institutions in Massachusetts which formerly housed juvenile delinquents has recently been converted to a halfway house for adult offenders released from the state reformatory. It has been staffed with custodial officers from the reformatory, specially trained to deal with offenders in an open setting. At a lunch there recently with prisoners and guards, the latter reported that what they were trying to do now in this newly established halfway house could never have been attempted within the reformatory. The interior regime of the reformatory would not permit it, tradition would not permit it, and the other old-line correctional officers would not permit it, because they have been so hardened and accustomed to systems of restraint, not treatment. The guards transferred from the reformatory to this halfway house were carefully selected from among those who had not yet been completely hardened by years of confinement with prisoners under repressive conditions. They had not yet been so brutalized that they could not adapt to a regime in an open institution that was without guards, without bars, and that operated with a minimum of regulations.

There is a pragmatic reason in addition to the humanitarian for urging an extension of alternatives to the traditionally walled institution. Figures have already been cited on the tremendous burden of the cost of crime which lies heavily upon all countries, regardless of their stage of development. Not included in those costs is the failure on the part of our fixed institutions to either reform, correct, or rehabilitate. The first truly scientific followup study of the graduates of one of the oldest and most respected reformatories discovered a recidivism rate of almost 80 percent.[37] Since then, successive studies have confirmed that upwards of 50 percent, ranging to a high of two-thirds of the men released from penal institutions, go back to lives of crime.[38] Of all men in the correctional institutions of Massachusetts, upwards of two-thirds had previously spent time in training schools when they were boys.[39]

No other institution in our society with such a consistently high rate of failure would be permitted to endure. Any hospital which received back over one-half of its released patients a few months later with the same conditions for which they had first been admitted, would certainly lead us to doubt their ability to deal with health problems. There are fallacies, of course, in comparing medical institutions with prisons. But hospitals are known to infect their patients with diseases they did not manifest when they came in—like those caused by strepticocci. The hospital is increasingly anxious to get people out as fast as they are capable of coping on the outside. So should prisons.

Brooke House, a halfway house for men released from Massachusetts correctional institutions, has been in operation since 1965. From this one center, its services have been expanded to include two residences for parolees, a drop-in center, a credit union (the first in the country in a halfway house for offenders), a drug-treatment program, a nonresidential walk-in center for releases from the county house of correction, and a facility which provides a 30-day housing service. Most recently it has undertaken a program for training personnel in the community correctional field [40]

"In July 1971, a comprehensive study was begun of the 58 men who lived at Brooke House in 1968. Follow-up now reveals that of these 58 men, 41 men (70.7) percent have not recidivated. This places the recidivism rate for the House at 29.3 percent—as against the overall recidivism rate in the state of 68 percent.

"Brooke House costs about $1,000 per man for the average of three months of residency, and successfully rehabilitates almost 71 percent of its graduates. The state correctional system costs about $13,000 per man (two years at $6,500 per year) and successfully rehabilitates only 32 percent of its graduates. The arithmetic shows that Brooke House costs run about $7,414 for each successful case, while the state system costs about $40,625 for each successful case."[41]

This simple arithmetic sums up the case for alternatives to traditional forms of penal treatment: the community cannot only deal with a large proportion of convicted offenders more cheaply than can any institution; it provides at the same time the surest crime preventive action, pointing the way back to a simpler time when society coped with the problems which arise from people living together. To round the argument out, it reflects the solicitude which should mark a humane society concerned for those who fail by reason of the larger failures of society itself.

NOTES

1. *Planning for Criminal and Juvenile Justice* (Los Angeles: Public Systems Research Institute, 1970).
2. *Summary of the White Paper on Crime* (Tokyo: Research and Training Institute, Ministry of Justice, 1973), Table 13, p. 28.
3. Oliver J. Keller, Jr. and Benedict S. Alper, *Halfway Houses: Community-Centered Correction and Treatment* (Lexington, Massachusetts: D.C. Heath, 1970), Chapter 6.
4. Benedict S. Alper and Jerry F. Boren, *Crime: International Agenda* (Lexington, Mass.: D.C. Heath, 1971), pp. 12–13.
5. Jacques Godechot, *The Taking of the Bastille* (New York: Scribners, 1970).
6. Lord Byron, *The Prisoner of Chillon and Other Poems* (1816) (Menston, England: Scholar Press, 1969).
7. Philip Slater, *The Pursuit of Loneliness* (Boston: Beacon Press, 1970), pp. 15–16.
8. Nathaniel Hawthorne, *The Scarlet Letter* (Boston: Ticknor, Reed & Fields, 1850).
9. Edwin M. Schur, *Labeling Deviant Behavior: Its Sociological Implications* (New York: Harper & Row, 1971).
10. Testimony of Dr. Don Hardesty, before the United States Senate Subcommittee on Juvenile Delinquency, Washington, August 27, 1970.
11. *Furman* v. *Georgia,* 92 S. Ct. 2726 (1972).
12. In Japan, a sentenced offender is deprived of his civil rights only for the duration of his imprisonment; these are restored to him upon release.
13. Statistic furnished by the Director, Research Training Institute, Ministry of Justice, Tokyo, May 1973.
14. Gresham Sykes, *Crime and Society* (New York: Random House, 1967), p. 166.
15. Harry Elmer Barnes and Negley K. Teeters, *New Horizons in Criminology* (Englewood Cliffs, N.J.: Prentice-Hall, 1945), p. 107.
16. *The Open Correctional Institution in Asia and the Far East* (New York: United Nations Report No. TAO/AFE/14, January 28, 1965).

17. "Homenaje al Coronel Montesinos," in *Revista de Estudios Penitenciarios* (Madrid: Dirección General de Prisiónes, Vol. XVIII, No. 159, October–December, 1962).

18. John Vincent Barry, *Alexander Maconochie of Norfolk Island: A Study of a Pioneer in Penal Reform* (London: Oxford University Press, 1958).

19. McKelvey Blake, *American Prison: A Study in American Social History Prior to 1915* (Montclair, New Jersey: Patterson Smith, 1968), p. 26.

20. David Rothman, *The Discovery of the Asylum* (Boston: Little, Brown, 1971), pp. 440–41.

21. B. Hollants, *Social Action and Welfare in Belgium* (New York: Belgian Government Information Center, 1950); John D.J. Moore, "What Geel Means to Me," *Look Magazine*, May 23, 1961; Matthew P. Dumont, "Is St. Dymphna's Tradition Doomed?" *Context*, Vol. II, No. 2 (Fall 1961), pp. 11–14; Jan Sjöby, "Extraordinary Ordinary Town," *International Herald Tribune*, November 30, 1973.

22. See Leslie Wilkins, *Social Deviance, Social Policy, Action and Research* (Englewood Cliffs, New Jersey: Prentice-Hall, 1965), p. 102.

23. Henry Greenbaum, ed., *The Practice of Community Mental Health* (Boston: Little, Brown, 1970), see also David Landy and Milton Greenblatt *Halfway House* [U.S. Dept. of Health, Education, and Welfare] (Washington: U.S. Government Printing Office, 1965).

24. David J. Rothman, "Of Prisons, Asylums, and Other Decaying Institutions," *Public Interest* (Winter 1972), pp. 3–4.

25. *Non-Institutional Treatment of Offenders in Japan* (Tokyo: Rehabilitation Bureau, Ministry of Justice, 1970), pp. 18–19.

26. *Summary of the White Paper on Crime*, op. cit., Table 20, p. 34.

27. Information furnished by the Research Training Institute, Ministry of Justice, Tokyo, May 1973.

28. Note by the Secretary General of the United Nations, *op. cit.*, p. 20.

29. Statement by Connecticut Commissioner Francis H. Mahoney, quoted in *Impact* (Raleigh, N.C.), Vol. 1, No. 6 (June–July 1973), p. 1.

30. State Reformatory for Women, Skowhegan, under the Department of Mental Health and Corrections.

31. *National Prison Statistics* (Washington: Bureau of Prisons, April 1963).

32. *Kriminal Varden* [The Correctional System] (Stockholm: National Correctional Administration, 1971), p. 12.

33. Ibid., 1969, p. 15.

34. Leslie A. Bostic, "Effective Treatment Programs in Halfway Settings for Delinquent and Pre-delinquent Youth," in *Proceedings: Seventh Annual Interagency Workshop* (Huntsville, Texas: Institute of Contemporary Corrections and Behavioral Science, June 1972), p. 198.

35. George Bernard Shaw, *The Crime of Imprisonment* (New York: Philosophical Library, 1946), p. 18.

36. Eleanor Glueck and Sheldon Glueck, *Later Criminal Careers* (New York: Commonwealth Fund, 1973), Chapter 10.

37. Ibid., *500 Criminal Careers* (New York: Knopf, 1930), pp. 201–202.

38. Gresham Sykes, op. cit., p. 7.

39. Cited in a speech by Dr. Jerome Miller, Commissioner, Massachusetts Department of Youth Services, at Boston College, May 18, 1972.

40. Massachusetts Halfway House, Inc., *Annual Report* (Boston: MHH, Vol. III, No. 3, January-February 1973), p. 8 [307 Huntington Ave., Boston, Mass.]. It is interesting to note that the bad-debt rate amounted to 5.6 percent of the total loans made as against a bad debt rate of 7 percent on federally granted student loans.

41. Ibid. (Vol. II, No. 2, April 1972), p. 5.

Chapter Three

Alternatives to Jail Detention— Awaiting Trial

THE COMMON JAIL

After arrest, the next step confronting an accused defendant is the likelihood of a period in jail awaiting trial (unless he is otherwise freed while he awaits court action). If he is appealing the decision of the first court which has heard his case, he is similarly detained. It should be made clear at this point that although jails do contain some persons on short sentences, their main function is to detain people for court action, whereas prisons are used to confine long-term prisoners.

In recent years there has been much argument over the role of the jail in the control of crime. Because some persons released on bail have committed additional offenses while their original case was still pending, there has been a movement to detain persons who are deemed to present a continued danger to the community or are suspected of intent to commit a new offense, under what is called "preventive detention." The constitutional implications of denying a suspected offender the right to bail because he *might* commit additional crimes while he is awaiting trial on the instant offense are grave. There is the added difficulty that psychiatry has not yet developed any precise device for predicting future "dangerous" conduct, as has been pointed out in a recently published debate.[1]

So far, the District of Columbia is the only jurisdiction that operates under a law which makes it possible to detain a suspect preventively, if the court determines that he should not be allowed at large pending his court hearing. Otherwise, and in other jurisdictions, the only reason defendants may be detained is to assure their presence in court on the appointed day. Persons charged with a very heinous crime may have bail set at a million dollars or more. Some jurisdictions do not permit release on bail of anyone charged with such offenses.

25

Conversely, if the defendant can put up the bail bond, or raise it from others, or procure it through a bondsman by putting up a percentage of the bail set by the court, he can go free.

This is a critical area in the criminal justice system, because for many defendants, jail is their first exposure to imprisonment. The following instances were cited by President Johnson following the signing of the Federal Bail Reform Act of 1965: "(1) A man spent two months in jail before being acquitted. In that period, he lost his job, and his car, and his family was split up. He did not find another job for four months. (2) A man could not raise $300 bail. He spent 54 days in jail awaiting trial for a traffic offense, for which he could have been sentenced to no more than five days. (3) A man was jailed on a serious charge brought last Christmas Eve. He could not afford bail and spent 101 days in jail until a hearing. Then the complainant admitted the charge was false." [2]

About half of all persons put in jails are there for the first time. It is therefore important to determine what sort of a place the jail is, generally speaking. Before doing that, it is necessary to assert one of the very basic principles of the common law with reference to offenders. Of ancient origin, it has been won only after long struggle, starting with the nobles who pried the Magna Carta out of King John in 1215 at Runnymede. It is written into the Bill of Rights in our own Constitution, and stands today as a cardinal principle, though often lost sight of and disregarded. This is the *presumption of innocence.* Every person charged with a crime is presumed innocent until and unless he is found guilty by due process of law—that is, by a procedure which protects his constitutional rights. While this presumption is cavalierly regarded in some places and at certain times, it is one of those precepts whose meaning becomes clearer when confronted with its opposite: what would it say about a society which operated on the presumption that every accused was guilty until he had proved his innocence?

"No matter which is the alternative," points out a recent report from Venezuela, "the truth of the matter is that the State should compensate the individual for the time spent illegally in jail (a form of kidnapping) and for the material and moral damages that confinement caused him. If not, we are confronted with a clear violation of Human Rights and the Venezuelan Constitution." [3]

It is asking too much to expect that we will ever get 100 percent compliance with the principle of the presumption of innocence, so that every arrested person is treated as if he were completely innocent. The presumption may not carry too much weight when in order to make an arrest a police officer must presume guilt, given reasonable or probable grounds for believing that an offense has been committed by a particular person. But because this is so at the arrest stage does not mean that we should not insist on respect for the principle at every subsequent stage. Immediately after arrest, the presumption must stand. The manner in which presumably innocent persons are received and treated in our jails awaiting court action would seem to give the lie to the viability of that presumption, by reason of the low level of care and treatment extended to persons detained there.

To what degree is that presumption honored in the places where persons are detained while awaiting trial? The following description is only the most recent of a series of critiques of jails which goes back at least 200 years to the time of John Howard.

"In April, 1972, Judges Spaeth, Smith and Williams found that detention in all three Philadelphia Prisons constitutes cruel and unusual punishment, and ordered the Philadelphia Prisons to comply with the law . . .

"The judges found filth, rats, roaches and intolerable living conditions.

"Such elements as food, clothing and shelter are inadequate. The daily food budget of 96¢ per day, per inmate, is not sufficient to provide a decent diet. The food is prepared in unsanitary conditions. Provision for special diets (to meet medical or religious needs) is poor. Clothing is inadequate, and laundry services are so poorly managed that most inmates do their own by hand. Cells are poorly heated, poorly ventilated, and often leak water.

"Minimal hygienic needs, such as soap, toothpaste, toothbrushes, deodorant, and towels are only sometimes issued on arrival, and must be purchased thereafter.

"Medical and dental services are dangerously scarce. Inmates must pay for fillings and other dental work apart from extractions. Without $20 in his account, one cannot even receive an eye examination, much less glasses. There is a backlog of 300 people waiting for consultation services at Philadelphia General Hospital." [4]

There was a time—not long ago—when there was little hope that traditional police use of the third degree, the forced confession, the application of physical brutality and even torture to "get the accused to talk" would ever be abandoned. Yet in the few short years since the Warren Court reasserted the protective clauses of the Bill of Rights with regard to due process, police practices have been improved in many jurisdictions. The accused today may not be subjected to the third degree, he must have counsel and access to outside communication. The change was brought about by citizen campaigns, by civil liberties groups, and by socially-minded lawyers. The recent cases brought before the courts, especially the federal bench, asserting jails to be places of "cruel and unusual punishment" may mark the ushering in of a new day in the long and brutal history of these places.

Meanwhile, the magnitude of the jail problem may be seen from the fact that in 1960 there were in the United States over 10,000 local jails and 3,000 county jails.[5] In Massachusetts, approximately 24,000 persons are released in a year from jails and houses of correction (county institutions)—

ten times as many as are released from state prisons and reformatories.[6]
In Illinois, forty times as many men pass through jails and lock-ups pending
trials as pass through the penal institutions for sentenced prisoners: 160,000
as against 4,000.[7] Hans Mattick, one of the co-authors of the report just
cited, who had been for some years Assistant Sheriff in Chicago in charge of
the Cook County Jail, describes the jails as "the Cloacal Region of American
Corrections"; in simple language, the jail in the United States is a sewer, as was
the Cloaca Maxima in Rome in ancient times, and up to today.

An American Friends Service Committee study of 600 inmates
awaiting trial found that one-third of them had been locked up for three
months or more, 23 for more than a year, and 4 for more than two years.[8]

Some notion of the costs of jail detention may be gathered from
the estimate by the President's Commission report that supervision of detainees by just one correctional officer requires approximately five full-time
officers working 40 hours a week, at least $30,000 annually if each officer
receives $6,000.[9] These costs should be increased by the inflationary effect
on prison administration—like the cost of living generally—in the past seven
years.

Jails are chiefly for detention, but more than one-half of the inmates of local and county jails are there for reasons other than conviction of a
crime. A national jail survey in 1971 discovered 8,000 juveniles in confinement.[10] Sometimes both accused and sentenced persons are not fully segregated from one another, but are forced to mingle with one another, at least
for some portion of the day.[11] "Few responsible jailers have ever asserted
that a short jail term will have a constructive influence on such problems, and
most jailers will admit that such [short] sentences tend to exaggerate the very
condition they are designed to ameliorate."[12]

Said the President's Commission Report in 1967: " There is a
need to incarcerate those criminals who are dangerous. . . . However, for the
large bulk of offenders, particularly the youthful, institutional commitments
can cause more problems than they solve. Institutions tend to isolate offenders
from society both physically and psychologically, cutting them off from
school, jobs, families and other supportive influences and increasing the probability that the label criminal will be indelibly impressed upon them."

"A released defendant is one who can live with and support his
family, maintain his ties to the community, and busy himself with his own
defense by searching for witnesses and evidence and by keeping in close touch
with his lawyer. An imprisoned defendant is subjected to the squalor, idleness
and possibly criminalizing effects of jail."[13]

Clarence Darrow said of them, seventy years ago: "There should
be no jails, they do not accomplish what they pretend to accomplish. If you
would wipe them out there would be no more criminals than now. They

terrorize nobody. They are a blot upon any civilization, and a jail is an evidence of the lack of charity of the people on the outside who make the jails and fill them with the victims of their greed."[14]

In Massachusetts, in the old city of Salem, the county jail has two wings, a modern and a not so modern. The new section was built in 1880, the older section in 1830. Both wings are still used today to house people presumed to be innocent.

But there are factors other than the humanitarian to consider when alternative forms of control are advocated. The economic factor is one. Loss of productivity results when a person who is charged with an offense is locked up in a jail. If he does not work, his family has to be supported—most likely from welfare funds. There is the further expense of feeding and guarding him. For all these costs, there is no offsetting benefit. Therefore, from the economic point of view alone, it can be argued that no person should have his life disrupted by being locked up in jail awaiting trial or appeal unless there is a very substantial reason for doing so: namely, that he may otherwise not appear for trial.

While cost is an important factor in keeping persons out of jail who can be otherwise handled, in cases of drunkenness—much of it chronic—this cost factor is multiplied by as many times as an individual public drunkard comes into and passes through the criminal justice system. The cost factor in recidivism was the subject of a recent study in Los Angeles County, where the Antelope Valley Rehabilitation Centers received in 1967 a total of 1,198 drunkenness offenders from the courts. The study compared the number of drunk arrests of a sample accumulated during the year preceding the arrest of an individual with the number of arrests for the same offense during the year following his discharge. For the sample of 713 men (out of the total received in 1967) who have been referred to rehabilitation rather than being committed to jail, recycling through the courts was reduced by 46 percent during their first post-treatment year, a reversal of what had previously been an opposite trend. In terms of dollars saved, the study concluded that greater savings were realized through reduced arrest and arraignment frequencies than through reduced jail time, itself a saving. At the end of the first post-treatment year, estimated savings to the justice system ranged from 69 percent to 95 percent of what it cost to operate the rehabilitation centers. This figure does not include costs or savings attributable to arrests for other offenses, the wages earned by men who would otherwise have been jailed, or welfare payments that would otherwise have been received.[15]

There is the further fact that approximately one-half of all persons who have spent time in jail are ultimately dismissed or released by the courts. Thereafter they find themselves back on the street: because the charges against them have been dropped, or they are found innocent, or placed on probation, with or without a suspended sentence. It is difficult to think up a convincing answer to the question of why a person should be locked up *before* trial when in one-half of the instances, he is not sent to prison *after* he has been tried. At least one-half of the entire cost of keeping people in jail is thus wasted, to say nothing of the consequent disruption to the families and the employment of people thus detained.

Any measures that can be taken, therefore, to keep people out of jail, to keep them on the street, will save them from the brutal experience of living in a dirty and overcrowded place where they are demeaned and made less than human as a consequence of their detention. It will save them from idleness and the greatest sin in the world—boredom.

In most jails, men spend as much as 22 hours a day by themselves—alone—doing absolutely nothing, in their narrow cells. One of the reasons for riots in jails, as in prisons, is boredom, which can arouse to the point where people will kill or take a chance on being killed, if only to have some activity, some excitement, some use of their bodies and minds.[16] Health is adversely affected when the only exercise is walking around in a small enclosed area. The food is universally dreadful.

The Charles Street Jail in Boston was built in 1848. Detainees complain that it is bug-ridden, and until recently, pigeons could fly in from the outside while the men were eating. In 1972 the detainees brought a class action suit before the federal district court, and through counsel asked the court to determine that the conditions under which they were being kept constituted undue cruelty.[17] The basis of the suit was that because a person is detained for trial, even on most serious charges, he is not thereby—and in the process—to be held under conditions which violate the "cruel and unusual" provisions of the federal Constitution. the judge of the federal court, before whom the case was brought, decided to spend the night in the jail to see for himself what it was like. He evidently had some advance suspicion as to what he might experience, for he had the good sense to dine at an excellent French restaurant nearby before being locked up for the night.

In a footnote to his opinion, describing his one-night's stay, the judge wrote, "The noise seemed to increase after midnight and approached a virtual bedlam which lasted until dawn. At least a dozen radios, tuned to various rock music stations, seemed to be turned up to full volume; and for hours from a nearby cell, whether above or below we couldn't tell, a deep-voiced inmate, evidently deranged, shouted an obscene, incoherent monologue . . . ."

After the case was heard, that same judge handed down his decision ordering that after June 30, 1976, no inmate awaiting trial may be assigned to that jail, thus ending the ancient pile.[18] One of the issues which determined this decision was the court's finding that 85 percent of the jail's population had not been convicted of the offenses for which they had been arrested and awaiting trial. The judge also found that the conditions to which detainees were being subjected while being held for trial were worse than those of sentenced prisoners confined in the state's penal institutions. Pending abolition of the jail, the court further ordered mandatory physical examinations for all persons confined for more than one week and for all kitchen workers and food handlers; free institutional laundry and institutional clothing for all who needed it; free time outside the cell of no less than four hours each day, not including meal time; extension of hours for attorneys as well as for family and friends to include evenings, Sundays and holidays; access to unmonitored telephones, and only limited censorship of mail.

The possible implications of the state's refusal to provide a new or alternate facility may confront it with the possibility, quoted from the 1971 Arkansas case of *Hamilton* vs. *Love*: "If the state cannot obtain the resources to detain persons awaiting trial in accordance with minimum constitutional standards, then the state simply will not be permitted to detain such persons."[19]

Conditions such as were found and finally outlawed in this county jail are by no means uncommon, though they may sound notorious when described on paper. John Howard reported in England 200 years ago of a disease known as jail fever.[20] When Howard traveled from one jail to another to make his visits of inspection, he did not use the public transportation of that time, the stagecoach, because he smelled so badly from having spent time in jails that nobody would sit near him. He died of that same fever. So offensive was the smell of the jails of those days that when a defendant came into court to appear before the judge, the court officer would precede him, carrying a bouquet of flowers, to save the nose of the judge from the stench of the defendant.

BAIL VS. JAIL

Persons who are awaiting trial on bail, or on recognizance (their own word, or the word of another, trustworthy, person) that they will appear for trial when wanted, walk into the courtroom on their own, accompanied, if by anyone, by their lawyers, family and friends. They will have had an opportunity to bathe, to put on fresh clothes and eat breakfast before facing the ordeal before them. The next defendant who comes into court comes in not from the street, he comes in from the jail. He probably wears the same clothes that he was picked up in by the police weeks—or even months ago. He has no hot water; the food he has eaten has been of bad quality and poorly prepared. He has not been out in the fresh air and the sun, so he looks gray. His appearance before the court gives a first impression of an unhealthy man, not a very personable man—whether he is truly guilty or not—because of the way he has been treated while he was awaiting trial. When he appears in court—pale, thin, and badly shaven—he presents the image of a man not quite so easily presumed innocent as the one who comes in off the street looking neat and fresh. In the county court house in Dedham, Massachusetts, up until about eight years ago, defendants who were free on bail entered and took their seats in the open court. But a defendant who was held in jail came in through the back door and sat in a cage in the court room. What is the likely effect on judge or jury of seeing a man in a cage, and how can a man be presumed to be innocent if he has to be kept in a cage in the court while he is standing trial?

THE JAIL AS TEACHER

One of the most vicious effects of a jail experience is that it exposes people— especially the first offender—to a course of higher education in crime. Any number of persons, especially young persons, become professional auto thieves and burglars while they are awaiting trial. A fifteen-year-old boy interviewed in an adult jail, on a charge of having stolen more than 70 cars, freely described his early experience. The first auto he stole when he was 15 had the keys in it. Arrested and sent to jail to await trial, he was taught by the other inmates how to steal a car without keys, thereby becoming a professional auto thief.

A young college student, arrested and jailed after participating in an antiwar demonstration, was approached by his cellmate who was awaiting trial on a racket charge, to join his organized gang. When the young man refused, he was threatened with reprisal. He finally agreed, reluctantly, when he knew that he would appear in court before his cellmate, and would be out and away before the latter would be released.[21]

Truman Capote tells the true story of the frightful murder of an entire family by two psychopaths released from the Kansas State Penitentiary, who had learned from another prisoner the location, the name, the floor plan of the house, and the daily schedule of a rich farmer in that State.[22] When the two left the penitentiary, they went to his farm to get his money, and failing in that attempt, slaughtered him and his wife and two children.

When people are placed in confinement, society runs the risk of improving their education and making them more efficient burglars, thieves, or counterfeiters—or even murderers—than when they first went in. We cannot do away with all jails or jail detention for all defendants any more than we can do away with imprisonment for all prisoners. But the more people are kept out of institutions, the less is the state paying to educate people to be better criminals than they were before.

Homosexuality is a problem in all institutions, jails as well as prisons. Many young boys are introduced to homosexuality by force for the first time in jails, where they might not otherwise have had that experience. "Scottsboro Boy" describes the practice of forced submission of younger boys and men to the protection—and sexual exploitation—of the older, stronger, and more ruthless "husbands" in an institution in the South. "A gal-boy would spend a few years like that in Ardmore. Then they would let him out, maybe when he was twenty-one or so. That is why, I later learned, the Negro sections of the Northern cities have so many gal-boys in the streets today. The Southern prisons breed them." [23]

SPEEDY TRIAL

Given these disadvantages, what can be done to reduce the necessity for detention in jail? One of the first steps to be taken is speedy trial. If some of the money presently spent on jail detention, on imprisonment, on the police, or on arrests for offenses that are really not a menace to society, could be applied to speeding up the trial process, it would greatly reduce the necessity for keeping people in jail. Some detainees await trial for two and up to three years. Part of that delay is occasioned by obstructions of the defense counsel, part by the prosecution. If the cost of keeping just one man in jail for two or even three years were spent on judges to speed up the process, how many additional cases could be cleared from the docket with those same dollars? Speedy trial, as Beccaria has said, like sureness of apprehension, is one of the most important factors in reducing crime. It is no surprise, therefore, to read of a move to limit by law the length of time a person may be detained in jail.

Trial within sixty to ninety days is adequate, because the greater the lapse of time between arrest and trial, the greater is the chance that the truly guilty will escape. The public and the prosecutor is not so interested after 90 days as when the offense is first committed; witnesses move away, die, or forget; the victim after 90 days may not be so insistent in having his assailant brought to trial. Immediacy diminishes with the passage of time.

The confidence of the general public in the criminal justice system is based on the assurance that when a crime is reported, the police will make an arrest, and the suspect will be speedily tried. Anything which weakens that assurance—police inefficiency or corruption, or failure to bring a suspect to book—will inevitably lead to a decrease in the number of offenses brought to police notice. Criminals who are aware of the hesitancy of their intended victims to report crimes can only be emboldened to commit further criminal acts.

FEUDS IN PAKISTAN

The adverse effect of delays in hearing cases, particularly murder cases, is described in the following statement made by a Deputy Inspector of Police in Pakistan. The circumstances of life in his country resembles ours not at all, especially in the prevalence of feuds between families, which does not wholly deprive the following statement of relevance at this point.

"Crime in Pakistan is on the increase like in many other countries: though the rate of increase is very low. Beside corruption in the lower ranks of police, and unemployment, the major cause of increase in offenses against persons is the inordinate delay in the trial of cases. This has an adverse affect for reasons more than one.

"To begin with, 85 percent of the people in Pakistan live in villages. The society is homogeneous. Their love of hatred lasts for years unless it is settled by local interference or by a quick process of law. In case a person is murdered or grievously hurt, the accused is normally arrested quickly and sent for trial. Due to acute shortages of magistrates/judges, such cases linger in the courts for months together and sometimes for years.

"I can safely say, basing my remarks on my twenty years stay in the police, that a big percentage of my offenses against the person is due to personal enmity and delay in trials. I can at this stage quote a specific instance.

"In September 1970, I was asked by the Governor of Punjab to visit the jail in Gujrat, a district in Punjab, which has the highest number of murders in Pakistan. The Governor had received numerous complaints from the jail inmates. As I went to inspect the jail, I received a large number of written applications from those under trial. They had only one grievance— that their cases were pending in courts for the last two to three years. I examined the statistics and found that there were nearly 300 murder cases pending. The District has two Session judges to try these cases. By rough estimate, an accused arrested today would come up for trial only after four years. What happens under such a situation is known to all the District Police: there is a chain of murders. I remember that in one case there had been five to six murders in a family—one as a result of the other."[24]

On a recent visit to an institution in Japan which houses both sentenced prisoners and persons detained for trial, a young man from Hong Kong, charged with violation of the narcotics law, was found to have been awaiting trial for nine months. Like others in the same plight, in the same wing, he spent all but forty minutes of the day behind a locked door in a cubicle. Other detainees were reported to have been jailed as long as thirty-two months. When asked the reason for the limited period allowed for exercise, the warden replied that he did not have sufficient personnel to supervise a longer period. The reason given by him for not permitting any association between persons awaiting trial was that "they might destroy evidence." But the presumption, to be properly regarded, can only suffer when those who have yet to stand trial are—as in this instance—given no benefit of the doubt by being locked in their cells for twenty-three and a half hours a day. The sharing of a common law procedure—though, in this instance, not the tradition— does not seem to mitigate the inhumanity of cellular confinement anywhere.

Since 1947, Japan is committed to the principle of the presumption of innocence. Their expert and intensive prosecutory procedures, screen out almost one-third of accused penal code offenders for suspension of prosecution on various grounds. The public prosecutor has the power to decide whether or not to prosecute, even though there is sufficient evidence to secure a conviction, but his actual decisions are not as capricious as may appear from this simply stated fact. His ruling is subject to review, after it has been made, on the basis of the offender's character, age, previous record, offense, and circumstances under which it was committed. The degree of harm caused the victim and society, the degree of premeditation, the offender's willingness to make restitution and the attitude of the victim are all weighed.

Decisions by the public prosecutor to suspend prosecution are reviewed by a citizens' "Committee for the Inquest of Prosecution." Members are drawn by lot from a list of citizens of the district covered by the particular court. The choice resembles the procedure for naming grand jurors, on which it was patterned. Should the committee determine that the prosecutor's decision to suspend was not justified, they may recommend to the Chief Prosecutor's Office that the case be reexamined. A victim in any criminal case, or any other citizen, may also appeal to the committee for a review of the case. It is reported that of some 2,000 such appeals in a recent year, 10 percent were recommended for prosecution.

This unique system of submitting the discretionary decisions of the prosecution to citizen review is said to have the full support of the Japanese public. One reason may be found in the fact that prosecutors, unlike elected district attorneys in the United States, are specifically trained professionals, appointed civil servants serving without regard to party or to electoral results. Their status is, thus, similar to that of Japanese judges who are also appointive officers of the court.[25]

BAIL REFORM

Bail is an ancient way of assuring the appearance in court of the defendant, because if he is going to suffer the possibility of monetary loss, he will be more likely to appear for trial. Bail is also one of the most discriminatory practices to be found in the criminal court process, flagrantly favoring the well-to-do. If the defendant is ultimately acquitted, poverty alone has, in a sense, been made a crime punished by an irretrievable loss of liberty, often for a substantial period in the company of convicted criminals. Considerations such as these prompted Justice Douglas to ask, "Can an indigent be denied freedom, where a wealthy man would not, because he does not happen to have enough property to pledge for his freedom?"[26]

A recent study answers this question. Based on an analysis of cases coming before the lower criminal courts of metropolitan Boston in 1969, the study discovered that poor defendants (those earning less than $75 per week), were found guilty in 59 percent of the cases, while the nonpoor (those earning more than $100 per week) were found guilty in only 40 percent of the cases. Twice as many of the poor as the nonpoor received jail sentences; 25 percent as against 13 percent. These are the results of the hearing of the charges against them. But, while they were waiting for their hearings, 25 percent of the poor defendants were committed to jail for failure to make bail, compared to 19 percent for the nonpoor.[27]

In Philadelphia, a recent study of jail defendants by the highly respected Pennsylvania Prison Society concludes that "for those who are incarcerated pending trial, the major crime is usually poverty. Being behind bars makes it impossible to raise money for a private attorney, forces families on welfare, and makes it virtually hopeless for the defendant to assist his attorney in the preparation of a defense to his case. Private counsel are unwilling to return to the prison for multiple conferences and trial preparation. The trip out to Holmesburg Jail and back may consume an entire day for an attorney. Often, only the defendant himself knows how to reach and can convince his witnesses to come forth to assist him in his defense. Being in prison prior to trial provides a distinct and unjustified advantage to the prosecution and a disadvantage to the defendant."[28]

The result of such findings across the country is a spate of different schemes to make bail more easily available, less profitable to private bail bondsmen and others with an inside track, at the same time assuring the appearance in court of defendants when their cases are called. Instead of paying a bail commissioner 10 percent of $1,000 of the bail set by the court, for example, for which the bail commissioner promises to pay that amount to the court in case the defendant defaults, the bail-cash law works on a different basis. On a bail requirement of $1,000, the defendant gives the court $100 (10 percent), or $50 (5 percent), and then if he does not show up in court, he is responsible for the rest of his bail. If he does show, his deposit is returned to him. This is one very good way of making it possible for people who are not rich to be free while awaiting trial. One variation or another of this bail-cash deposit system is now in effect in a growing number of jurisdictions.

Another progressive trend in recent years, notably exemplified by Illinois, requires a cash deposit from the defendant for whom a money bail has been set.[29] He may gain his release by depositing with the court 10 percent of the amount. Under this system, when the defendant returns for trial, the clerk returns to him 90 percent of his original deposit. As an alternative, he may deposit the full amount of bail in cash, in securities, or double the amount in real estate.

Illinois considers their deposit system a success in that the rate of default under the plan is reported to be no greater than under the professional bail bond system which it has replaced. In the Massachusetts pilot program, patterned on that of Illinois, the cash deposit was 5 percent of bail with the total returned to the defendant when he shows for trial. Preliminary results indicate a lower rate of defaults under the plan as compared with the previous year: in one court the default figure dropped from 19.7 percent to 16.2 percent; in another, the drop was from 24.2 percent to 18.3 percent. This bail-cash-deposit system has eliminated the need for reliance on the professional bondsman—a prime source of corruption of criminal justice—in the areas where it exists.

The Vera Foundation in New York has helped to reduce the detention population under a pioneering experiment which permitted persons who could not afford bail to live at home, pursuing their ordinary routine, and to come into court on the day their case is called on the basis of a simple summons.[30] Describing 25,000 defendants in sixty similar projects throughout the nation who were released without bail for a four-year period, it is reported that only 400 of them, or 1.6 percent, did not return to stand trial.[31]

RELEASE ON RECOGNIZANCE

Another historic form of release awaiting trial is through recognizance—that is, release on one's word, on one's honor. It derives from the same source as does the oath in court, as "parole," which is used for after-care, originates from the French, meaning literally, "I give my word." Release can be granted to a defendant on his own word, or on that of a reputable person, his employer for instance, that he will appear in court when wanted, in lieu of being confined.

"In Oklahoma a program has been developed which permits a defendant to be released into the custody of his attorney. Excluded are persons with previous felony convictions, and those convicted in the previous six months of an offense involving moral turpitude. Failure to produce his client in court results in removal of the attorney from the approved list. Nearly 200 defendants a month gain release through this program, while during its first nine months only 13 attorneys had their names removed from the list."[32]

Additional release alternatives applicable to all offenses except those punishable by death are based on the principle that a charged person should be released on his personal recognizance unless a judge believes that this will result in the risk of his defaulting. For example, the Massachusetts Bail Reform Act of 1970 provides that the court which admits a person to bail should consider such factors as the nature and circumstances of the offense charged, family ties, financial resources, employment record, history of mental illness, reputation, length of residence in the community, record of conviction or flight to avoid prosecution, and failure to appear in court. The act provides that a defendant's ties to his community, rather than merely the seriousness of the charge against him and any record of past convictions, are the important determinants in any decision whether to detain or to permit release.

The basic provisions of this Release on Recognizance Act (ROR) are also in effect in New York state.[33] There, however, jail officials must formally verify the basic information on the defendant by telephone or personal followup, and on the basis of those verified responses, recommend to the court either release or nonrelease. The defendant recommended for pretrial parole after verification stands a two to three times greater chance of being released without bail than one who is investigated and not so recommended.

Under another related program—conditional or provisional release—the court may restrict the freedom of a released defendant by requiring him to maintain contact with the court or other law enforcement agency or impose other appropriate conditions such as release to the custody of a third person or agency-organization, halfway house, mental health clinic or hospital for psychiatric, medical or counseling aid, a police or probation officer. The judge determines the method of release and the frequency of contact required. Failure to abide by any of the conditions for release would be communicated promptly to the court which would immediately attempt to locate the defendant and demand either bail or commitment to jail detention.

For any of these release programs to operate effectively, the court must be provided with complete and reliable information both on the defendant and on the availability of community resources. An information collection and verification procedure as provided in New York's ROR program can be used to gather information on provisional release resources in order to develop a list of potential sponsors for released defendants, including such persons as lawyers, ministers, and employers who may be willing to stand surety for a specific defendant.

Other forms of diversion from jail include halfway houses, where persons awaiting trial may spend their time instead of in jail. Such places provide a modified form of supervision to the offender with a minimum of restriction. They are not incarcerative nor do they convey any implication of punishment. Persons awaiting trial who are not regarded as bailable can be supervised during their free periods of time such as weekends and holidays; they are free to work or go to school during the day with a minimum of disruption to their ordinary lives.

"The further development of halfway houses, and their establishment in more and more communities, would not only be an enormous aid in enabling jails to restrict their functions to detention purposes only, but would be an important element of jail reform in its own right, even if the traditional jail functions were not basically changed. A convicted prisoner who is remanded to a halfway house does not experience the sharp break in family and community ties experienced by the jailed prisoner, but he is under restriction of movement and effective supervision during the period of his sentence. If he were sitting in jail in idleness, he would be of no use to himself or others and would not be preparing for future responsible citizenship in the community. Nor would he be able to support himself and his family, or pay his debts, or accumulate any savings. The use of halfway houses, to which prisoners can return after working hours and on weekends, provides a more flexible and civilized facility for selected offenders. It offers the opportunity for counseling and guidance so that the prisoner can contribute to his own rehabilitation. By allowing the inmate to work and distributing his earnings according to some agreed-upon formula, he can help to defay the costs of his own maintenance, prevent his family from having to go on welfare, and thus save the jailing jurisdiction the expense of his incarceration. Such a system would also help the prisoner to maintain his self-respect. Altogether, the combination of the halfway house and a work-release program would reduce the high recidivism rates produced by the traditional maladjusting jail experience.

"At present, work-release programs have been well developed in four states, with highly encouraging results. In one evaluative study, it was found that of 1,700 Minnesota misdemeanants whose work-release sentences terminated in 1965, only 9 percent failed to complete their sentences successfully, and 74 percent retained their jobs."[34]

The extension of rights to sentenced prisoners is considered later in this book. It may be well to point out here, however, that as there is no law which denies the vote to persons accused of crime, nor even to convicted misdemeanants, as distinguished from felons, there is no reason why such persons should not be permitted—even encouraged—to register and to vote. It is a simple matter to arrange for registrars to be admitted to the jail to register its inmates, and the same efforts which are made to enable old people and shut-ins in nursing homes to cast their ballot could by the same system—and for the very same reasons—be introduced into jails for detainees, and for misdemeanants under sentence.

As this is being written, the Connecticut Commission of Correction has announced that the century-old jails in Hartford, New Haven, and Bridgeport are to be shortly replaced by community correctional centers to house inmates in a variety of release programs such as those described in this chapter.

NOTES

1. Jack Landau, "Preventive Detention: Public Safeguard," and Alan Dershowitz, "Preventive Detention: Social Threat," *Trial Magazine* (December-January 1969-1970), pp. 23-26.
2. *Bail and Summons: 1965* (Proceedings: Institute on the Operation of Pretrial Release Projects, New York City, Oct. 1965; Proceedings: Justice Conference on Bail and Remands in Custody, London, 1965; published, August 1966), p. xxii.

3. Rosa del Olmo, "Sentencing Practices in Caracas: Venezuela's Penal Courts," *International Journal of Criminology and Penology,* Vol. 1, No. 1 (February 1973), p. 49.
4. Pennsylvania Prison Society, "Jails" (Philadelphia, February 1973), p. 3 (dup.).
5. Gordon Misner, "Recent Developments in Metropolitan Law Enforcement," *Journal of Criminal Law, Criminology, and Police Science* (January–February, 1960), p. 502.
6. Information furnished by the Massachusetts Department of Corrections.
7. Hans W. Mattick and Alexander B. Aikman, "The Cloacal Region of American Corrections," *The Annals* [Philadelphia], Vol. 381 (January 1969), pp. 109–118.
8. Pennsylvania Prison Society, op. cit., p. 4.
9. President's Commission on Law Enforcement and the Administration of Justice, *Challenge of Crime in a Free Society* (Washington: U.S. Government Printing Office, 1967).
10. Department of Justice, Press Release, Washington, January 7, 1971.
11. At the Adult Correctional Institution at Cranston, Rhode Island, for example.
12. Mattick and Aikman, op. cit., p. 115.
13. President's Commission on Law Enforcement, op. cit., p. 9.
14. His "Address to the Prisoners in Cook County Jail, Chicago," (1902) (Corinth, Vermont: Black Mountain Press, 1969), pp. 8–9.
15. David B. Coffler and Robert G. Hadley, "The Residential Rehabilitation Center as an Alternative to Jail for Chronic Drunkenness Offenders" (unpublished paper, 1971), p. 7.
16. Bruce L. Danto, *Jail House Blues* (Orchard Lake, Michigan: Epic Publications, 1973).
17. "Friends of the Court." Included: the NAACP Legal Defense Fund, the Civil Liberties Union, and the Massachusetts Law Reform Institute.
18. Opinion and order of Judge Arthur Garrity, Jr., in the U.S. District Court of Massachusetts, Civil Action 71-162-G (June 20, 1973).
19. Ibid, footnote 8.
20. John Howard, *State of Prisons* (New York: Dutton [Everyman's Library], 1929).
21. From a personal communication to the author.
22. Truman Capote, *In Cold Blood* (New York: Random House, 1965).
23. Haywood Patterson and Earl Conrad, *Scottsboro Boy* (New York: Bantam Books, 1962), p. 68.
24. Habib-Ur-Rahman Khan, participant from Pakistan at the 33rd course at UNAFEI, to the author.
25. From a lecture by Toshihiko Tsubouchi, Public Prosecutor, on "Suspension of Prosecution in Japan," UNAFEI, 15 May, 1973.
26. *Bandy* vs. *United States,* 81 S. Ct. 197, 198 (1960). Less than a year later in *Bandy* vs. *Chambers,* 82 S. Ct. 11, 13 (1961), Mr. Justice Douglas said, "Further reflection has led me to believe that no man should be denied release because of indigence. Instead . . . a man

is to be released on 'personal recognizance' where other relevant factors make it reasonable to believe that he will comply with the orders of the court."

27. Stephen R. Bing and S. Stephen Rosenfeld, *The Quality of Justice in the Lower Courts of Metropolitan Boston* (Boston: Lawyers Committee for Civil Rights Under Law, 1971), pp. 125–126.

28. Pennsylvania Prison Society, op. cit., p. 6.

29. Ronald Goldfarb, *Ransom* (New York: Harper & Row, 1965).

30. "Bail in the United States" [Report to the National Conference on Bail and Criminal Justice, Washington, May 1964] (New York: Vera Foundation, 1964).

31. D. Freed and P. Wald, "Bail in the United States" (1964), cited in Jane H. Stein, John M. Flackett, Benedict S. Alper, Martha L. and Elliot R. Rothman, *Metropolitan Boston Detention Study* (Boston: Center for Corrections and the Law, Boston College Law School, November 1972), p. 99(n).

32. Ibid., pp. 64–66.

33. Ibid., p. 67.

34. Mattick and Aikman, op. cit., p. 111.

Chapter Four

Alternative Programs within the Jail

Given a certain proportion of persons who cannot be released on their own recognizance, or that of other persons, who are for whatever reason not considered suitable for release on bail or to the supervision of a half-way house in the community, then commitment to a jail—for as short a period of detention as possible—is the only remaining alternative. It has been pointed out in the preceding chapter that incarceration itself produces severe and traumatic consequences for almost all inmates. The objective of programs in pretrial detention is to reduce these detrimental effects by providing nonpunitive, service-oriented detention. One of the first requirements of any jail program is to provide reception procedures and record-keeping which will help to determine the needs of detainees for possible services, and to inform them of the availability of such services.

What more can be done to improve the condition under which such people are confined? Must the jail be nothing better than, in Mattick's terms, a sewer? Must it be a place where people deteriorate physically and emotionally, where unrelieved boredom inevitably prevails? Or can it be made a passably decent place where persons presumed to be innocent are held for trial? One of the difficulties is that while he is held in jail, no detainee can be compelled to work. Forced labor may be a condition of sentence, but it cannot be of detention. That is why the task of maintaining the jails is done by prisoners under sentence. They live in a separate wing of the jail and perform the necessary work which detainees cannot be forced to do.

All that can be required of a person detained for trial is that he keep his person and his quarters clean and in good order—to wash, to make his bed, to keep clean his cell. Beyond that, a man's time is his own—a bleak, unrelieved stretch of futility, anxiety and boredom. To lock people up in their cells for 22 hours a day is to provide the conditions under which they will challenge authority if only because they are given all day long to conspire against the administration, to plot escape, to exchange information about crime. Jails foster trouble, if they do not actually create it, when they do not fill the nonsleeping hours of the inmates' day other than by locking them up. Except for custom, there is no reason why a healthy adult should be compelled to keep the hours of a schoolboy by turning off his light at 9 or 10 p.m.

Many other simple programs are being made available in some advanced jurisdictions. For example, persons confined in jails worry about their families; yet most jails make no provision for the families of detainees. We do not normally regard the jails of Dickens' England as particularly enlightened or humane, yet these permitted—and made provision for—the wives and children of a detained man to live with him in jail.[1]

SOCIAL, COUNSELING, AND LEGAL SERVICES

Some jails are introducing the services of social workers or counselors to help prisoners to deal with real and pressing problems relating to their families on the outside. Many such families are on welfare. Furnishing social work services in the jail does two things. First, it helps the families on the outside, and second, it eases the mind of the prisoner inside, who is awaiting trial and worrying about them. Volunteers for such counseling services can be found among students in social work, sociology, psychology, and counseling who seek opportunities to do field work.

Closely related to this is the provision of legal services to help jail detainees with problems not related to the criminal charges under which they are being held. A defendant who was arrested, for example, on a larceny charge, may have his own lawyer or a public defender to represent him. The jail cannot be expected to furnish such criminal legal defense services. But the same detainee may have an automobile bought on installment and may be as worried about losing it as he is about the outcome of his trial. Or his wife may be threatening a divorce, and he may fear that while he is in jail he will not be properly defended. He may have a problem with the Veteran's Administration, or the welfare department; he may be anxious that if his rent is not paid his furniture will be tossed out and he will lose a place to live. He may have a case pending against him in the civil branch of the court and be unable to appear to defend himself. In-house legal services on the civil side can help prisoners with these problems. Whether of a casework or legal services nature, they can reduce anxiety and fear and help to fill the defendant's life with constructive activity, with the direct and immediate result of making the administration of the jail that much easier.

Inherent in the failure to introduce programs such as these in the great majority of local jails is the vestige of the philosophy which led to the creation of the penitentiary: if persons who have committed an offense

against society are isolated from their fellow men, relieved of the obligations
of normal living, they will utilize the resulting free time constructively. Given
an opportunity to ponder on their wrongdoing, they will come to understand
and admit their guilt, make their peace with their maker, exorcize the devil
within them—and go and sin no more. That is why the Bible was the only
book, and the minister the sole visitor permitted to persons in confinement.
The parallels between that approach to the errant criminal and the life of the
silent monk are too obvious to be more than cited—even to the similarities
in architectural arrangements between the celibate monastery and the cellular
penitentiary.

This same basic attitude still guides almost every jail in America.
Lack of imagination, a fundamental disrespect for—and fear of—inmates, plus
a scarcity of funds for such noncustodial purposes, is only the outward evidence
that the jail of today continues to pattern itself on a model that is hundreds of
years old.

The popular interchangeable usage of the words "jail" (properly:
for presumed innocent persons awaiting trial) and "prison" (properly: for
sentenced persons), as is pointed out at the beginning of Chapter 3, is an exact
reflection of an actual situation: that the public, no less than the criminal
justice administrator, regards all those caught up in the system—whether accused
or convicted—in much the same light, and treats them all alike. There *is* no perceptible difference to the inmate between being in a jail or in a prison in
America today. The implications of this fact run through the entire court-correctional process, up to and including the practice of plea bargaining.[2] At
the same time, this process makes a mockery of the avowed presumption of
innocence by failing to distinguish in any way between close confinement of
persons only *charged* with an offense and those persons who have been *found
guilty* and sentenced to imprisonment.

It has been noted that a man cannot be forced to work when he is
detained in a jail. Nor can he be forced to learn, either, any more than a student
can be made to study in school. But opportunities can be provided for him to
do so if he wishes. There are men awaiting trial in jail who will take advantage
of such opportunities if offered, if only because they have nothing else to do with
their time. Forward-looking jails are therefore introducing well-stocked libraries
containing not discards, but modern books on subjects in which prisoners may
be interested.[3]

The late Malcolm X describes his early life—he was a "bad hombre"
who went to the penitentiary after conviction for burglary. There he was exposed to good books in the prison library, which had been donated by a
generous citizen. For the first time in his life, Malcolm was exposed to philosophy and science, and as he states in his autobiography, these books changed
his life.[4] There may not be many prisoners who have that degree of intellec-

tual interest, but certainly there would be more if there were more decent
books for them to read.

Some jails provide the services of an inmate librarian, a job for
which he is not paid, which he cannot be forced to do, but one which can at
least interest him. In the Middlesex County Jail in Massachusetts, through an
arrangement with the local public library, any person in jail can order any
book he wants. Each of the correctional facilities in the state of Connecticut,
including the smallest, has been making an entire law library—on microfilm—
available to all inmates. The program was the result of federal court decisions
ordering inmate access to adequate legal source materials.[5]

EDUCATIONAL, MEDICAL, AND DRUG PROGRAMS

In many cities of the North, there are large settlements of Puerto Ricans, as
there are Mexicans in the Southwest, who have difficulty with the English
language. It is difficult enough for them to find employment; if they get into
trouble and land in jail it is seldom that they find a Spanish-speaking guard
or other staff person. Here is an opportunity to help them to learn English as
a second language. This is but one example of the kind of programs which
can be made available to persons awaiting trial so that their period of detention may be used constructively. Such language teaching is done by volunteers.
As with many other programs for filling the days of persons in jail, they do
not require money. They require organization, the desire to make the necessary
arrangements, above all an attitude which is neither denigrating nor discriminatory towards persons in confinement. The Sheriff of one of the most enlightened jails in the country, where most of the programs herein described are now
in operation, refers to his inmates as "Gentlemen," and makes it a point to
call as many as possible of them by their first name.[6]

At the same time that Spanish-speaking inmates are taught English
in some jails, their instructors, some of them students of education, learn how
to teach English; this program gives them the opportunity to gain experience,
a not unimportant advantage. Considering the low educational level of most
persons confined in jail, it would appear desirable, in addition to helping relieve
the boredom of the jail, to extend the programs of short, intensive courses in
basic subjects, leading to a high school equivalency diploma, as is done in a few
jails across the country.

Recreational opportunities, athletic programs, radio, television,
movies, arts and crafts, cards, dominoes, puzzles, checkers and chess can be
made available as well. These programs need only nominal supervision by the
jail staff: part-time assistance can be provided by inmates as well as by volunteers from outside the jail.

It is a requirement of any detention system that children not be
mingled with adults. This has been a goal for penal reformers for 200 years,
but is yet to be attained in too many jurisdictions. As recently as 1967 it was
reliably reported that "an estimated 100,000 juveniles are detained in jails
and similar facilities for adults in the United States each year. . . . Only three
jurisdictions, Connecticut, Puerto Rico, and Vermont, can actually claim that
their jails are never used for children."[7] The struggle to keep children out of
such places is unending. In Massachusetts in 1970, despite statutory restrictions,
instances of fourteen- and fifteen-year-old boys being confined in a county jail
resulted in a court hearing in which the judge reasserted the ban.[8] Children
should only be detained when they cannot be kept at home, for whatever
reason, or in special juvenile detention quarters or in foster homes.

The constructive use of this period while awaiting court hearing
is well illustrated in Israel. Group sessions are part of the presentence investigation procedure for juvenile offenders. The group, most often composed of an
offender and his accomplices, meets for two or three unstructured discussion
sessions. During the first, the aims of the investigation are explained and the
offense itself discussed. In the following sessions, topics introduced by the
leader include parental reaction to the offense, school experiences, sibling
relationships, and after-school activities. These are not presented in any order
and the youngsters are free to introduce new topics. The final session usually
terminates the investigation and preparation for court hearing.

"The group discussions allow the social worker to see the juvenile
in a situation akin to his day-to-day life, especially his peer relationships. It is
also possible to learn,through the group, about the interaction that led to the
offense and the roles the various members played in it. The group-session
information has been found to be a useful supplement to data collected in
interviews and home visits."[9]

Among adult offenders, alcoholism is a serious problem; many detainees in our jails are there for drunkenness—either awaiting trial or on short
sentences, or for alcohol-related offenses. Local chapters of Alcoholics Anonymous are established in some jails to take up some of the slack time of inmates,
and if only incidentally, to extend a helping hand to them.

In recent years drugs in some jurisdictions have eclipsed alcohol
as a condition related to crime—either directly in the violation of a narcotics
law, or as a stimulus to the commission of a property offense in order to get
money to support a habit. Between 1970 and 1972, the percentage of drug
users among persons detained in one county jail surveyed increased from 25 to
63 percent.[10]

Advantage could be taken of the presence of men in jail awaiting
trial to help them with their problems, with pharmaceutical and psychological
aids. Admittedly, the success rates of such programs is not very high. But if

these services are made available in the jail, it gives the detainees something to do. At the same time, such programs may provide some positive and construc tive steps leading to the prisoners becoming interested in a program of therapy; some may even be encouraged to continue it after they are released.

In addition to alcohol and drug dependency, many offenders in jail suffer from untreated medical conditions. Jails should take advantage of that opportunity to focus on early detection of health problems at the time of confinement, with the capacity to carry on further diagnostic evaluation as a minimum. The most fundamental medical need in jails is to prevent the spread of disease. Beyond that, there is need for such services in jail because of the clear relationship, in a perceptible percentage of prisoners, between physical conditions and crime.

Throughout this discussion runs a serious question: why should free benefits, which are not given free to noncriminals, be extended to people who are accused of breaking the law? This argument cannot be lightly dismissed. But if a commitment exists in the society to control and prevent crime, then the investment of money in repairing people who come into custody through the accident of arrest, is a more effective expenditure of public funds than spending it to keep those same people locked up for years.

While it may not be fully justified on other grounds, perhaps it can be justified, at the minimum, on an economic basis. Instead of expending funds merely to keep a person confined, which serves only to secure his body, their application to repair the damage that has taken place in his life is one way of trying to insure that he will not be a threat to society again.

The same argument holds for inmates with emotional disturbances. Many people who get into trouble because of psychological difficulties come to public attention only when they are charged with an offense. But if advantage could be taken of the opportunity to extend psycho-therapeutic services to these people when they first come to public attention by reason of apprehension for an offense, two purposes will have been served: reduction of the level of emotional disturbance so that they become easier prisoners to handle: and the help given them may help keep them from commiting other crimes.

Given the dire state of municipal finances, and the distorted distribution of national tax revenue for a variety of destructive and military purposes rather than for human services, it may be unrealistic to expect even the most meager appropriation for such programs.

But there are other areas of jail life which do not require large expenditures to bring about a change in customary procedures, specifically in the area of communications. Persons at liberty may not appreciate what it means to have restraints on their communication with others, which is one of the most destructive aspects of jail detention.

The overwhelming preoccupations of persons awaiting trial are, understandably, how long they are going to be detained, and what will be the

outcome of their day in court, when it comes. If they have families, they
are anxious about them. Yet most jail regulations strictly limit communication
with the key persons in the inmate's life—his lawyer and his wife and children.
His mail is censored—both ways; the telephone calls he may make are usually
limited to emergencies.

Jails which have abolished censorship of mail—except for examination of incoming letters for contraband—do not report any increase in escapes
plotted by correspondence. Reasonably free and direct access to public telephone service—as through a central switchboard—for outgoing calls, and for
limited incoming calls helps to remove a prime source of the anxiety and
antagonism of inmates. There is no reason why persons presumed to be innocent should be limited to one or two visitors a week. The extension of visiting
schedules to make possible evening hours for husbands, wives and children
to spend some time with their relatives in jail may require some extra effort
by the custodial staff, but the returns in terms of helping to maintain normal
family relationships would more than offset it.

COEDUCATION IN JAILS

Some of the volunteer teachers in jails today are young women. This is a
hitherto unheard-of arrangement, because one of the traditional penalties of
being locked up is complete and absolute segregation from persons of the
opposite sex. But if persons in jail are not supposed to be there as punishment
because they are only awaiting trial, there is no justification—other than precedent—for cutting them off from all contacts. Denial of freedom is, by itself,
the supreme deprivation. Very few people, if any, would accept an invitation
to be a guest in the penthouse suite of the finest hotel in town, at no expense
for food or any other need, with freedom to do anything they like—except to
go out, to have unlimited company, or to associate with persons of their
own choice.

Imprisonment is punishment enough without adding to it. The
inmates are under the control of those with power to order their lives in every
respect. As the basic fact of imprisonment is compounded by additional restrictions and deprivations, it begins to border on the sadistic. One difficulty
with jail detention, as with corporal punishment, is that most human beings,
when they have another under their complete control, tend to take advantage
of that power. Since the purpose of confinement before trial is supposed to
be nonpunitive, jail restrictions should extend no further than to maintain
security, health and order.

In an institution composed solely of males or females there is an
inevitable tendency toward homosexuality. This is at least somewhat alleviated by the presence of women and men in the institution—as teachers or as

classmates. From a purely administrative point of view, control is eased when individuals are not completely segregated.

A jail in the Midwest is providing classes in education subjects for both male and female inmates, taught by both men and women.[11] They are also allowed to sit together to see the movies. When men are permitted to sit with women in classes, they are both better motivated to study and to participate. The sheriff who began the program also reports that the idea originated with female detainees who wanted the same educational opportunities as those given to the men.

The program started with a basic adult education course of six men and six women, conducted five days a week for one and a half hours a day. Attendance is reported to be better in this than in the other jail programs offered. "Allowing inmates to have some contact with members of the opposite sex allows them more easily to make the transfer from the institution to a more natural environment such as that they will face when they are released."

Where more than one jail serves the needs of a large metropolitan area, including more than one jurisdiction, regionalization of detention facilities makes possible a pooling of resources and the introduction of a more complete program of services than any one jail can offer by itself.

It is good to be able to report that in at least one county under bold leadership, most of the programs described in this chapter have been combined in one jail, which both serves—and draws upon the facilities of— a total community. Rehabilitation programs, composed of representatives of various agencies and organizations from the area surrounding the jail conduct, through the person of the intake referral coordinator, an interview with each incoming inmate: to acquaint him with the services available, and to ascertain which of these he may need or be able to benefit from.[12]

Thereafter, services offered by the jail include the following: classes taught by certified teachers from the local school district, ranging from instruction in basic reading and writing skills to high school equivalency examinations, which are administered by and at the jail.

Drug-abuse programs offer services including individual and group psychotherapy, medical services, including in-patient detoxification. Vocational services of counseling and placement for inmates with drug or drug-related problems are also available. The drug program makes available the services of liaison workers between the jail and the community as part of the after-care program, including at least five community agencies which specialize in drug care.

The Community Health Center cooperates by offering psychological, counseling and recreational therapy. The local Tri-County Council on Alcoholism offers an alcoholic program in conjunction with the rehabilitation services of the state Department of Education. Volunteers help in a long list of activities: sewing classes for female inmates; library services, tutorial assistance, and editorial assistance in the publication of the inmate periodical. The jail physician devotes 70 percent of his time to assisting inmates, and works closely with the drug and alcohol staffs.

Most institutions, whether jails or prisons, provide radios and even television sets for their inmates, usually for passive diversion. This jail is unusual in that it is equipped with a comprehensive audio-visual system complete with control room and studio, making it possible to provide inmates with a wide range of educational experiences available through commercial programming, educational TV and tapes, opportunities for educational programming during weekends and other times when instructors are not available; the ability to attend class for those otherwise unable to do so due to sickness or security considerations; a vehicle for artistic and self-expression through the use of in-jail inmate-produced "mini-productions," a concept seen as valuable for improving the self-image of inmates and thus contributing to a more positive mental attitude; physical fitness exercises, including isometrics, which can be done in the inmate living areas with a minimum of supervision, in the belief that physical conditioning contributes to the receptivity of detainees to rehabilitation efforts.

NOTES

1. See his *Little Dorrit* (New York: Walter Black, 1940), p. 78.
2. Abraham S. Blumberg, *Criminal Justice* (Chicago: Quadrangle Books, 1967), esp. pp. 104–105, 183.
3. See Lesta N. Burt, "Keepers of Men Need Keepers of Books," *Crime and Delinquency,* Vol. 18, No. 3 (July 1972), pp. 271–283; William R. Coons, "Books and People Behind Bars at Attica," *Wilson Library Bulletin* (March 1972), pp. 614–619.
4. Malcolm Little, *Autobiography of Malcolm X* (New York: Grove Press, 1965), esp. pp. 151, 172–175.
5. *NECC News* [Boston, New England Correctional Coordinating Council], Vol. 1, No. 10 (April 1973), pp. 3 and 4.
6. Middlesex County House of Corrections, Billerica, Massachusetts.
7. "Corrections," in *Task Force Report* (Washington: President's Commission Report on Law Enforcement and Administration of Justice, 1967), p. 24.
8. Opinion of Middlesex County Superior Court Judge Levin Campbell, August 25, 1970.
9. Zalman Gordon, "Group Work and Juvenile Offenses," *Probation* [London], Vol. 17, No. 3 (1971), pp. 81–84.
10. Stein, et al., op. cit., p. 77–78.
11. "Coeducational Classes Start in Ingham Jail" *The State Journal* [Mason, Michigan] (February 4, 1973).
12. J. Frank, "Ingham County Jail Inmate Rehabilitation Program," Mason, Michigan, February 1973 (dup.).

Chapter Five

The Traditional Institution

SENTENCES

After a defendant—who may have spent time in a jail much like those described, without the benefits, perhaps, of the kind of programs suggested in the preceding chapter—is found guilty and sentenced to imprisonment, he is likely to find himself in an institutional setting not much different from the short-term place of confinement he left behind. In some instances he may be given credit for time previously spent in jail while awaiting trial or sentence. In most jurisdictions he will be eligible for consideration for parole after he has served one-third of his sentence, unless his offense was one involving arms, or where a serious degree of violence was used in its commission, in which instance he may not be eligible until two-thirds or more of his sentence has been served.

Prisoners in the United States receive among the longest and most drastic sentences in the world.[1] By contrast, a "serious" offense in other countries is punishable by much less severe, shorter sentences. In Greece, Norway, and Switzerland, for example, a serious offense carries a sentence of no more than one year's imprisonment or deprivation of liberty; in France, serious offenses are punishable by a sentence involving loss of civil rights; in Germany, such offenses are punishable by solitary confinement (reclusion) or by imprisonment for nine months; in Austria, the severest on the Continent, a serious crime is punishable by a term of imprisonment over five years.[2] Of over 9,000 persons admitted to correctional institutions in Sweden in 1971, 66 percent were under sentences of less than four months, 10 percent to less than one year.[3]

Of some 3,000 men and women in the prisons of Holland, 80 percent are currently serving sentences of less than six months duration, and only 42 have terms of more than five years. The concomitant figures on prisoner ratios are highly relevant: with a population of 13 millions, there are 22 people in prison per 100,000, in contrast to 309 per 100,000 in the

United States. "A prison sentence does little to resocialize a person," states the vice president of the Hague Court, "it more likely leads to rancor and bitterness. . . . A heavy sentence keeps a person out of possible mischief longer, but it merely postpones and aggravates the problem of recidivism." [4]

The deterrent effect of very long sentences is highly questionable. If the threat of the death penalty is not sufficient to prevent murders—especially those committed in passion—what can be said of the sentences meted out for very, very long terms? A judge in a Dallas court was reported in June 1972 to have sentenced a heroin pusher to 2500 years. Concurrent life sentences are sometimes handed out. Twenty- and thirty-year sentences for armed robbery and drug offenses are not uncommon. Beyond what point does the fear of punishment fail to deter? There is the story of the felon standing before the judge in Old Bailey in London, who had just sent him away for 200 years—"Your Honor," he is reputed to have said, "I'll never do it." Beyond what point does imprisonment—if an institution should succeed in helping a man to straighten himself out—have any rehabilitative effect, if a man does not have a chance to go out and prove himself capable of leading a law-abiding life? At the other end of the scale, what value is there in the short sentence—the thirty, sixty, or ninety days, the six months so easily imposed on convicted offenders? The only sure result obtained by incarceration is that for the time he is confined, the offender is restrained from further wrongdoing—on the outside. If the stress were placed on seeing what can be done to permit readjustment to take place in the community, with prison as a last resort, and long sentences only in the extreme, the whole area of sentencing and of incarceration would receive a fresh new look.

Meanwhile, and as things stand today, after a convicted defendant has been handed his prison sentence, the place he will serve it is consonant with the severity of his punishment. The following pages will describe the sort of places he lands in and what the chances are of his being helped to understand and solve some of the problems which may have led him into criminal activity in the first place.

PRISONS, TRAINING SCHOOLS, AND RECIDIVISM

"Riots, work stoppages, hunger strikes in prisons across the nation have opened the eyes of even the most myopic to the shocking and degrading physical conditions to which prisoners are subjected. From Attica we learned that men work for twelve hours a day in temperatures of often more than a hundred degrees, are permitted but one shower a week, one roll of toilet paper every five weeks. We heard the prisoners' vivid descriptions of rotting food, roach-infested cells, and gross medical neglect—all ruefully acknowledged by the prison administration and confirmed by subsequent official investigations." [5]

It is not surprising that institutions which treat their inmates in such fashion—whether these be children in a juvenile training school or adult felons in a maximum-security prison—should fail overwhelmingly to correct, treat or rehabilitate. They also bear responsibility for the 80 percent of all serious crimes that are committed by persons who have served time in them.[6] The evidence is so overwhelming on this score that it is difficult to select from the abundance of reports which confirm it. A selection is made from among only some of the most recent of such statements.

The Director of the Training College of the Danish Prison Administration has put it succinctly: "Prisoners are forced to live a frugal life with poor clothes, a Spartan diet, sexual abstinence, regular habits with more hours for sleeping than normal adults, little exercise and fresh air, and are prevented from taking any responsibility for showing initiative. They live according to norms, discipline, and internal rules of punishment which are out of date in the outside world. Such an artificial and unnatural way of life is expected to help them lead a socially acceptable and noncriminal life in the ordinary community after release."[7]

The result of that "unnatural and artificial" life on the after careers of persons released from it is strikingly revealed in such followup studies as that made of inmates received into Canadian penitentiaries in 1961: no less than 77.2 percent of them had served previous sentences of imprisonment.[8]

The following is a description of the county training schools of Massachusetts, places 100 or more years old, which received boys (only) who were sent to them for reasons of truancy, runaway, school offenses, and stubbornness: "Reform school inmates are fed and housed, and to some extent, clothed. They receive a minimum of medical and dental attention. They go to classes where some who cannot read are taught to read and write. They learn a few skills, though these are of little use upon release. They have no privacy and virtually no personal possessions. They spend months or years in a situation of almost total conformity and irresponsibility with no chance to develop independence of thought, or self-reliance. They do not learn how to handle money—to earn it, or even to spend it. They are isolated from their families by a system which permits two parental visits per month. They are isolated from outside friends . . . they never meet or associate with girls. They go out with no resources into a world that is totally strange. It is no wonder that so many of them graduate to become inmates of our correctional institutions."[9]

It is heartening to report that as a result of the work of such committees as the one here cited the three remaining schools were closed down by vote of the state legislature, and the boys placed back in their own communities.

A study conducted by the Federal Bureau of Investigation, based on the nearly 18,000 persons arrested for federal criminal offenses in 1963, reports that 55 percent of them had been rearrested three years later. Approxi-

mately 52 percent of those who had been arrested for robbery and 45 percent
of those sentenced and then paroled had been rearrested within two and a half
years after their first arrest. Of the persons who at the time of arrest were
under thirty, more than 60 percent were rearrested.[10]

       The statistical rationale for granting to youthful offenders up to
their early twenties a larger measure of special handling to reduce their tendencies toward recidivism may be found in the following: "Youths 16 to 23
are a significant group in the offender category: in 1964 they were 12.9 percent
of the total U.S. population and were responsible for 27 percent of total
arrests in the U.S. These youths commit largely minor or less serious crimes:
of the 1,259,206 arrests in 1964, 24.8 percent were in the major crime area.[11]
When the upper age of 23 is increased by only two years, a startling jump in
crime rates is noted: of all arrests for index crimes, petty larceny and negligent
manslaughter (in 1968), three-quarters were of persons under 25 years old.[12]

       There is "increasing evidence that the younger the individual when
he first turns to crime, the greater [is] the likelihood that he will become a
recidivist."[13] It follows that the lower the age at the time or arrest or confinement in institutions, the higher seems to be the rate at which, after release,
young people engage again in criminal activity.[14]

       According to Dr. Jerome Miller, recently the Commissioner of
Youth Services for Massachusetts, the recidivism rate for committed juveniles
was 80 percent; and the earlier they were institutionalized, the greater were
their chances of ending up in prison in adulthood.[15] How much this may
be due to failure on the part of these schools to train or educate, as against
what the boys and girls learn from one another of criminal matters, is not
easily determined.

       "Though recidivism remains the most commonly used measure
of correctional programs, there is intense and widespread disagreement over
its adequacy and usefulness. Furthermore, lacking a uniform operational
definition of this statistic, comparison of studies is rarely possible. It is not
surprising that estimates of national or state rates of recidivism vary widely.
Most estimates place the rate in excess of 60 percent."[16] However, all
reports indicate that 40 percent of the country's 343 publicly operated reform
schools, housing over 50,000 children at any one time, are overcrowded; the
average length of stay is 9.9 months, and the annual operating expenditure
averages $5700. They share several common characteristics:

1. They are expensive.
2. They are populated by children of the poor; children of middle and upper
    class parents can purchase a number of alternatives to reform school.
3. They aren't institutions of learning because they don't teach subjects, but
    rather obsolete skills which anchor the youth to the bottom scale in the
    job market.

4. Their professional personnel are generally of low caliber.
5. Recidivism is directly proportionate to the length of time they spend in the institutions.
6. Jobs in the schools are political appointments.[17]

      "With the exception of Indian massacres in the late nineteenth century, the State Police assault which ended the four-day [Attica] uprising was the bloodiest one-day encounter between Americans since the Civil War." [18] The national attention which was thereafter drawn to Attica should not obscure the fact that since that tragedy, as prior to it, the same conditions go on in similar prisons all over the country all the time. Only when conditions become so unbearable that riots result, are they brought dramatically to public attention. Eighteen months after Attica, in the State of New York, at Great Meadows Correctional Facility, more than one-half of the 1,358 inmates engaged in a nonviolent protest, after their most recent attempt to make known their grievances. Foremost is the fact that overcrowding and limited facilities leave 300 inmates with nothing to do: no educational classes, no work in vocational shops, or in the soap or furniture factory. This leaves these 300 men locked up in their cells for twenty-two out of twenty-four hours of the day. "Another problem is the remoteness of the prison. Family visits are difficult for New York City inmates, and blacks and Puerto Ricans are regarded with suspicion in nearby towns. There are no blacks or Puerto Ricans among the 268 correctional officers and 155 civilian employees of the prison."[19]
      It is difficult to escape the conclusion that by permitting such practices as these to continue, after they have been repeatedly brought to public attention in brutal and irrefutable fashion that the entire citizenry is in the process brutalized as well. Its brutalizing effect on the correctional staff would likewise seem inevitable—if only out of understandable fear and consequent self-defensiveness. If it is true that absolute power corrupts absolutely—as may be seen in persons in control of prisons—then its counterpart should hold true for prisoners: their absolute powerlessness is corrosive of them as well. Just as the taking of human life, whether by capital punishment or as recorded in victorious "body counts", cheapens the value of all life.
      From all we know, it is clear that the act of incarcerating a person will impair or destroy whatever potential he has for a life free of crime, and that regardless of the form of treatment while he is in prison, the longer he is kept there, the more he is deteriorated, and the greater the chance of his becoming a recidivist. *Time* magazine recently carried a story about a man who had committed a series of brutal murders and was being held for trial under $1 million bail. The news account detailed his early life. At the age of five, he was sent to an institution. At age 15, he killed both of his grandparents, called his mother to confess what he had done, and was released from the youth authority after treatment. When he walked out of the prison camp where he

had been confined in 1967, he said as he left: "I do not want to go out there. I do not think I can make it out there."[20] Looking back, it would appear that nothing much was done at this point beyond recording his expressed feelings of inability to cope with the pressures of the outside, in the way of helping him to adjust to the world which he so feared, on which he vented himself so cruelly.

Admittedly, one of the factors which makes any kind of individualization impossible in our penal institutions is their mass, congregate nature— their enormous size. Many prisons have a capacity in excess of 1,000; there are not a few which run much higher. Joliet accommodates almost 5,000; Texas is reported to be building a new prison with a capacity of 4,000. Sweden, by contrast, with 452 juveniles in confinement, divides them among 22 institutions, an average of less than 25 in each.[21]

Any regime which seeks to bring conformity through the application of fear cannot reach or correct the causative or precipitating factors which induced a person to commit crime in the first instance. Fear and confinement, like physical punishment, may bring about outward agreement in an institution, but its effect on the recipient is to teach him to mask his true feelings of revenge, to teach him to bide his time. A person who has been involved in criminal activity for a long time, whether young or adult, very soon learns to express outwardly in his actions what he knows is expected of him, while inside he remains untouched. In fact, he may be more firmly and strongly confirmed in his decision to break the law because he has conned society into believing that he is conforming, when inside he is no different from what he was before—if not worse.

We have high rates of recidivism because we parole prisoners from institutions because they have lived up to the regulations for the period prescribed. They have not hit a guard, they have gone to work, have been respectful, have kept their cell clean, said "yes sir," and "no sir," in the right tone and to the right people. So outwardly they were eligible for parole, while behind the conforming conduct they evidently remain the same. When they get out on the street, when it is no longer necessary to conform, they revert back to what they were before, because inwardly the system of treatment or confinement did not alter the basic dynamics of their lives. The motivation for their antisocial behavior remains untouched; frequently it is strengthened. All that we have succeeded in doing while we have them in confinement was to make them good actors, dissemblers and hypocrites in order that they may be seen to have behaved as was expected—or demanded—of them.

An unpublished New York State survey of the effectiveness of most treatment programs—for offenders of all ages—based on a review of 231 researches, concluded in the words of one of its co-authors, "I think it is fair to say that there is very little evidence in these studies that any prevailing mode of treatment has a decisive affect in reducing the recidivism of convicted offenders. . . . Little has appeared since completion of the study to contradict its conclusion, and recent evidence indicates that incarceration is even more damaging than we thought."[22]

A committee of the Council of Europe, in a report on alternatives to prison, recommended to governments that they consider making provision in their own legislation for new measures designed to avoid imprisonment, particularly imprisonment of first offenders.[23]

SWEDISH PROPOSALS

One of the first governments which seems to have acted in accordance with this recommendation was that of Sweden, which has recently released the report of its Commisson on Criminal Care.[24] This contains a series of proposals to be put into effect during a five-year period, beginning in 1974. They will not be submitted to parliament for legislative action until reactions have been received from "various interested bodies."

Two of the commission's main proposals are worth quoting in full: "In the future, the building of institutions should concentrate on small, local institutions and the renovation and rebuilding of those small institutions which already exist. The building of large institutions should cease completely. The size of large institutions reduces the possibilities for personal contact between offenders and personnel and makes individual treatment more difficult." These proposals are based on certain agreed-upon findings by the commission, the first of which is that: "As a rule, deprivation of freedom does not improve an offender's possibility of adapting to a life of freedom." The commission added that although it is not known to what extent more intense and effective care brings good results in noninstitutional settings, "there is a broad agreement that from an individual and preventive point of view, care of criminals in freedom gives a better result than that in an institution"; and that such care is both more humane and less costly than institutional care. Therefore the commission recommended that institutions should be used only for the most "complicated cases," concluding that the aims of criminal care in Sweden should be to facilitate the adjustment of offenders to society, to reduce isolation and discrimination in work, education, housing, and the finding of jobs so that they can make a reasonable living.

In December of 1972, the American Assembly of Columbia University devoted its forty-second session to the topic "Prisoners in America."[25] Their first recommendation reads: "States should abandon large congregate institutions for sentenced offenders. Few offenders require confinement in maximum security facilities. If incarcerated at all, most should be assigned to a diversified network of smaller group facilities and nonresidential community-based services."

The second recommendation of the assembly is no less direct, perhaps even drastic. "It must become firm public policy to avoid further construction of adult prisons, jails or juvenile training schools. Resources should be allocated for more adequate alternative programs and services as well as for the repair of existing facilities to make them habitable. Present changes in correctional policy have not run their course. Plans for new construction must be deferred."[26]

No building is harder to adapt to another purpose than a prison that is no longer needed. Nobody wants to buy it. It is not good for investment or speculation. It is one of those places that can only be improved by tearing it down.

THE MYTH OF CLASSIFICATION

Despite its respected place in penal administration, classification seldom implies much more than an estimate of a prisoner's "dangerousness" and his likely response to custody and control. Historically it is as old as the prison where it was first applied in 1821.

"The Auburn System, which developed in Auburn Prison in New York, used a congregative and solitary confinement plan. Because of the negative results of having prisoners work and sleep in groups, on the one hand, and in solitary confinement on the other, the New York legislature attempted to deal with the problem through a classification system. Inmates were divided into three groups which ranged from the most to the least hardened criminals. The most hardened prisoners were subjected to confinement to their cells day and night without work. The philosophy being identical to that of the Pennsylvania System; that of meditation. The less incorrigible were confined for part of the day and allowed to engage in labor and recreation during the second part. The third group involved the most hopeful group of men. This group was allowed to work together during the day and was housed separately at night. Silence was enforced at all times to prevent the contamination of one inmate by another. This system is the forerunner of the maximum, minimum and medium security grading system employed in our penal system today."[27]

In effect, all that classification does is to fix the mode of treatment available to offenders on the basis of spatial predeterminations. If a certain number of spaces in maximum-security facilities are available, it is inevitable that enough bodies will be found to fill them, under what may be termed a penal Parkinson's Law. This law tends to operate to classify prisoners in the direction of maximum security for several reasons: because the facilities are available for a certain number of people who can be classified as requiring maximum security; and because in classifying, the tendency is to bear down mainly on the factor of security. In this way, the prison administrator is less likely to make a mistake than the other way around, which is more chancey.

Classification can take on more than this usual connotation when the classifiers have a range of facilities to which they may assign offenders, after a period of observation, testing, interviewing and orientation. For example, in New York state, the Elmira Reception Center, after two months of pre-liminary study of the offender, determines which of the twenty-one available and diversified institutions in the state's correctional system he should be transferred to. These facilities vary from small work camps of a forestry or conservation nature to vocational training centers, reformatory and medium-security installations, to centers for the defective and the criminally insane, and, as a last resort, to maximum-security prisons.

Pending the Supreme Court decision on capital punishment, men under a sentence of death were kept, in most penitentiaries, one to a cell, in what is called death row. After the decision was handed down, they were re-leased into the general prison population. It is difficult to follow the logic of this operation, given the fact that the inmates involved were the same men after the decision as before it.

To be consistent, all murderers and persons serving life sentences would be given the strictest kind of confinement. But many such persons are, in practice, among the easiest prisoners to deal with. If those under life sentence do not require maximum security, it is difficult to understand why so many other prisoners, not under life sentences, are placed in maximum security. Lowering that denominator, scaling down what constitutes "dangerousness" or security requirements, means, in the end, the necessity for a high degree of psychotherapeutic care for those who remain in the maximum-security class. This is not meant to imply that only the psychotic offender should be kept in institutions or that only the hard-core felon should be given therapy, but rather that a very much higher percentage now in minimum and medium security may be placed safely in the community rather than being imprisoned, with the end result that institutions become increasingly selective.

Limited availability or diversity of facilities, coupled with the attitude which applies the highest factor of security needs common to a few inmates need not, as it now does, determine the manner in which the great majority, or at least a very large number of them, are today unnecessarily tightly confined. If that sounds like a very pleasant but unrealistic formula-tion, perhaps a recent incident will confirm its reality and practicability.

NEW ZEALAND'S EXPERIENCE

In 1971, in New Zealand's Paremoremo maximum-security prison, there accumulated a sizeable number of difficult prisoners who had been assigned to the maximum-security wing for extended periods of time. The conditions under which they were kept seem to have constituted "maximum-maximum" conditions. The unrelieved close confinement restrictions led to increasing unrest, to a point so critical that the government assigned the state ombudsman to inquire into it. His preliminary report concludes: "Finally, we think that too many medium (or less) security risks are confined in this maximum security prison. This is unfair to the men concerned, depriving them of the opportunity to rehabilitate under more open conditions and with at least some better opportunity for contact with people and with nature in the form of grass, plants and animals. Even for maximum security risks, to spend nearly three years under such conditions, as is the case with some, must have a dehumanizing effect, however necessary this type of confinement may be deemed to be. All these men eventually leave prison, and society should use great efforts to see that they do so under circumstances which will render their return less likely." [28]

The policy appears to have continued unchanged despite this recommendation, resulting in further disturbances within the prison—work stoppages, fires, and riotous conditions not unlike what has taken place in our own country recently.

A private citizens' group which gave testimony during the inquiry came to the same conclusion that "the only real solution was to abandon the whole concept of a maximum security prison on the pattern of Paremoremo. Many of the inmates . . . did not require to be in a maximum security prison . . . ." [29]

"Maximum-maximum" is the last full measure of security—the point at which no more pressure can be applied without permitting some outlets for release of that pressure. Without an atmosphere—and the opportunity—for working things out, the more inevitable is frustration and the greater the possibility that ultimately it will find its release in destructive outbursts. The provocative effect of "escape-proof" penal facilities was proven during the famous Alcatraz riots of 1946, which led to the ultimate abandonment of "The Rock."

Considering how frequently Sweden has been cited in these pages as a leader in progressive penal matters, it is all the more pertinent to cite an incident which recently occurred there. On the night of August 17, 1972, fifteen men escaped from Kumla, considered the most closely guarded prison in Sweden. The escapees included two Croatian nationalists sentenced for the murder of the Yugoslav ambassador in Stockholm, and a well-known bank swindler. While they were still at large, two of the escapees telephoned a newsman on a leading Stockholm newspaper and gave their views on the security wing where they had been confined. One, who had spent the first two years of his sentence in solitary confinement, is quoted as saying: "My time there affected me so negatively that I had to escape. I got to a stage where I had to try to change my existence for the day I eventually got my discharge. . . . I haven't got out to commit any crime, if that's what anyone thinks." Said the other: "The majority of us are admittedly entirely normal, sensible people, but there were those who were growing absolutely desperate from their treatment. . . . The worst thing was the almost total isolation. . . . We also felt a pressure from the incredibly hard climate at the wing, the tense relationship with the staff." Asked if he preferred his present life as a fugitive to being locked in the security wing, he replied: "It was the only conceivable solution just now, when one is no longer functioning as a human being."[30]

These last words seem like an echo of the slogans raised by the inmates at Attica less than a year before. There, such a point of desperation was reached that the inmates preferred to risk death rather than to live any longer under the inhuman conditions to which they were being subjected.[31]

Every penal institution has a small number of extremely difficult men who act in response to a high degree of instability, even of psychopathy. Instead of spending as much money as we do to keep such persons in maximum confinement, and increasing the pressure on them as they badger and bedevil their administrators, if the same amount of time and effort were expended on those who require not more serious confinement, but some skilled professional intervention, we might begin to see some de-escalation of today's prison paranoia and its tragic results.

DENMARK'S CONTRIBUTION

That such a notion is not beyond the realm of possibility may be seen in the work of the well-known Danish psychiatrist, Dr. George Stürup, who for twenty-five years has dealt with the criminally insane, the violent assaultive types who present a serious menace to society. After ten years, 90 percent of such men who leave this treatment center in Herstedvester are crime-free.[32]

Stürups' approach has a great deal to teach us about how to deal with the seriously disturbed offender. His thesis is, in effect, that no one is "untreatable." He makes two other remarkable points which anyone concerned with offenders might well ponder and put into practice. First, there is very little difference between those whom we imprison for crimes and those who treat them. Except for accident—the circumstances of birth or fortune—many of those who are the jailers could be the jailed. A certain degree of humility marks this approach, one not ordinarily found in people engaged in prison work. His second point is that the therapist does not attempt to intervene in the life of the prisoner in order to change his attitudes to conform with those of the therapist. The function of the latter is, rather, to unlock the barriers which prevent a prisoner from helping to cure himself, because in the long run each of us is, or can be assisted to be, his own therapist.

That this idea is gaining ground in the United States may be seen from the following excerpt from an article by a perceptive writer in this field. "Unquestionably, the increased emphasis on community treatment of all offenders, particularly youth, will lead to an increasing proportion of those eventually committed to state institutions having severe emotional and psychiatric disturbances. The need for psychiatric services will continue to grow, and the gap between the state correctional system's need for these services and its ability to provide them is likely to widen.

"The degree to which the correctional system is able to deliver needed psychiatric services will hinge upon its increased ability to attract professionals in the fields of psychiatry and psychology. . . . In developing specialized psychiatric treatment, correctional institutions recognize that: (1) a high level of administrative attention and support is necessary for specialized psychiatric treatment programs to function effectively; (2) a psychiatric treatment program must have the capability to handle those disturbed wards who display aggressive or assaultive behavior. . . ; (3) specific policies and procedures . . . between the psychiatric treatment program and the larger correctional system which it serves must be developed and carried out.

"If correctional systems continue to receive increasing numbers of seriously disturbed offenders, they must develop their capacity to: (1) provide psychiatric diagnostic, and prescriptive services . . . , present specific program recommendations for treatment; suggest individualized methods and approaches . . . and provide paroling authorities with that information necessary for release considerations; (2) provide those treatment services necessary to achieving a client's . . . ability to effectively function when returned to the community."[33]

This is, perhaps, the point at which to record the fact that with all the talk that goes on in conferences of correctional experts and in their professional journals regarding the value of psychotherapy and the need to employ it within our penal institutions for the truly difficult cases, there were, in the year 1954, only twenty-three full-time psychiatrists employed in the federal prison system, to deal with 162,000 inmates. On the basis of a forty-hour week, each inmate could have received 82 seconds per month of psychiatric care. On the same basis, the sixty-seven psychologists and psychometrists would be available to each inmate for 4 minutes per month; institutional parole officers 6 minutes; and chaplains, 10 minutes.[34] The dollars saved by the placement in the community of only four prisoners who are now in prison would pay for the services of one psychiatrist where he is most needed and can be most effective—in our prisons.

Classification in the past has paid little more than lip service to the basic differences in what is, in fact, a most heterogenous population—the inmates of any given institution. By emphasizing the elements of custody and security, administrators have looked to their classification officers for guidance as to which inmates were trustworthy and who constituted the potentially most dangerous threats to safety and good order. The accuracy of case studies and the verification of basic material on offenders has been carried to a very high point of excellence in many prisons. But the measures and programs available within the institution to carry the results of these case studies into practice—except for the factor of security—are so limited that despite the completeness of the knowledge which may be gathered as to any one offender, there is little in the institution which is thereafter geared to his needs and potentialities.

Security is the talisman, the area which is always adequately manned; it never suffers from want of whatever the latest gadget may be for cowering men and wiping them out if need be. Prison industries may operate with equipment and at a level which is twenty years behind the times, but the tear gas, the riot cars and equipment are of the latest model available.

Recently there has been brought forward a typology of offenders, based on the social maturity of the offender, his ability to get on with his peers, and his potential for adapting satisfactorily to social demands. While designed for juveniles, it has within it possibilities of adaptation to the adult offender as well. The emphasis on the value of classification not solely for security purposes, but for therapy as well, is cogently brought forward in the following by Marguerite Q. Warren, a pioneer in the field: "There is a growing awareness that the heterogeneity of offenders has importance in the treatment approach used. Numerous typologies of offenders have been developed and currently, throughout the world, there is considerable interest in the possibility of developing, in a systematic way, differential treatment strategies for the various types of offenders. Still undetermined, however, is the kind of classification frame of reference most useful in developing differential treatment strategies.

"In assigning an offender to a particular program there is advantage in tailoring the environmental atmosphere, the selection of a staff worker (his characteristics and style), and the treatment method . . . to his particular needs. Use of a typology or classification system can make this feasible. Preliminary findings indicate an advantage to homogenous grouping of offenders placed in appropriate treatment climates."[35]

The possibilities of utilizing some kind of typology of offenders, like the above, to place prisoners in appropriate educational and vocational programs, is limited only by the availability of such programs in most penal institutions.

CONTRADICTIONS IN CORRECTIONS

One of the basic reasons for the failure of penal institutions is the unresolved conflict between various philosophies and attitudes as to their purpose. If as many contradictions existed in the field of education as to its basic purpose, it would probably be impossible to teach children even how to read or write.

Despite national differences, the educational systems of the world have a fairly clear idea of what they want their children to learn: certain basic skills, literacy, language, culture, a view of the world, and, at the appropriate time, some vocational or professional training for a later economically productive life, with satisfaction both for themselves and for society. Differences may exist as to methods, approach, programs or emphasis, but as to the basic purpose of education, there is little doubt. It is not urged as the first purpose of education that schools should control the young, or make them exactly like their teachers or parents, or to close their minds. Quite the contrary, the attempt of our model schools is to open young people up to the possibilities in the world and within themselves.

When it comes to institutions which imprison people, the primary aim is punishment, even though all but a few of those so punished are ultimately to be set free. The general and cynical acceptance of this fact is dramatically illustrated by a recent news account, which tells of an 84-year old woman, who after spending thirty-nine years in a state hospital, was finally declared competent to stand trial. In 1933, estranged from her second husband, she had shot and killed him and thereafter shot herself over the heart in an attempted suicide. This failed, and the court committed her to the state hospital.

The District Attorney informed the press that the woman would not be prosecuted, the indictment would be nol prossed. "The interests of justice have certainly been served in this case," the D.A. announced, "She has been incarcerated for thirty-nine years." To which the assistant superintendent of the mental hospital added: "She is not a menace to society."[36]

As long as such vengeful attitudes are maintained by officials charged with the custody of sentenced offenders, our peno-correctional institutions will continue to fail, in a sizeable percentage of instances, as places for the resocialization of offenders. John Conrad, in his study of prisons across the United States and the north of Europe, concludes that the message of all these places is punishment.[37] Until we deal in some kind of forthright manner with the ancient dilemma of *why* we punish, we shall not resolve the conflict nor the inconsistencies in our approach toward the sentenced offender.

Born into all humans is the instinct to hit back when hit. It is found in children who have not yet been socialized; it is not uncharacteristic of many adults. It is an important part of man's innate defensive equipment; without it, the species would probably have long since died out. But when born into a society, and become, as a result, committed to an unwritten social contract, without the formality of signing it, we agree that if we are attacked, we will not reciprocate; we will leave that to government. In exchange, society pledges to protect our property and persons against assault, against theft, against murder. That is why criminal cases are not tried in the name of the victim, it is the United States government against the thief or murderer, it is the State of Ruritania as prosecutor vs. John Doe.

At a primitive level, revenge is still a private matter. Until recently in Kentucky, feuds between families persisted generation after generation. They handled justice at their own level. This exists to this day in a primitive tribe in New Guinea, only recently discovered when an airplane flew over an uncharted valley where a tribe of people were discovered living as they did in the Stone Age.[38] But in this society, the only pursuit is war. The men wage it, the women have the babies, and do most of the simple agricultural tasks. While the two rival camps are derived from the same tribe, they are divided into two warring gangs who play for very high stakes—their lives. And it does not matter in this society whom you kill, whether a grandmother or a newborn baby, the winning side gets credit for that as a victory. They then return to their huts for a feast of pork and sweet potatoes and celebrate. The other side then has its turn to kill. The men on both sides spend all their time sharpening their spears and standing watch. There is nothing romantic about this unspoiled way of life, it is the rawest possible system of taking justice into one's own hands.

Civilized societies require that their members yield up to the state that power of revenge, but in the process the members do not rid themselves of the instinctive reaction to hit back when hit. That remains, and goes far to account for the sadism, for the desire for revenge which sanctions the death penalty and the brutality in imprisonment. If it is impossible ever to remove or diminish this in individuals, it cannot be diminished or removed from society, either. Punishment down through history can be described as the institutionalization in society of the totality of our individual feelings of revenge.

There is hardly a person who has not—at one time or another harbored a desire to kill, or even expressed it openly—seriously or in jest. When a particularly vicious act has been committed against a victim, even a person not related to us, this feeling of revenge then arises and dominates one's individual thinking and is expressed in a desire that the offender be harshly dealt with. It is the rarest person who will stand up in court and ask for mercy for someone who has grievously harmed, or even killed, someone dear to him. Most of us clamor for the state to take the kind of action we would take if we could get hold of the assailant—if we were strong enough. So if we criticize the state for dealing punitively with offenders, it is well to remember that this is only the extension—the institutionalization in government—of what lies within ourselves, deriving from the instinct for revenge. It is not easy to root out that desire or, at times, even to control it. But in criticizing those who impose punishment in the name of the state, it is well to realize that it is being imposed in the name of all those who, deep within themselves, cry out for the punishment of others.

By influencing government to relax its most brutal exercise of the power to punish, we shall have gone far to reduce brutality in our midst, in the same way that the abolition of the death penalty helps to appreciate the sanctity of all life.

Penitentiaries were replaced by reformatories, industrial schools are today called training centers, punishment came to be called corrections, later rehabilitation; today the "in" word is reintegration.

But juvenile crime is still juvenile crime, even if it is called delinquency. The search for new terms is only an attempt to find a more palatable term for imprisonment and for punishment, because this or that word has gone out of style. The penitentiary of two centuries ago set out to make penitents. The reformatory, 100 years later, was pledged to reform: that had a better sound to it. Anyone—whether visitor or inmate—who today enters one reformatory, and one prison, in almost any country of the world, would be hard put to describe the difference between them as to what goes on inside. The difference in label affects neither the content nor, as we have seen, the resulting product.

There is much useful new information from the behavioral sciences which has not yet found its way into places which deal with offenders. It was not much more than seventy years ago that the criminal was first brought under any kind of clinical examination, just as psychiatry in the nineteenth century paid little heed to scientific attempts to discover why people became psychotic. A lot of hair-splitting went on in arguing about the classification of psychotics, in a manner reminiscent of the way theologians used to argue about the number of angels who could dance on the head of a pin. Freud was a pioneer in clinically examining the dynamics of human conduct. Lombroso came on the world scene almost coincidentally, and for the first time in criminology, a physician put the criminal on the dissecting table, and with scalpel and microscope set out to discover if criminals were a different breed of man.[39] The world has long since questioned Lombroso's conclusions, but we commend him for the first time emphasizing the clinical nature of the criminal disposition in the same way that Freud sought for the motivation of human conduct in the psyche of man. Both Lombroso and Freud have had many detractors, but the contribution each made to an understanding of the motivations of human conduct and the dynamics of the human personality have not yet made their way—in approach, attitude or application—into the administration of most of the training schools and prisons of the world.

With all the knowledge since accumulated about individual dynamics and motivations, the criminal justice system applies very few of those findings to the understanding of human conduct leading to programs for dealing with the results of such motivations. The term rehabilitation leads many prisoners to ask how they can be *re*habilitated when they were never *habilitated* in the first place.

The latest term is reintegration—to prepare the prisoner to return to society with some confidence that he is not only himself whole and complete, but that he can become one with society. The term iself has a decidedly progressive and humanitarian connotation. But it is doubtful whether the inmates see any basic resulting difference in the manner in which they are treated.

NOTES

1. "American statutory sentences are generally twice or thrice as long as those of other countries—even authoritarian countries—even though American prisoners, on the whole, serve only from one-half to two thirds of their sentences." "A Program for Prison Reform" (Cambridge: Roscoe Pound-American Trial Lawyers Foundation, 1973), p. 34.

2. "Suspended Sentence, Probation, and Other Alternatives to Prison Sentences," (Strasbourg: Council of Europe, European Commission on Crime Problems, 1966), p. 11 (Austria); p. 58 (France); p. 64 (Greece); p. 95 (Norway); pp. 109-110 (Switzerland).

3. *Kriminal Varden* [The Correctional System] (Stockholm: National Correctional Administration, 1971), p. 9.

4. W.F.C. Van Hattum, quoted in *Newsweek,* January 15, 1973, p. 26.

5. Jessica Mitford, *Kind & Usual Punishment* (New York: Knopf, 1973), p. 169.

6. Ramsey Clark, *Crime in America* (New York: Simon & Schuster, 1970), p. 39.

7. B. Paludan-Muller, "Modern Methods of Treatment of Offenders," *Federal Probation,* Vol. 36, No. 4 (1972), p. 37.

8. Alistair W. MacLeod, *Recidivism: A Deficiency Disease* (Philadelphia: University of Pennsylvania Press, 1965), p. 70.

9. Mary B. Newman, *The Newman Committee Investigation into Conditions in Training Schools in Massachusetts* (Boston: State House Library, 1971).

10. *Uniform Crime Report,* 1970.

11. Milton Luger and Elias B. Saltman, "The Youthful Offender," in *Task Force Report: Juvenile Delinquency and Youth Crime* (Washington: President's Commission Report on Law Enforcement and Administration of Justice, 1967), p. 120.

12. Norval Morris and Gordon Hawkins, *The Honest Politician's Guide to Crime Control* (Chicago: University of Chicago Press, 1969), p. 35.

13. Alistair W. MacLeod. *op. cit.,* p. 71.

14. Daniel Glaser, *The Effectiveness of a Prison and Parole System* (New York: Bobbs-Merrill, 1964), p. 19.

15. Brian Vachon, "Hey, Man What Did You Learn in Reform School? Well, uh, How to Disconnect a Burglar Alarm," *Saturday Review,* September 16, 1972, pp. 69–76.
16. Ibid.
17. Ibid.
18. William L. Wilbanks, *Federal Probation*, Vol. 37, No. 1 (March 1973), p. 3. See also *Attica: The Official Report of the New York Commission on Attica* (New York: Bantam Books, 1972), p. 187.
19. *New York Times,* March 4, 1973.
20. *Time Magazine,* May 7, 1973.
21. *Kriminal Varden,* op. cit., p. 10.
22. Robert Martinson, Douglas Lipton, and Judith Wilks, "Treatment Evaluation Survey," cited in a press release from the Legal Aid Society of New York City, May 14, 1973, p. 1 (mimeo).
23. "Suspended Sentence, Probation, and other Alternatives to Prison Sentences," op. cit., p. 6.
24. "Proposals for Reform of Swedish Criminal Care" (Stockholm: Royal Ministry for Foreign Affairs, Information Service, September 1972) (dup.).
25. "Report," Harriman, New York, Arden House of Columbia University (no date), p. 6.
26. Ibid.
27. Evelyn Friedman, "The Forgotten Woman: The Development of Women's Prisons in New York and Massachusetts," Boston College, Department of Sociology, November 1973, p. 9. (Unpublished).
28. "Report by Sir Guy Powles and Mr. L.G.H. Sinclair into Various Matters Pertaining to Paremoremo Prison," Auckland, 21 January 1972, p. 16 (dup.).
29. Ibid., "Auckland Prison (Paremoremo): A Report," Wellington, 15 March 1973, Appendix A (dup.).
30. *Dagens Nyheter,* Stockholm, August 29, 1972, as quoted in *The Swedish Dialogue* (Stockholm, The Swedish Institute, 1973), pp. 16, 17.
31. *Attica,* op. cit., p. 456.
32. George K. Stürup, *Treating the "Untreatable"* (Baltimore: Johns Hopkins Press, 1968), p. 217.
33. Stephen Golden, "Treatment Programs for the Emotionally Disturbed Correctional Client," *Youth Authority Quarterly,* Vol. 25, No. 4 (1972), pp. 17–21.
34. Albert C. Schnur, "The New Penology: Fact or Fiction?" *Journal of Criminal Law, Criminology and Police Science* (November–December 1958), p. 331.
35. *Correctional Treatment in Community Settings–A Report of Current Research* (Washington: U.S. Government Printing Office, 1972).
36. Associated Press Dispatch, July 7, 1973.
37. John Conrad, *Crime and Its Correction* (Berkeley and Los Angeles: University of California Press, 1967), p. 204.
38. Peter Matthiessen, *Under the Mountain Wall* (New York: Viking, 1962).
39. Cesare Lombroso, *L'Homme Criminal* (Paris: Alcan, 1887).

Chapter Six

Variations on Traditional Prison Programs

Up to this point the main stress has been on the antecedents and status of today's prison world. This chapter will set out a range of schemes and programs which are currently in operation in the United States and in other countries. These are presented as a review of the possibilities which are available for experimentation in the field of institutional custody, and are not meant to serve as models to be imported or applied without modification to other places unless they can somehow be related to local conditions. Traditional values and customs are ways of looking at the world and responding to it. To attempt to adapt an idea from somewhere else simply because it sounds good without making sure that it fits the conditions of a particular jurisdiction is a distortion, in the end to be repudiated in the same way that a sound organ transplanted into the body of another person is ultimately rejected because it is not consonant with whatever may be the makeup of that other human being.

Many of these new ideas are modifications of old ones. All of them go in the direction of the open institution, the easing of restrictions and the treating of people in confinement, whether these be children or adults, in humane and nonoppressive fashion. Most of these can be viewed as modifying or enriching—or replacing—traditional programs within institutions.

FURLOUGHS AND FAMILIES

The furlough is one of the most widespread of the newer modes of providing to men in custody an opportunity to prepare themselves for release by permitting them to leave the institution for family visits, interviews with employers or other constructive purposes. A furlough is not to be confused with the kind of leave traditionally permitted to a prisoner, usually only to attend the sickbed of a close relative, or the graveside of one who has died. Prisoners on this kind of leave are customarily under guard or escort.

"The Federal Bureau of Prisons embarked on an experimental furlough program under the Prisoner Rehabilitation Act of 1965 which authorized unescorted furloughs to federal prisoners for a variety of purposes and allowed selected inmates work releases for employment or study in the community with continuing residence in the institutions. As of June 1, 1966, 650 prisoners were in the work release program and 436 had completed work release assignments; 180 prisoners had been granted unescorted furloughs to visit dying relatives, attend family funerals, and seek employment prior to release. None failed to return to prison on schedule."[1]

A furlough program has been in operation in Pennsylvania since October 1971. In the first year of operation, 4250 prisoners were released on furloughs into the community for a combined total of 16,000 days, an average of almost 4 days each. Only 37 did not return at the appointed time—less than 1 percent—and only 17 were charged with criminal activity while they were out.[2] Furloughs are an accepted practice in the correctional systems of at least six countries, in addition to the United States. In the United Kingdom since 1951, leaves of up to five days have been granted to men toward the end of their sentences in order to enable them to prepare themselves for conditions of release. Denmark grants furloughs only to certain inmates—those confined to workhouses, and juveniles—while Switzerland limits home visits for periods up to 24 hours. Germany grants the same privilege for up to seven days.

In this, as in many other correctional matters, Sweden is the most flexible—and unorthodox. Their prisons grant furloughs at fairly regular intervals: the first after six to ten months of confinement, with later leaves scheduled at four-month intervals thereafter. The first furlough is for 48 hours (plus travel time); subsequent visits are for three days. Toward the end of the institutional period, leaves for longer than three days are granted. Swedish prison authorities report that in 1970, a total of 14,281 furloughs were approved. Of these, 9 percent did not return within the prescribed time, an additional 4 percent abused the privilege for reasons of other misconduct, such as intoxication by drugs or alcohol, or criminal activity.[3]

When the prison administration in Sweden undertook to apply the social insurance system which prevailed outside the prison to the men inside it, it was discovered that the law required two weeks vacation for all persons registered under it. Some men who participated in the system were not considered good enough risks to be permitted to enjoy their vacation period without supervision, which resulted in the establishment of vacation camps specifically for them.[4]

"Furloughs can help cut down violence inside the prison, allow an inmate to look for a job or to find a place to live as he nears parole, and give him a chance to spend a night with his wife. . . . In prison a man is torn between abstinence and homosexuality," remarked the Secretary of the

Massachusetts Department of Human Services, in a statement defending the furlough system in that State.[5] This program began in November of 1972. Of more than 3,000 men released on furloughs (of from 12 hours to 7 days) since that date, 98.7 percent have returned without any incident in the community coming to public attention. Among eighty lifers released from the medium-security institution at Norfolk Prison Colony in Massachusetts, only one failed to return, as was the case with twenty-five lifers released on home leave from the nearby maximum-security institution at Walpole.[6]

Twenty-nine of the fifty state departments of corrections which responded to a recent questionnaire reported that they currently have some kind of furlough program in operation, and sixteen indicated that they had plans for such programs under consideration. California reported an absconder rate of 1.7 percent for prisoners released on furlough, compared to 0.2 percent in Florida, 0.4 percent in Michigan, and 1.3 percent in both Oregon and Washington. Only six states gave the negative response that they did not intend to initiate a furlough program.[7]

Much is heard these days about conjugal visiting, compared to which the furlough program is broader and more flexible as a means of assist-ing in the rehabilitation of the prisoner. Fourteen states prohibit family visits. California and Mississippi permit conjugal visiting. Oregon permits short visits of six hours, accompanied by a sponsor; 30-hour week-end furloughs in Hawaii, one week-end a month in North Carolina.[8] Objections raised against con-jugal visits are that it discriminates against the unmarried inmate; it is em-barassing to the wife, and perhaps to other inmates; it is hardly the equivalent of a program of community involvement or setting in which relations between men and women normally take place.

There are other parts of the world where conjugal visiting is permitted, but they rouse the suspicion that they are in effect a system of licensed prostitution, in which the warden plays the part of the public pro-curer. Some may regard this as hardly the most enlightened way of dealing with the sexual problems of prisoners, to say nothing of the propriety of grant-ing the warden that kind of a fringe benefit.

By way of contrast, in the Middlesex County House of Corrections in Massachusetts a short-term county prison—a system of week-end furloughs for prisoners has been in operation for the past three years. The sheriff prefers not to occupy the house which is one of the perquisites of his office, and he turns it over to those inmates who have established good records of conduct, and who wish to maintain good relations with their families. Such inmates are permitted to leave jail during the weekend, to walk across the lawn, and to spend the weekend with their wives and children—not just a conjugal visit, but a family visit. The inmates' wives cook in the sheriff's house, the families have picnics outdoors, go on walks, and swim in the small pond on the institu-tion grounds. On Monday morning, the prisoner comes back to jail and the family goes back home. This plan has been in operation since April of 1970; the sheriff reports that there has not been a single escape so far by any prisoner who has been granted the family furlough privilege.[9]

New Zealand has under consideration a plan to permit first offenders who are married to go on home leave for three days—plus traveling time— every four months. A projected work-release program would permit prisoners to go out on daily parole to outside employment. From their wages, at regular outside rates, they would be expected to pay room and board as well as to contribute to the maintenance of their dependents. Post- and pre-release hostels are projected, and plans are being considered for preventive and remedial work with inmates, including marital counseling and reconciliatory programs.[10]

A recent news story reports on a prison in Toluca, Mexico, where prisoner relations with his family are given top priority in preparing him for return to society.[11] "The involvement of the family in the life of the prisoner is considered of critical importance by prison officials. They feel that if the prisoner can rely on his family, he will have less need for his guard and this lessens the chance for situations in which guards may exploit prisoners."

"Moreover, as long as the prisoner's woman (be she legal wife or otherwise) remains loyal to him, there is a vastly reduced chance that he will be approached to have a homosexual relationship, nor would he likely initiate one out of desperation, say prison officials. No guard can violate a prisoner's privacy during a conjugal visit, unless he is summoned. If the couple has an infant, it will remain in a crib in the conjugal room with them overnight. Older children will spend the night in a separate section, to be reunited with their parents the following day."

The majority of the men committed to Toluca Prison are convicted of violent crimes, 68 percent of them after heavy drinking. The prison is described as "an expression of Mexico's lack of faith in institutions," which would appear to be confirmed by their reported recidivism rate of only 2.08 percent among those released from confinement there.

In England, in the Parkhurst Prison at Newport on the Isle of Wight, the authorities have set up an overnight stay center for the accommodation of prison visitors.[12] When the family comes to see the prisoner, they may have had to travel a long distance. The overnight stay center is equipped for sleeping, with lockers and lamps, and a kitchen. During the period between January and December 1970, bed and breakfast were provided for 415 adults and 145 children. The cost was 87 pence for an adult (approximately $2 U.S.) and 50 pence per child. An interesting feature of this plan is that a number of the advance bookings were made by wives who wanted to meet their husbands at 7 o'clock on the morning of their release from prison. The prison encourages this practice as an aid to family unity, where the wife cares enough to call for the husband, and they go home together. This is in marked contrast to the usual prison practice of turning a man out of prison at the gate, alone, with a few dollars in his pocket.

British prison authorities in some instances grant a subsidy for the trip of the wife to visit her husband in the institution, including vouchers for railroad travel. They also provide child-care facilities at the institution while the wife is visiting.

There are many prisons where children under a certain age are not permitted to visit their parents or brothers. Other institutions require six months to elapse after commitment before a child can visit his father. Children under certain ages are not permitted in certain hospitals for fear of contagion, and the same kind of argument could be made for keeping children away from the prison. But what does a mother do with her children if she wants to visit her husband, if she cannot find or afford a babysitter, or if there is nobody at home to take care of them? The prison can provide facilities for caring for the children of women who come to see their husbands, and also arrange for private quarters for husband and wife to meet in. This provides a situation where the two can discuss present and future plans with more privacy and intimacy than is possible in the usual prison visiting room. This same institution suggests, as well, that during these family visits, the guards be less obtrusive, so that they intrude less on the privacy of husband and wife.

Such emphasis is important, because we know that the relationships which the prisoner has with the outside—particularly those with his family—very often make the difference between a good record or a recidivist record after release. Many prisoners have no families, are not married, are "lone sticks." We cannot expect the prison to make up for such lack in a man's life. But if we dealt adequately with all those men who started out with good family situations, and helped to maintain them to the best of our ability, we would go far to prevent the recurrence of criminal careers. If we cannot do this for all, because all do not have good family relationships, we can at least start with those who do have, and make sure that the period of confinement maintains that relationship and does not destroy it for them. We all know of men who go to prison, leave a fond family behind, but who are away so long, and have so little contact, that one day they receive a so-called "Dear John letter"—"I am divorcing you and will marry somebody else because I cannot stand this separation any longer." In such ways as those described above, the institution can help to maintain a stable family relationship which is one essential element of a good rehabilitative program.

This same concept of imposing some penal sanction without complete disruption of normal life and ties in the community is contained in a scheme to give youthful offenders a taste of detention (i.e., imprisonment) by requiring that week-ends and two evenings a week be spent in the institution. The concept may be extended, as well, to adults.

At the Japanese maritime academy for young offenders, elsewhere described, when a young man is released from the institution, both staff and inmates line up and applaud as he walks out to the car waiting to take him to the station. The departure resembles an honorable discharge from the service (from conditions perhaps not so honorable—imprisonment) but the aim is obviously to make the moment of release a commendatory and memorable occasion. This is a very different thing from having the prison gates swing open to eject a man into the world with a feeling that he is as unwanted there as he was in prison.

WORK RELEASE [13]

In 1913, in Wisconsin, a little-noticed law was passed and became operable in that state. The concept embodied in that law, which has become known by the name of the state senator who introduced it—Huber—has since been extended, at an increasingly rapid rate, to twenty-seven other states. Seven other states authorize work-release programs in city or county institutions. Most simply described, it permits a man to leave the prison each day of the working week to go to a job, which is paid at the prevailing wage rate. At the end of the day he returns to prison, and spends his nights there, as well as his weekends. The prison usually houses the work-release prisoners in a separate wing or section of the institution to limit the possibilities of contraband or of messages being passed. Most importantly, under this program, a prisoner can now have not only some meaning to his life, but he escapes the monotony of the institution, and at the same time earns some money—to pay for his keep, to save for his release, and to help support his family. His weekly check is paid over to the institution for distribution in this fashion. One of the great advantages of this plan over and against industrial programs within the institution is that it obviates the installation and maintenance of expensive facilities and equipment which would have to be constantly modernized. The problem of how much to pay a prisoner for prison work is also avoided. He receives full wages on the outside, and the problem of being exploited by prison industry, or competition with free labor or unionized workers is done away with.

A followup study of the after careers of 2,360 minimum-security inmates of the Santa Clara County Jail in California between 1968 and 1970 confirms the value of work-release programs. Specialized vocational rehabilitation service resulted in a much smaller proportion of work-furlough releases who were reconvicted than for those inmates who had served their entire sentence in confinement.[14]

Selection of prisoners for work release can be initiated in several ways. The inmate can himself propose the possibility at the time of sentence or after he has begun serving it; the sentencing judge can suggest the possibility, or even include a recommendation for it in the sentence; or the prison staff may initiate the idea. The prison must approve work-release candidates, selecting them on the basis of their discipline and responsibility.[15]

Help in finding a job comes from various sources: a friend or family member, or the inmate may resume the job he had before he was sentenced. Most work-release jobs are obtained by the prison or by parole officers. Some states house work-release programs in special community correctional centers under state or county control, such as in a nearby jail; some stay in halfway houses.

All of the states charge work-releasees for room and board. Extension of the release concept to enable a prisoner to attend educational or vocational-training classes in schools in the community is a variation of the basic work-release concept.

WORK

Connecticut plans to have every qualified inmate in the state's prisons involved in a work or educational release program by 1976, and boasts that no other state "will be able to touch that." Such programs of study-release or work-release help to solve the problem of work within prisons. Most inmates do not do much beyond maintenance jobs. The easiest way to keep them busy is in polishing floors, cleaning windows, laundering their own clothes and those of the staff, and taking care of the garden of the warden's wife, plus food preparation. This kind of busywork can keep a large proportion of the population occupied all day long. At the end of such a day, they will have learned nothing. They may have kept the institutions clean and fed after a fashion, but their day will have been one of boredom.

With imagination, the most menial work can be made meaningful. For example, industrial cleaning has today become big business, most of it done under outside contract, rather than by employees of an institution or of an office building. In the past, the only people who took those night jobs were women, alcoholics—and ex-convicts—because these are the lowest and most marginal. But as commercial and industrial cleaning has become increasingly specialized and professionalized, it is better paid than before, and persons who hold these jobs or serve as contractors can earn better than a minimum wage. There is no reason why, in prison, the job of cleaning and maintenance cannot be used to teach men, and thus qualify them for such skills after their release, by training them in the uses and care of technical equipment. It is reported that some who have graduated from these programs have set themselves up after release as cleaning contractors, employing others. There are many places where other skills are taught. For example, in the Federal Correctional Institutions at Danbury, Connecticut, contracts are arranged between the institution and outside companies to train men in computer skills. This is also being done in the Central Prison in Teheran, Iran, where such training is currently made available for both men and women inmates.

It is not likely that the day will ever arrive when the basic conflict between prison administrators and prisoners will be resolved. The prison staff think always in terms of security and keeping men in; their charges have but a single thought: when will they get out?—by escape, or by official release processes. One of these processes is parole. But one of the realities which men face when they come before a parole board is that these boards change in their membership. They also change in what they are looking for—it frequently depends upon what the prevailing "gimmick" is. If education is the big thing and a man comes up for parole consideration who has done well vocationally, they may ask: "What have you done about completing your high school equivalency?" Well, the man was busy learning welding, so the board says, "Go back and get your high school equivalency and we will reconsider you." By the time he comes up for parole again having completed his high school equivalency, the game has again changed and the board asks: "Really, you don't have a vocation; why don't you go back and learn some welding?" A man does not know until he appears before the parole board what the latest standard is or what the prevailing emphasis is going to be at that particular time.

A recent development in Minnesota promises to resolve that conflict. It may be too new to evaluate, but it is at least an attempt to answer some of the problems of internal control, custody and discipline within the institution. Its emphasis is on a common goal: cooperation between administrators and inmates in looking toward release. Under its "contract system," every inmate newly received at the institution sits down with a committee— what would normally be the classification committee—and works out an agreement with them as to what he will do to earn his release over two years, or four years, or whatever the period may be, within the limits of his sentence and parole conditions. At the end of the negotiations, all three parties—the inmate, the administration, and the parole board—sign a formal contract that binds equally all three signatories.

The contract provides that if the offender lives up to his part of the bargain, the administration promises to put at his disposal the means necessary to attain his objectives, and the parole board agrees to release him if the institution says he has fulfilled his commitments.

Following are some of the sorts of things an inmate may pledge to do: "To demonstrate my willingness to handle stress without assaultive behavior and to learn to assert myself in a verbal manner, I will attend a weekly debate club for one year with 80 percent attendance. I will improve my general attitude and work reports to at least three (on a scale of five) for the upcoming quarter of January through March. To demonstrate an increased sense of responsibility and reliability, I will remain in my institution assignment job for a six months period with 80 percent attendance, and at least average grades."[16]

Once a man in prison can be offered something more than the traditional programs of carpentry, cement work and the stamping out of license plates (which is nowhere a function of private industry), the only limit to his learning the occupations of the future is set by the ingenuity and the imagination of the prison administration. For example, the Draper Correctional Center [17] provides training and placement of youthful inmates for jobs as combination welder, small electric appliance repairman, and technical writer, given together with intensive counseling and schooling in basic education courses. In the City of Boston, the largest employer is the field of health services—hospitals, medical schools and laboratories. To meet their needs, the Massachusetts Department of Public Health is just now setting up programs in prisons for training in the techniques and skills which may lead to health careers for inmates on work-release and parole status.[18] The response of many of the prisoners to this opportunity has been enormous. At the same time it helps to recruit and train workers in an understaffed, expanding field. Experiments such as these are taking place all over the country.

The prisons of Sweden, like those of Japan, are geared to a program of full employment, of keeping prisoners busy, in sharp contrast to most prisons in the United States, where unemployment or under employment is the rule—with the resulting feeling among the prison population of having nothing to do, of being neither wanted nor needed.

If work is for free men and women on the outside a basic rationale for living and for placing life in a positive setting, how much truer must it be for persons in confinement who exist with not much more than constant restrictions upon their lives and activities? The more men can be kept constructively busy, the less self-centered they will be, the lower will be the impetus to provocation or paranoia. We put men in prison for hard labor, but do not provide them with either the tools, the programs, or the incentive to labor even lightly. The classic cartoon shows convicts in striped suits splitting blocks of stone with a sledge hammer under the glaring sun. There is no longer much of that going on today. At the same time, around the world there is not enough significantly useful, truly productive work being offered—or done—in most prisons. So anything that can be done to provide prisoners—most of whom are unskilled and casual laborers—with opportunities to engage in meaningful work, to learn skills and work habits which can make them self-supporting when they are released, can at the same time repay the state some of the costs of confining and training them.

Sweden today shows what can be done when the work program in correctional institutions is geared to an emphasis on realistic training for employment after release. "Institutional care implies a policy of full employment. Every able-bodied man who can work a normal 40-hour week is required to do so, the sole exceptions are made for offenders pending trial, and the ill or disabled. For a total potential institutional population of 6,000, about 4,000 openings are available in industry and another 1,000 in rationally operated farming and forestry. The remaining clientele are put to simpler tasks in cells (these are chiefly for remanding persons awaiting trial who wish to work) or to kitchen and maintenance duties.

"The workshops at the new institutions are fully comparable in every respect with their counterparts in civilian life. Even the older institutions do their utmost to organize their work programs in accordance with present-day manufacturing principles.

"The purpose of the employment program is to facilitate the inmate's integration in a civilian working situation after his release. This is achieved by training the inmate in a working environment and under *working conditions that approximate as closely as possible the situation in the outside world.*

"Employment is available in shops for the production of various kinds of mechanical products and for television, radio and automobile repairs, in factories for prefabricated houses, furniture, interior fittings and rough carpentry, in tailoring shops, and in laundries and other shops for the manufacture of different kinds of industrial products.

"Another area of employment is the building industry, including the repair and maintenance of the installations of the Correctional Administration and the construction of buildings for the administration and other contractors.

"A third line is agriculture, which offers jobs in crop husbandry, animal husbandry, dairy and chicken farming, market gardening, various kinds of forestry and the sawmill industry, as well as in road-building and construction.

"Handicrafts and occupational therapy provide opportunities for inmates who are not capable of working under industrialized conditions.

"The value of products manufactured in fiscal year 1969/70 amounted to 77 million Sw. kr. Five million working hours were required to achieve this result."[19]

PAY

To this should be added the statement that Sweden is now experimenting with a plan to pay full wages to prisoners, the equivalent of what a worker on the outside would receive for the same production—in quantity and in quality. The scheme may seem to be a radical one. Yet the Secretary of Labor in the Johnson administration brought forward the proposal that men in prison should be covered by the Social Security System, with their contributions to it deducted from their prison pay. If after they had been released, they later found themselves unemployed, they would then be granted unemployment insurance, coverage of which had been deducted from the wages paid them while they were in prison.[20] The idea was never carried into effect.

The Swedish plan of full employment of prisoners is consonant with its not intruding on the scheduling of other correctional activities, such as education classes, vocational training or therapy sessions. In the past year the prison administration has taken another long step with the initiation at Tillberga open prison, 75 miles west of Stockholm, of a scheme whereby prisoners who work in prison industries will receive the "same wages as are standard on the labor market outside," for work in the manufacture of pre-fabricated houses, or in mechanics.

"Piece-work wages and hourly wages using the labor market system are calculated on the basis of average wages. During the experimental period the prisoners were exempt from income tax. Thus their wage scale corresponds to what a wood-products industry worker would earn after withholding tax is deducted. This means that Tillberga wages are estimated at 8–10 kronr per hour ($1.70 to $2.10). Deductions for meals are made at the same rate as that for the personnel. After deductions for meals, the prisoner is allowed 25 percent for his personal use. The remainder is set aside for savings and to cover his personal financial problems.

"An important goal is to get the prisoner to clarify his present financial situation and to learn to plan his economy with an eye to the future. Thanks to the higher wages he earns at Tillberga, he should be able to improve his situation prior to being released, for example by paying off his debts in whole or in part, or by paying rent on an apartment which he might otherwise forfeit. He should even try to save enough to support himself and his family during the first weeks after his release. The prisoner should plan his budget himself. He will be encouraged and given an opportunity to contact his creditors and, when necessary, make agreements with them on conditions for repayment. The guiding principle is that the prisoner himself should take the initiative and feel responsible for his future. The duty of institution personnel is to gain his confidence and assist him through advice and guidance.

"What is hoped will be the main result of the Tillberga experiment is a reasonably good financial and social situation for the prisoner when he is released. This should have a favorable influence on his readjustment to society and reduce the risk of a relapse into crime.

"Participation in the Tillberga experiment is voluntary. All prisoners in all institutions in the country have been informed of the experiment by means of a specially printed folder. They have been given an opportunity to request transfer to Tillberga, at the same time agreeing to accept the conditions set by the experiment."[21]

The regulations governing the wage payment plan also provide for overtime to be paid at rates which are 50 percent above the regular pay schedule. This is a far cry from the usual payment for prison work in most places—35¢ a day, or 50¢ a week, or a few dollars a month. Based on wage rates in the United States, if the same principle of full pay for full production were to be applied to prisoners, of the basic minimum wage, or even up to 6 dollars an hour, that would mean paying prisoners up to $200 a week for doing the same jobs as on the outside. The notion is not so madcap when the bookkeeping is examined, however. Income taxes are deducted from their wages, which go to the federal and state governments, unemployment insurance and social security are deducted, even medical-care insurance. But instead of the family receiving $100 a week from welfare, the prison pays them out of the man's wages. Some of it goes to him, some of it goes into his savings account, which is given to him when he leaves. Meanwhile he is charged room and board.

The bookkeeping thus comes out about the same as it does now. In the end, perhaps, the man does not have much more left than if he were paid only pennies a day plus "gate money" when he leaves. But there is a tremendous resulting difference between being treated like somebody on the outside, like a productive person, and being given a hand-out from the state. A man who goes out on parole, goes on welfare if he is out of work because he does not share in the national unemployment insurance plan. There is a difference between being on welfare and being the recipient of unemployment insurance because one is entitled to it, under a plan to which he has contributed while he was working in the institution. Acceptance of the bookkeeping means acceptance at the same time of a principle that is more important than the purely financial: that a prisoner is being treated as a member of society, and not as an outcast, as an object of charity, rather than as a person with benefits coming to him as a matter of right. The men who rioted at Attica prison demanded that they be treated like men, at the same time that they demanded better food, and more frequent showers. But their main demand was that they be treated like men.

That the principle of full pay for a full day of prison work is gradually gaining ground may be seen in the policy declaration of the National Council on Crime and Delinquency, whose Board of Trustees recently urged "the introduction of federal and state legislation requiring that an inmate employed at productive work in a federal, state or local institution shall be paid no less than the minimum wage operative nationally or in his state.

"We urge legislators and administrators to adopt and support the foregoing policy and we call on civic organizations and the general public to demand its implementation."[22]

EDUCATION

Few people in prison have graduated from high school. Their average level of education stands at about the ninth grade. One of their basic difficulties is this low educational level, which makes it difficult for them to make a good life for themselves on the outside. So the period of imprisonment should be utilized to raise the educational level of those who have been disadvantaged before they came to prison. Considering the length of time that has elapsed since the first school was opened in the first prison—the Walnut Street Jail in Philadelphia in 1784—education within prison walls has been abysmally slow in developing.

"This was followed by a few elementary courses in New York in 1801, Pennsylvania in 1844, and at Auburn and Sing Sing Prisons in 1847. In 1870, a school system was established at the Detroit House of Correction, and the nation's first reformatory at Elmira, New York, opened a vocational trade school six years later. Prison instruction continued to be scanty however. During the 1870s, almost half of all prisoners in the United States were reported to be illiterate.

"The modern trend in correctional education began in 1929, and by five years later, approximately 60 percent of all inmates in federal institutions were enrolled in some kind of educational work. Thereafter, emphasis began to be centered on social education activities and problems of motivation, and during the 1940s forums, current events and discussion groups, and debates and lectures were introduced.

"By 1957, more than 40 percent of the federal prison inmate population were enrolled in correspondence courses, and a few received college credit for the courses taken. The 1960s saw the introduction of college programs in Illinois, Texas, California, Oregon, and the District of Columbia."[23]

The realization began to grow that education had a significant role to play in the resocialization of offenders. "At the Patuxent Institution for Defective Delinquents at Jessup, Maryland, forty-three students are enrolled at the elementary level, sixty-eight at the junior high level, and forty-six in high school classes. Eight full-time teachers instruct twenty-four courses. In Florida's correctional institutions, prison schools operate on a continuous twelve-month schedule, and new students are admitted each week. College-level instruction has been provided for four institutions by two junior colleges. As of 1970, more than one-half of Florida's inmate population were involved in some form of academic education."[24]

In the Bordentown Reformatory in New Jersey, in the Draper Correctional Center in Alabama, in the Canadian Penitentiary Service in Ottawa, educational programs are introduced into prisons to help raise the educational level of prisoners.

The University of Victoria, according to a recent report, has entered into a contract with the Department of the Solicitor General to provide four university courses for 40 or 50 inmates at the British Columbia Penitentiary—English, history, psychology, and sociology. A fifth course, when added, would provide prisoners with a full year university program, for credit.[25]

"In 1967 the Upward Bound Oregon Prison Project was developed at the State Penitentiary in Salem to provide inmates with educational opportunities which would enable them to further their education after release. In 1968, after an evaluation of its worth as an education program, the project was named NewGate. By September 1971, six NewGates had been established in Oregon, Colorado, Kentucky, Minnesota, New Mexico, and Pennsylvania. NewGate's uniqueness consists of the linking of three components, guidance, counseling and college-level education into a single comprehensive program within the institution, and continuation of these programs outside the institution. A fundamental operating principle brings community resources and people into the correctional program and develops community-based systems into which student-inmates can move upon release. Although measures of success for NewGate are difficult to develop, results so far are encouraging. Of the inmates released through NewGate, less than 15 have been convicted of new offenses or have been returned to the institution for parole violation."[26]

The Massachusetts STEP Program (Student Tutor Education Project) was begun in the maximum-security prison at Walpole in 1968 as an experiment, to determine if there were prisoners with sufficient intellectual potential, regardless of previous academic achievement, who would be interested in a program of study within the prison which might motivate them to continue their education. The teaching staff, all of them with graduate degrees, are expected to spend some time in individual educational counseling. Up until late 1972 the program was sponsored by Brandeis University; thereafter, the funding came from three private foundations and from federal sources. This made possible the expansion of the program to the medium-security institution at Norfolk, and the assumption of sponsorship by the University of Massachusetts. While the program has evolved through various stages of development and change, it is currently offering two full years of academic study, leading to the Associate in Arts degree.

The program operates on an annual budget of $50,000, and since its beginning has served 334 inmates, of whom 80 have since been released on parole. Of those, 20 percent (16) have been returned for new offenses or parole violation. But of that same 80, 12 are known to attend or to have attended colleges or universities. This program offers a real upward movement in the lives of men enrolled in its courses. Starting in January of 1973, nine STEP prisoners on study-release are being bussed daily to and from the University of Massachusetts.[27]

"College-level instruction in correctional institutions is growing at a rapid rate. Programs are presently operating in California, the District of Columbia, Florida, Illinois, Kansas, Kentucky, Maryland, Michigan, New Jersey, New York, Ohio, Oregon, Texas and Washington. Although they now serve a relatively small number of inmates, it is estimated that approximately

25,000 prisoners will be involved in college level programs in the near future."
[28]

Progressively-run training schools, whether under private or public
auspices, have for some years organized their educational program within the
school under the control of the local public educational authority. This forces
the institution to bring its standards, its curriculum and the qualifications
required of its teachers up to the level of public schools on the outside. The
idea seems to be catching on in adult institutions as well, for a recent report
from Massachusetts suggests the creation of a special school district to provide
training for prison inmates. The purpose here is to upgrade education for
prisoners, a much needed step. A mere 1 percent of the annual state corrections budget went to education of prisoners in the preceding year. Those who
teach in prisons averaged $2,000 a year less than comparable public school
teachers, and of their pupils, 80 percent lacked a high school diploma.[29]

The boldest scheme for making college-level education available
to persons in confinement is contained in a recent press release from the
State University and the Department of Correctional Services of the State
of New York. The joint announcement described a coeducational program
which was to be introduced into an existing correctional facility, renovated
to accommodate some 200 male and 50 female students. It is described as a
"combination prison college," to "make it possible for more prisoners to
move back into society and lead productive lives . . ., to educate them in the
broader sense and give them a better self-image." The college would offer a
broad liberal arts program, completely tuition-free, leading to an associate
degree, and guaranteeing the right to transfer academic credits earned to other
colleges in the State University system after release.[30]

PRIVACY AND IDENTITY

What of other restrictions on prisoners? One of the great deprivations placed
upon them is the right to send and receive mail. Although the longer a man
is in prison the more letters he may receive and send, all incoming and outgoing
mail in most institutions is censored. The fear, obviously, is that escape plans
will be hatched by correspondence, or that under the stamp of an incoming
letter some grains of LSD will be hidden.[31] Therefore all mail is opened—
outgoing as well as incoming—and if a prisoner writes something critical of a
guard, that letter may never reach its destination. We are gradually doing away
with these unnecessary invasions of privacy, which demean and dehumanize
the prisoner, which deprive him of privacy from the moment he enters the
institution.[32] The problem of the self-identity of prisoners is involved in
the imposition of many unneeded restrictions in prisons which, as Erving Goffman has pointed out, are "total" institutions—like mental hospitals and the

Army, and have complete control over the lives of inmates.[33] A man coming into prison is literally stripped of everything which connects him with the outside world—or reminds him of it. His hair is cut and he is put into a uniform which is not worn on the outside, and from then on, he is a number, the object of a depersonalized regime designed to make it impossible for him to retain his identity as an individual.

In the maintenance of some relation with people on the outside lies one of the few ways of supporting his ego and the continuity of his life. If you worry about contraband, if you worry about the contents of letters coming in and out, then open the letter in the presence of the prisoner, and if you find contraband you can tell him so at once, and use that as a disciplinary measure against him. So much of his privacy has been taken away from a prisoner in the institution that he must be left some means to hold on to the threads of the contacts he has with the outside. After all, the end of imprisonment—to put it at its best—is ultimately to return the prisoner to the community, socialized. If we interfere completely with this contact with the outside, on the grounds that it is necessary for security, we make it more difficult and not less difficult for him to maintain his contact with the outside—and with his sanity.

About a year after the United States became involved in World War II, there was a great shortage of manpower. Under an Army regulation dating back to 1878, men with prior felony records were barred from induction. This regulation was suspended, and the Federal Bureau of Prisons proceeded to enlist in the armed forces men who were released from federal and state institutions on parole. They entered the army like any other inductees. As a result of this program, some 50,000 to 60,000 men who would not otherwise have entered the armed forces were accepted, thereby permitting an equal number of workers with necessary skills to remain at their jobs of war production.

When the war was over, a survey of prisoners released into the army discovered that the record of heroism and bravery in action attained by soldiers and sailors released directly from prison was equal to that of men who had not served time. And their records of court martials, bad conduct and dishonorable discharge did not differ markedly from that of other recruits.[34] When it is realized that these men were under the handicap of a prior criminal record, it might be said that they did better than the average, because many of those who were paroled into the armed forces had histories of aggressive behavior, were assaultive, were a "danger" to the community— the very qualities the army sought for its soldiers. If there could be evolved a peacetime equivalent to the army, for many of these men society would be preventing criminal careers in the first place, and would at the same time benefit from their efforts.[35]

Young people in today's world have a basic need to test themselves under adventurous conditions, to grow up in a society which seems to them at times to be overregulated. When they do not follow the normal approved modes of life, and seek for excitement or challenge, they are punished for their "delinquency." Maybe it is society's fault that it does not provide peaceful and acceptable noncriminal ways for them to test themselves. Under the Outward Bound program, a few young people have lost their lives. But young people daily lose their lives by accident and by suicide in large numbers because life is not rewarding or because they search for relief from the humdrum of life.

Pennsylvania, where 200 years ago the Quakers founded the first penitentiary, has experienced trouble in its jails and prisons—riots and disturbances of a violent nature. The newly elected Governor of the state has given his attention to these problems.[36] Pennsylvania is the only jurisdiction in the world to adopt, in their entirety, the Standard Minimum Rules for the Treatment of Prisoners, which were first formulated in 1926 by the League of Nations.[37] Consonant with these rules, and in order to reduce disciplinary problems within prison, inmates are now permitted to wear their hair as they choose, and to grow beards and moustaches. Prisoners may also correspond without censorship. Incoming mail is checked only for money, drugs, or other contraband. Telephone calls from inmates to members of their families at times of emergency or for special occasions are encouraged. Visiting rooms are being refurnished in informal living room settings. Longer and more frequent, even some evening, visits are permitted. Prisons normally do not permit evening visits, so that a friend or a wife must come in the daytime when the staff is on duty, leave his or her job, and perhaps lose a day's pay. When you think of it, evening visits are a sensible relaxation of an age-old rule.

Restrictions on incoming publications have been relaxed: most prisons accept books and magazines only if they come directly from the publisher, in order to make sure that they do not contain contraband. Only material containing hard pornography or believed to be a serious threat to the prison is excluded. Commissaries now offer a much wider selection of goods. Medical and dental care is being improved and expanded. Food preparation and service are being made more appetizing. The bad food which is served in most prisons is one of the most frequent single causes for disturbances. Good food is not necessarily a matter of expense, because given the same basic materials the difference lies chiefly in preparation and serving. Mealtime can be a social affair, except in those prisons where silence is enforced in the mess hall. Like many other programs described here, the decisive factors in improving the prison regime are not matters of more money, but of more attention, concern, and serious interest.

Administrators of prisons regard the serving of meals purely as a routine stoking function, to be kept at a minimum. Properly viewed, preparation and serving of food in an institution can be seen as an opportunity for

training of inmates in the culinary arts. There is a tremendous demand throughout the world today for good chefs. Food served in prisons could be used not
only to feed the inmates well, but as a means of training them for professional
careers in restaurant and hotel work.

PRISONERS' RIGHTS [38]

Rights for prisoners seems at first blush to be a contradiction in terms. What
rights do prisoners have?[39] Under our law, generally, upon conviction of a
felony, a person loses all of his civil rights. While such felons are paying the
price under custody in an institution, how dare they talk about human rights?
In many instances, persons who have served a long stretch in prison, after
release on parole, never entirely recover their civil rights. In a sense they carry
with them to the grave a life sentence, some of it spent in the institution and
some of it spent on the street. An imprisoned felon loses the right to vote, he
will have difficulty in getting a driver's license, he cannot be a barber, a TV
repairman, an electrician, nor can he hold public office or get a civil service
job—for the rest of his life. He cannot even return to visit a friend in prison,
because he is required when he signs the visitor's roster to declare whether or
not he has ever been convicted of a felony. A man who spent nineteen and a
half years in three institutions was ultimately paroled, and today is completely
and successfully rehabilitated. Married, with three children, he holds a responsible and well-paid position. Elected to a national committee for penal reform,
he must obtain the permission of his parole officer before he may go out of
state to its meetings. This is always granted, but he must, each time, nevertheless submit to the indignity of asking for permission, and will continue to live
under such restrictions for the rest of his life, until and unless pardoned.[40]
        Prisoners are deprived of many rights between arrest and sentence.
When arrived in the prison, they have no rights whatsoever; the rights of the
presumption of innocence have at this point been exhausted.[41] But today
a change is coming about, and prisoners are starting to demand and receive
many rights which were previously denied. The Constitution forbids the use
of cruel and unusual punishment, the imposition of any form of treatment
which a court may deem excessive or discriminatory. In the recent Supreme
Court decision with regard to the death penalty, that penalty was generally
determined by the court to constitute cruel and and unusual punishment, for
one thing because it was inequitably applied to the poor and to members of
minority groups.[42]
        Similarly, in a class action suit brought against the administration
of the Suffolk County jail in Boston, already cited,[43] the impetus for the
successful court action arose as a way of reasserting constitutional guarantees
for prisoners, at the same time that it struggled for the redress of the grievous
conditions imposed upon detainees in jails and prisons.

Up until recently, the practice of criminal law has been at the bottom of the legal profession. The most highly esteemed lawyers are those who "have traditionally concerned themselves with only one sector of the world in which the law operates, the sector of commerce. . . ."[44] The criminal lawyer is generally looked down upon, unless he handles those clients who pay him large fees. George Bernard Shaw once said that the status which a man occupies is determined for him by his clients. A banker or stockbroker whose customers are investors is at the top of the professional ladder. But a criminal lawyer, who deals with thieves, rapists, pimps and arsonists cannot reach such high social status, unless he is a Clarence Darrow or an F. Lee Bailey, and gets one-hundred or two-hundred thousand dollars for defending rich lawbreakers. Otherwise he tends to be—if only slightly—identified with the kind of people he represents.

Recently, with the growing emphasis on civil rights and the suits of prisoners for their constitutionally guaranteed rights, the status of the criminal lawyer seems to be rising. Many young lawyers are going into this field out of the same desire to devote themselves to public service that brings other young people to work with delinquents, drug addicts and the mentally retarded. They are putting that desire—plus their legal training—to work in a variety of ways. One of these is by listening to prisoners' complaints, and then doing something about them.

For while men who work in the free world can come home and take out on their families and wives the frustrations of the day, thus enabling them to cope with the day's problems, and help them to face tomorrow, in prison there are no such channels for release of tension. Thence derives the pattern of the prisoner with a grudge, with an *idée fixé,* which is necessarily directed against those in closest proximity to him—guards and other prisoners. Out of this need to find some means of letting himself be heard, of having someone to listen to, of overcoming the complete powerlessness of the one prisoner against the massive prison world, have come in recent years several sources of relief.

In the Rhode Island Correctional Institution at Cranston, a legal assistance program is now in its third year.[45] The program was initiated because a majority of the inmates could not afford private counsel, in answer to their many requests for legal assistance. It is funded by the Law Enforcement Assistance Administration, and staffed with thirteen law students, under the supervision of a full-time member of the Bar and of the professor in criminal law and procedure at Boston College Law School, where the program originated. The program serves the legal needs of prisoners in a variety of ways. The state pays only the automobile mileage of the law student-advocates, otherwise their services are free, in return for which they get experience on the job. The uniqueness of the program lies in its concept of an "in-house" full-time law office with a resident lawyer assisted by a highly motivated staff of volunteer law student interns.

An even more comprehensive program is now operating in the prison system of the District of Columbia, which controls over one thousand young prisoners between the ages of 18 and 26.[46] A half-dozen trained lawyers, with an equal number of law students and other professionals, have here for the past two years, through a specially created Center for Correctional Justice, conducted a unique experiment. Most simply put, their aim, as trained outside listeners, is to hear the legal problems of their youthful prisoner clients, and then to negotiate directly with the administration for their amelioration or solution.

Training for the job, for the Center's staff members, includes intensive preparation, plus a day and a half locked up in the facilities where they will later serve. By the end of its first year, the Center had served over 500 cases in the three kinds of legal service offered. Some inmates may feel that there has been injustice in their trial or sentence, which is referred to a public defender's office.[47] Civil problems which have merit are likewise referred to the local government-supported legal services agencies.

The most novel aspect of this service is in the third area of their work: dealing with individual or group complaints against conditions within the prison. The Center team attempts to work these out with the prison administrators, and to date have not required the services of outside arbitration. Inmate complaints arise from such areas as transfers, parole conditions, and possible errors in length of sentence. Group complaints are handled in a committee composed of prison inmates and officials on such matters as visiting hours, special religious requirements, commissary items and accessibility, and medical services. One of the important characteristics of this service is that it is run as an outside agency—it is neither the creation nor the creature of the correctional system nor of the prisoners themselves.

PRISON: THE OMBUDSMAN

It is this same objective and neutral feature which is embodied in the position of the ombudsman, so-called, which is receiving increasing attention as an effective means of dealing with justified prisoner complaints, and thus preventing riots and disturbances. The term is of Scandinavian origin and means a specifically appointed government official, free of any specific departmental connection. He is the freely roaming ranger within the governmental table of organization, with no fixed schedule, precise job description or boss—except to make himself available to receive complaints and to handle them unofficially, informally, equitably, without going through the bureaucratic process. His office is that of a nonjudicial but impartial advocate—an arbitrator in the best sense of the word. He is a combination of a lonely-hearts column and a fix-it shop, operating in a computerized society. The role of the ombudsman is much discussed these days for the amelioration of the "snafus" of government in its noncriminal functions. It is all the more required within the prison world

where, as has been pointed out, there exist few outlets for expressing exaspera-
tion or aggravated frustration in any kind of acceptable or constructive fashion.

We were all scarred by Attica: the nation as well as the correctional
field. At the last minute, on an emergency basis, all kinds of visiting groups
came into that prison. The membership and compositon of some of these groups
may have been criticized for one reason or another, but outside groups had
to be brought in at the final critical moment to listen to prisoner complaints
and carry them forward to somebody else to deal with. Had there been somebody at Attica to whom the inmates could have spoken beforehand, it might
have provided the safety valve which could have prevented the outbreak of
that catastrophe.

The first ombudsman program in the United States was proposed
by the Philadelphia Foundation to be staffed by the Pennsylvania Prison
Society. Unfortunately, the project was not carried through, and within a
month of its proposal, "the inmates staged a nonviolent peaceful hunger strike,
during which time most of their demands were recognized as valid but have
not yet been met. . . ."[48]

There is little doubt but what the ombudsman will be an increasingly valued and valuable member of prison staffs, as evidenced in the state
of Minnesota, which has just appointed a complete staff, including an ombudsman, together with a deputy, three investigators, and three secretaries. The
function of this office is to receive, investigate and act on complaints emanat-
ing from prisoners—and staff officers—at the state's correctional institutions
and prison camps, though it is expected that the greater part of their attention will be devoted to inmates of the Stillwater maximum-security prison.
Complaints will cover such matters as dissatisfaction with work and other assignments, instances of racial discrimination, and questions regarding prison
regulations. It is reported that in the short time since the service was established, the number of complaints to wardens, the commissioner of corrections,
and the governor of the state has dropped markedly. Connecticut seems to be
following suit with the establishment of a pilot ombudsman program in selected
correctional institutions to deal with the grievances of inmates, in the expectation that in time the program will serve all the correctional institutions
of the state.[49]

A UNION FOR PRISONERS

Meanwhile, prisoners in other places have not waited for this kind of relief,
and just within the past two years have begun to form a union of prisoners.
Started in Rhode Island, the National Penal Reform Association (NPRA) has
been in existence since the fall of 1971.[50]

As an indication of the growth of NPRA, it held a banquet to
celebrate its first anniversary, with almost 100 guests in attendance, including
state and local officials. At that time, NPRA announced its sought goal of

$60,000 to help find jobs and housing for released prisoners, to finance half-way houses and college education for parolees, and work-release programs to help inmates support their families. Through the efforts of NPRA, the correctional institution where it was organized has become the first prison in the country to hire inmates under the minimum-wage law: two are clerk-typists, and four others work on the association's newsletter.

At least one administrator of a state correctional system has vowed that he would resign rather than deal with such a union of prisoners. But forty years ago, some leaders of the automobile industry made the same threats about the new CIO union, only to retract them. Today, the United Automobile Workers has become one of the largest and most effective bodies representative of workers, and has helped to bring stability to the industry.

It is safe to say that not many years from now, unions of prisoners will become an accepted and established feature within penal institutions. It has already begun to spread to four other New England states. A parallel may be seen between this development and the inmate council founded by Thomas Mott Osborne in Sing Sing, which was called the Mutual Welfare League.[51] It was at this same time that some large employers, afraid of the growing power of unions, began to organize—and to finance—employee groups known as Mutual Benefit Societies, or Company Associates. Today these company unions have been supplanted by trade unions, organized and financed by such groups as the retail clerks, while postal workers, teachers, police and hospital aides have joined into unions to represent and bargain for their members.

"Concerned about getting the institution stabilized and reducing confrontation between inmates and staff," the charter of the NPRA states as one of its main purposes, as well as the promotion of modern, progressive and creative changes in the prison systems of the country through nonviolent action.[52] It is interesting that prisoners should emphasize the nonviolent aspects of their programs. The union of prisoners is undoubtedly one of the most revolutionary proposals that has been brought forward in the penal field. One of the advantages of the unionizing of prisoners is that it will bring about formal bargaining instead of the present private arrangements, which is precisely the reason why unions were formed in other areas. Negotiations will take place in such a way that the entire prison population will bargain together with the administration rather than, as now, permitting self-designated inmate representatives to deal privately—even secretly—with guards and administrators to gain, perhaps, some minor concessions, in the process winning special favors for themselves. Not the least of these favors is the acquisition of power—even of life and death—over their fellow prisoners. The idea of inmates banding together occurs in most places on the basis of a prison subculture which frequently by force and often through nondemocratic means elects its leaders. Donald Clemmer has described this in extensive detail.[53]

There is a penitentiary in Kansas, in which unbelievable conditions were described before a Senate committee investigating prisons about a year and a half ago.[54] Here the prisoners ran the hospital, dispensed the drugs, the amphetamines and barbituates, to their friends—for a price. It went so far that the inmates, through their self-appointed leaders in the institution, actually drew up the daily schedule for the guards. And so bad were the conditions in that institution, and so many inmates murdered by other inmates, that in one year there were 300 reported instances of self-mutilation on the part of prisoners as a means of getting out of the general population into the hospital, or as a protest against the gangsterism of the inmate leaders. So if the idea of a union of prisoners is deplored, or viewed as anarchical, it is well to consider that prisoners have come together at other times, other places, and under other conditions, even to running what are called kangaroo courts, where their self-appointed leaders punish those who do not obey them by holding an informal trial and punishing the offenders. There have been instances of their carrying out the death penalty within the institution, without interference, even with the knowledge and covert approval of the administration anxious, above all, to maintain "security" with a minimum of disruption. A union of prisoners is therefore a salutary move that will permit them to band together for the defense of their common rights. By this means, the entire prison population will have access to all the information, all the rights, and everything that makes up the material of bargaining. As a result, official rules and regulations will be limited to those which have been hammered out by agreement between the keeper and the kept.

If everyone knows what the regulations are, and these have been arrived at by mutual bargaining, the possibility of personal grudge or animosity on the part of guards, leading to discrimination and enmity between guard and inmate, and between prisoner and prisoner, may not be completely eliminated, but it will certainly be reduced.

Some of the arguments against unions of prisoners are that, in the past, inmate council government schemes have largely failed, that inmates in positions of power are likely to abuse it, that prisoner decisions relating to authority and security may possibly lead to violence. There may be some validity in such arguments, but the following incident may indicate otherwise.

In December of 1972 a strike of prison guards was threatened in the correctional institution in Rhode Island, over a question of working conditions. Tension grew in the prison and the national guard was alerted. At this juncture, the union of prisoners—black and white—held a meeting. Their leaders went to the administration and pledged that if the guards went out on strike, they would police the institution themselves, would refrain from any acts to make life difficult for the warden, and that it would not be necessary to call in outside security forces.[55]

Some of the stated goals of the National Prisoners' Reform Association include the following: abolition of prisons to the greatest degree possible by use of furlough; hospitalizing the psychotic and the physically handicapped, and the use of halfway houses; doing away with jails for persons awaiting trial, except for the smallest percentage of those who require jail; paying minimum wages for all prisoners; dealing realistically with the problems of the country's penal system; and serving as an information center for spreading the ideas of prison unions across the country.

The other side of the prisoner union movement is the question of the relationship between the larger world of organized trade unionism and the walled world of the prison-worker. For many years the concern of American trade unions was to make sure that the products of prison labor did not compete with labor in the free market, under the contract system whereby private industry employed prisoners, paid them next to nothing, and sold their products at prices far below those of comparable items made by free labor.

The Swedish trade unions have had a positive attitude toward work in prisons, as may be seen in the cooperative agreement between them and the prison administration which provides that trainees who complete their apprenticeship in the construction field while serving their sentence will have their practical training continued by the union after release. At a number of institutions, special advisory councils, including, among others, the warden, a prisoner and a trade union representative deal with such questions as the work in the institution, working conditions and pay.[56]

COEDUCATION

One of the age-old problems in prison administration is the unisexual character of the inmate population and consequently of the staff. Juvenile institutions were the first to initiate the practice of appointing women as cottage mothers, matrons, and cooks. The practice has been recently greatly extended and today finds women serving in adult penal institutions in a very wide variety of capacities—not only as clerks and secretaries—but as counselors, teachers, nurses, social workers, and psychologists. There are two women commissioners of corrections in the United States—one in Louisiana, for female offenders, and a woman in Maine whose job as commissioner of corrections gives her supervision over both men and women, juvenile and adult. Sweden has for years had women as wardens in some of its male prisons.

In the Women's Reformatory at Framingham in Massachusetts, which now is becoming coeducational, the number of females in custody is gradually being reduced from 84 to 24.[57] As women are placed in halfway houses and other community settings, their places will be taken by specially selected male inmates transferred there from the reformatory for men. Men and women will have all their programs together; they will share in recreation and classes, eat together, and separate only at night.

Massachusetts does not stand alone in this respect. In Fort Worth, Texas, there is a coeducational program at a federal prison, established in 1972, the first such institution for adults in the United States.[58] It is geared toward rehabilitation, preparing 359 men and 81 women for return to the community. Those selected for the prison were within two years of release at the time, were not considered escape risks or predatory, and were willing to accept the restrictions of the program and participate in intensive training. The average stay is fourteen to sixteen months.

The "residents" wear street clothes rather than uniforms, are allowed free interaction (excepting sexual intercourse) with other inmates (male and female), and may have visitors five days a week. Sixty inmates qualify for work-release and study-release programs in the neighboring community. The twenty-six-building facility has classrooms where subjects ranging from simple arithmetic to college-level courses are taught, in addition to vocational subjects. There is also a twenty-five-bed hospital. Four building units house male prisoners, and one, locked at night, houses female prisoners.

After one year's operation, the warden has reported, "We have a lot of the same problems that other correctional institutions have—theft, drugs, fights, and keeping order, but our cases are on a far smaller scale. The basic theory on which we operate is a simple one. We believe that people are people first and prisoners second. There is more about them with which we can identify than condemn."[59]

In the past, there were only four or five juvenile institutions in the United States which were coeducational, but the movement is spreading there, too. One of the oldest juvenile institutions in the country [60] has been coeducational for years. Boys and girls mix freely in all of their daily activities, attend school, go to picnics, parties and dances together. The superintendent once remarked that he is satisfied if the pregnancy rate among his girls did not exceed that prevailing at the local coeducational high school.

In Singapore, where training schools for boys and girls are separate, the administration arranges joint picnics twice a year, combined athletic weeks, cooking competitions and the like. Incidentally, in one of the schools for boys, the woodworking classes are so organized that the piece of wood which one boy may be working on is destined to form a part of a piece of furniture, for example, that the others are preparing other parts for, so that the end is the result of a joint, cooperative effort.

The Minnesota Home School for delinquents, for some time coeducational, has recently undergone a change in the direction of more progressive treatment of its 150 boys and girls.[61] Unmanageable children were formerly confined to solitary lock-ups. This has been replaced by a "quiet room." If a child gets out of control, he and a staff member go into the room and stay together until whatever was the instigating issue has been resolved.

In the view of the state administrator of the Minnesota training school system, "Isolation is no way to control children. When the counselor and the youngster are forced to work together, it is amazing how much faster they find a solution to differences."[62] The shift from solitary confinement has been accompanied by more urban excursions and more liberal policies concerning runaways. "If a child wants to leave, we discuss problems and possible benefits. If he still chooses to leave, we give him bus fare so that he doesn't get hurt hitch-hiking."

In the first wedding ever conducted at the Adult Correctional Institution in Rhode Island, a former policeman serving a twenty-five-year sentence for murder, was married in the prison chapel. Families of both bride and groom were in attendance, as were many fellow inmates. After the ceremony, conducted by the prison chaplain, a reception was held in the prison yard.[63]

Some traditional ways of doing things, when stood on their heads, make sudden good sense.

NOTES

1. Milton Luger "The Youthful Offender," in *Task Force Report: Juvenile Delinquency and Youth Crime* (Washington: President's Commission Report on Law Enforcement and Administration of Justice, 1967), pp. 119–131.
2. J. Shane Creamer, "Rapping Toward Prison Reform," *American Journal of Correction,* Vol. 34, No. 5 (September–October 1972), p. 28.
3. *Kriminal Varden* [The Correctional System] (Stockholm: National Correctional Administration, 1970), p. 11.
4. Remarks by the Delegate from Sweden, Fourth United Nations Crime Congress, Kyoto, August 1970.
5. *Boston Globe,* April 13, 1973.
6. Ibid.
7. Carlson W. Markley, "Furlough Programs and Conjugal Visiting in Adult Correctional Institutions," *Federal Probation,* Vol. 37, No. 1 (March 1973), pp. 10–26.
8. Ibid. See also F.J. Verborgen, "Imprisonment and Conjugal Life"; in *Hartwick Review,* Spring 1967, pp. 67–68.
9. *Boston Globe, op. cit.*
10. J.R. Hannan, "Developments within New Zealand," Wellington, 1972 (dup.).
11. *New York Times,* quoted in *Newsletter,* International Prisoners Aid Association, Milwaukee, March–April 1973, pp. 5, 6.

12. "Survey Report: Family Visits to Prisons," London, National Association for the Care and Resettlement of Offenders (NACRO), 125 Kennington Park Road, London SE 11, July 1970 (dup.).
13. A nationwide "Directory of Work Release Programs and Personnel" is available from the Publications Office of the Center for Study of Crime, Delinquency, and Correction, Southern Illinois University, Carbondale, Illinois 62901.
14. Alvin Rudoff and T.C. Esselstyn, "Evaluating Work Furlough: A Follow-up," *Federal Probation,* Vol. 37, No. 2 (June 1973), pp. 48–53.
15. Elmer H. Johnson, "Report on an Innovation—State Work Release Program," *Crime and Delinquency,* Vol. 16 (1970), p. 417.
16. Communication from the Minnesota Commissioner of Corrections, December, 1972. Variations of this program are being conducted in Wisconsin (Fox Lake Correctional Institution), in Arizona (State Reformatory at Florence), and in California (Los Angeles City Community Center). See Leon Leiberg and William Park, "Towards Change in Correctional Manpower Services: Mutual Agreement Programming," 1973 (dup.) See also, "The Mutual Agreement Program," College Park, Md., American Correctional Association. November 1973.
17. In Elmore, Alabama.
18. Information from the Massachusetts Department of Public Health.
19. *Kriminal Varden,* op. cit., 1971, pp. 8–9.
20. Information furnished by the Secretary, Department of Labor, Washington.
21. "Stockholm: Information Service," Royal Swedish Ministry for Foreign Affairs, December 1972, pp. 1–3 (dup.).
22. *American Journal of Corrections,* Vol. 34, No. 4 (July–August 1972), p. 44.
23. Martin P. Haskell and Lewis Yablonsky, *Crime and Delinquency* (Chicago: Rand McNally, 1970), pp. 389–90.
24. The quoted paragraphs which follow are taken from Albert R. Roberts, *Source-book on Prison Education: Past, Present and Future* (Springfield, Illinois: Charles C. Thomas, 1971).
25. *Bulletin of the Canadian Corrections Association,* Vol. II, No. 4 (March 1973), p. 4.
26. Roberts, *op. cit.*
27. The information which follows was furnished by the Director of STEP, 10 Channing Place, Cambridge, Massachusetts 02138.
28. Roberts, *op. cit.*
29. Information furnished by the Massachusetts Department of Corrections, November 1973.
30. *New York Times,* October 24, 1973.
31. Mathew Muraskin, "Censorship of Mail: The Prisoner's Right to Communicate by Mail with the Outside World," *The Prison Journal,* Vol. 48, No. 1 (Spring–Summer 1968), pp. 33–39.
32. An exception—in this instance a commendable form of invasion of privacy—may be cited from Japan. Here, in the maximum-security custody

institution at Fuchu, which holds some highly disturbed, even psychotic offenders, a 24-hour close watch was inconspicuously kept on a prisoner suspected of suicidal tendencies. A small TV camera was placed in front of his cell connected to a view screen in the administration office of the prison. Here the officers on duty checked from time to time on the behavior of the prisoner against the possibility of his hurting himself or of attempting suicide. This is an admirable device for maintaining round-the-clock surveillance over potential suicides which should commend itself, if only by reason of its economic advantages.

33. Erving Goffman, *Asylums* (New York: Anchor Books, 1961).
34. Hans Mattick, "Ex-Cons Prove to be Good Soldiers; Prison Returns Fell to Record Low" *The Menard Times* [Menard, Illinois State Prison], Vol. 17, No. 2 (March 1, 1966), p. 8.
35. William James, *The Moral Equivalent of War* (New York: Harper & Row, 1970).
36. J. Shane Creamer, op. cit.
37. *Standard Minimum Rules for the Treatment of Prisoners, and Related Recommendations* (New York: United Nations, Department of Economic and Social Affairs, 1958).
38. Richard Singer, *Prisoners' Legal Rights: Bibliography of Cases and Articles,* (New York: Warren, Gorham, and Lamont, 1971). See also Sheldon Krantz, *Cases on the Law of Corrections and Prisoner's Rights* (St. Paul: West Publishing Co., 1973).
39. "The Emerging Rights of the Confined," Correctional Development Foundation, P.O. Box 752, Columbia, South Carolina 29202, is devoted to the conventional and legal aspects of prisoners' rights. See also Hazel B. Kerper and Janeen Kerper, *Legal Rights of the Convicted Offender* (St. Paul: West Publishing Co., forthcoming).
40. S. Krantz, R.A. Bell, J. Brant, and M. Magruder, *Model Rules and Regulations on Prisoners' Rights and Responsibilities* (St. Paul: West Publishing Co., 1973).
41. Mathew O. Tobriner, "Due Process Behind Prison Walls," *The Nation* October 18, 1971, pp. 367–69.
42. *Furman* vs. *Georgia,* 92 S. Ct. 2726 (1972).
43. Opinion and order of Judge Arthur Garrity, Jr., U.S. District Court of Massachusetts, Civil Action 71-162-G (June 20, 1973).
44. Charles Reich, cited in *Harvard Law School Bulletin,* Vol. 25, No. 1 (October 1973), p. 18.
45. John Flackett and John A. Murphy. "Prison Legal Services: The Rhode Island Experience," *Rhode Island Bar Journal* (January 1973), p. 409.
46. *Wall Street Journal,* April 6, 1972.
47. Ronald Goldfarb and Linda Singer, *After Conviction* (New York: Simon & Schuster, 1973).
48. Pennsylvanis Prison Society, *Report for 1973,* p. 11. *Transition* [Boston, Massachusetts Correctional Association], (March 1973), pp. 1, 4.

49. *NECCC News* [Boston, New England Correctional Coordinating Council, 14 Somerset Street] Vol. 2, No. 2 (July–August 1973), p. 3.
50. Adult Correctional Institution, Cranston, R.I.
51. See Thomas Mott Osborne, *Prisons for Common Sense* (Philadelphia: Lippincott, 1924), pp. 57–105, for Osborne's description of the Mutual Welfare League.
52. Copies of the Charter of the NPRA are available from the Chairman, Adult Correctional Institution, Cranston, Rhode Island.
53. Donald Clemmer, *The Prison Community* (New York: Christopher Publishing Co., 1940).
54. Dr. Don Hardesty, Testimony before the U.S. Senate Subcommittee on Juvenile Delinquency, Washington, August 27, 1970.
55. From information furnished by the Director of Prison Legal Services. See footnote 45, above.
56. "Proposals for Reform of Swedish Criminal Care"; see footnote 21, above.
57. From information furnished by the Massachusetts Department of Corrections.
58. Carlton Stowers, "A Co-Ed Prison Without Bars," *Parade*, February 11, 1973, pp. 8–9.
59. Ibid. For a similar point of view on the part of a prison administrator toward his prisoners, see George Stürup, *op. cit.*, esp. Chaps. 1 and 2.
60. The Weeks School, Vergennes, Vermont.
61. Connie Rosenbaum, "No More Teen-Aged Prisons," *St. Louis Sunday Post-Dispatch*, December 19, 1971.
62. Ibid.
63. Associated Press dispatch, June 4, 1973.

Chapter Seven

Alternatives Beyond Prison Walls

The subject of alternative institutions is marked by tremendous variety and experimentation because the area is today in what has been aptly described as a state of ferment. Preceding chapters have pointed out that the motivation for this ferment arises in part from a realization of the failure of the traditional fixed institution. Most new programs go in the direction of utilizing the community as a resource for dealing with offenders.

RESTITUTION AND FINES

It is difficult to understand why restitution is not more widely used as a form—or condition—of sentence. The majority of the offenses for which people are committed to prisons are the economic crimes: theft, fraud, robbery, burglary, and embezzlement, quite apart from those which use force or weapons in their perpetration. Restitution would appear to be one area where the *lex talionis,* the eye for an eye and a tooth for a tooth, is precisely appropriate. If a loan, freely made with honest intent to return it, is not repaid, the lender has a legal right to proceed against the borrower. It would seem to make sense to apply that same procedure in economic relationships where the "loan" is of an involuntary or fraudulent nature.

One of the first objections raised to the use of restitution is that if a man is unemployed, he cannot be expected to pay back the value of what he has stolen. Yet, in the field of nonsupport, if a husband refuses to pay for the support of his wife and family, the court can compel him to. If a man divorces his wife, she has a right to demand a specific court-determined amount as alimony. Whether he is employed or not, the divorced husband has the responsibility to pay that amount, and if he does not, he may go to jail. One of the standard conditions of parole from prison is that a man shall have a job before he is released. Parole officers and after-care personnel work to find jobs for such parolees. If the court uses its probation staff to collect domestic support orders in desertion cases, the same staff could be used to find jobs for persons who have been convicted of economic crimes, who could pay restitution without the necessity of being sent to prison as penalty. The use of restitution, especially in countries with high levels of employment, would appear to be a most desirable alternative to commitment to an institution, for many offenders convicted of economic crimes. In Argentina, Columbia, Norway, and Sweden, restitution has been made mandatory by law.

Fines and court costs are a way of recompensing the state for the cost of administering the criminal justice system. But seldom—especially in fraud and income tax cases—does the court impose on a convicted offender a fine that anywhere nearly approximates the amount of his "take." This being the case, it would be difficult to contrive a penalty more likely to serve as a deterrent to crimes against property than that of restitution—plus fines or court costs—to let a prospective thief know that he will be forced to repay his theft in full, to the victim, if he is known, and to the State otherwise—especially in tax cases. Orders of restitution, like orders of nonsupport for alimony, carry with them the sanction, whether implied or overt, of a jail sentence, and therefore anyone under court order to do so who did not make restitution could be committed as a violation of probation, or by revocation of a suspended sentence.

A novel scheme for meeting the objection that money penalties—fines and restitution—discriminate against the poor and favor the rich, is the recently developed "day-fine" system. This scheme graduates the severity of the fine in accordance with the earnings which a defendant receives for a day's work. For example, conviction for a misdemeanor might be punishable by the forfeiture of two days wages; a more serious offense might result in a fine of thirty days wages, and so on. As compensation varies according to the occupation or profession of the defendant, the scheme can be calculated to have an equalizing impact on all offenders, regardless of their economic status. This idea has been incorporated into the Latin American Model penal code, although it originated in Scandinavia.[1]

The law is notoriously slow in responding to changes in the world beyond the courts. In this respect it is worthy of note that in many jurisdictions the dividing line between misdemeanor or felony in crimes against property is often pegged at $50 or $100, below which a crime is a misdemeanor, and above, a felony. Considering the enormous increase in inflation in the past ten to fifteen years, it gives cause to wonder why these designations have not been changed—as for example, by incorporating a cost-of-living increase into them such as is done in social security payments, wage negotiations or welfare benefits. Fines have likewise remained largely unchanged on the statute books throughout this period. The astounding inflation which occurred immediately after World War II necessitated legislation in Japan in 1948 to increase by 50 times the upper and lower limits of fines prescribed in the Penal Code. These increased fines were again, in 1972, quadrupled as the result of subsequent economic conditions.[2]

It is difficult to counter the argument that persons who steal or destroy the property of others—whether private or public—should somehow be required to make good the losses they cause through some contribution of their own labor. This led to the West German practice, in the late fifties, of "requiring vandals, as part of their punishment, to work in their leisure time on projects of value to the community."[3] This precedent, and the South African and Danish practice of weekend imprisonment, led to the adoption in New Zealand in 1962 of the Periodic Detention Scheme, "designed to place an offender under a form of control which does not remove him from the community and yet is more coercive or supervisory than probation. The crux of the scheme is control of a significant and substantial part of an offender's leisure time.

"The scheme was first enacted in 1962 for the young offender between 15 and 21 years of age, and the adult was included in 1966. A young offender reports at a center early on a Friday evening and resides there until about noon on the following Sunday. In addition he reports to the center on an evening during the week and stays there for two or three hours. The adult offender reports for the day on a Saturday. All offenders under this scheme are expected to work hard on the Saturday but preferably on projects of benefit to the local community. For instance, offenders have worked at such places as an intellectually handicapped children's home and an old people's home. There is a counseling and educational program for young offenders in the evenings. The center is directed by a Warden who is assisted by his wife, and the Warden is responsible to the local head of the Probation Service."[4]

Persons who have been convicted of an indictable offense or have failed to pay a fine previously imposed by court order are eligible for this type of sentence. Periodic detention can run as long as a year, for offenses ranging from disorderly conduct to burglary, for both youths and adults.

HALFWAY HOUSES

Referral to—or reliance on—halfway houses has become almost a cliché in today's consideration of many sorts of problem groups, including juvenile and adult offenders. Basically, the halfway house is an alternative to institutional treatment, reflecting the growing realization that the great majority of offenders do not require institutionalization, that prisons create an artificial environment for socializing them. It is as much a matter of common sense as of statistical studies of post-release recidivism that offenders, especially those who would be deemed eligible for short sentences, are best treated—if satisfactory adjustment to society is the goal—in a setting located within that society, and not in isolation from it.

While there are almost as many different definitions as there are halfway houses, and these must total into the thousands today, they all have several basic features in common. In the first place, they are community-based, and located in neighborhoods which provide a range of resources with which the halfway house occupant can establish new ties, be integrated into the community, and thereby develop himself and his capacity for integrated living when released.

The origins of the halfway house idea can be traced as far back as 1880, when the Japanese first began it.[5] In this country, their origins may be found in the kind of Salvation Army type of refuge which appeared in the nineteenth century, first in Philadelphia and later in New York and Boston.[6] Since then, with the pioneering work at Ditmas House,[7] and of the Highfields Center, the halfway house concept has greatly broadened until today it is a well-recognized reliance for dealing in local settings with a broad range of individuals.

Much has been written about Highfields,[8] because here for the first time a program of guided-group interaction was combined with living and working in a residential center which was completely open. Housed in the Lindbergh estate in rural New Jersey, Highfields has become the prototype for innumerable other houses and programs which it inspired. Here, during a four-month period, a program of individual self-rehabilitation is carried on in an informal, even intimate setting with a population of about twenty boys. They live at the house and go out to work as a group under supervision on the grounds of a nearby state institution. Their work provides them with an activity which keeps them physically engaged and also furnishes the basic material of their nightly guided-group interaction sessions. Here the boys all confront one another—as a group—with a common set of experiences to draw on, and on which to rear a set of changed attitudes, values and relationships which are the essence of this type of therapy. The lower rate of recidivism at this institution as compared with that of the alternative—the reformatory at Annandale—has commended halfway houses, with or without guided group interaction, to correctional authorities everywhere.[9] Essexfields,[10] Southfields,[11], and Red Wing,[12] are some of the best-known of the Highfields protégés in this country; they have also been widely emulated abroad.

Halfway houses today serve both children and adults, offenders committed by the courts, alcoholics, the mentally retarded and disturbed, and drug addicts. Their auspices and programs are as varied as their sponsors. While most started originally as a result of the efforts of private persons, they are today funded by local, state, and federal authorities. Location is preferably in neighborhoods of the sort from which their residents come—neither too much better nor worse than the settings to which they will ultimately return.

Considering the wealth of available information on halfway houses,[13] it will be sufficient here to cite a few guiding principles. The first is that they be manned by competent and dedicated staff, which in many houses includes ex-offenders, and that everyone on the staff be somehow involved in the treatment process. The small size of the house makes it impossible for any staff member not to become so involved, thus creating the

possibility for a therapeutic milieu for the residents. This is in sharp distinction
from the regular run of training schools for children where therapy or treatment or counseling is the responsibility of the professionals, while the cottage
or maintenance or catering staff are expected to keep to their occupational
responsibilities and not to "meddle" in treatment, despite the obvious fact that
many of these people spend more time with—and therefore are bound to have
a greater influence on—the young people in their midst.

Florida opened its first community-based facility in 1968, Criswell
House, a center for male juvenile delinquents, with a twin orientation to personal
and community responsibility. Members of the community at the House must
attend classes during the day at a nearby public school. From its inception, the
program of the House revolves around the core of guided-group interaction,
based on the Highfields model. Since then the Florida Division of Youth Services
has established a total of twenty-five community treatment programs, utilizing
a reality-therapy guided-group interaction approach.[14]

By 1976, the division plans to have 54 community facilities in
operation, which will enable the program to come close to its goal of serving at
least 70 percent of all court-committed children within their own communities.

Youths have been admitted to the halfway house programs regardless of offense, including manslaughter, serious and long-term heroin use, arson
and other types of serious cases which are often excluded from open community
programs elsewhere.[15]

As has been reported in other jurisdictions, the cost of caring for
children in halfway houses appears considerably less than that of training
schools: the average daily cost per child in halfway houses in Florida is reported
as $13.11, as against training school costs of $19.37 per day.

Children committed to the Florida Division of Youth Services
spend less time in halfway houses—4.9 months—than they do in training
schools—7.9 months. Followup records kept by the division show that two-
thirds of those who graduated from their halfway house programs during a five-
year period are successful, success being defined as not having been arrested
subsequent to release resulting in an adjudication or conviction, and also no
post-graduate parole revocation during the period studied.[16]

SOME MAINE PRINCIPLES

Pharos House is an example of one of the most recently established halfway
houses, created by private initiative to provide community living for a group of
offenders selected as likely to respond favorably to its program. Individuals
who live within a twenty-five mile radius of the House are eligible for the
program.[17]

"The duration of the program is normally 90 days during which
time the resident acquires a job, builds up a savings account, develops leisure
time activities and establishes community relationships. The program includes

a curfew which begins at 11:00 p.m. and increases or decreases depending on attitude and behavior, a sign in/out procedure whereby the residents must account for their whereabouts at all times and participation in reality-oriented individual and group counseling. Other parts of the program include a mandatory evening meal, house chores and a $25 contribution towards room and board. The resident may pay this amount by working in the house for $2 per hour. Any use of alcohol, drugs or violence in the House normally results in automatic expulsion. If a resident permanently leaves the house without permission or is dropped from the program for frequent or flagrant violations of the program standards, the parole officer is notified. The Pharos House resident has the same responsibilities to his parole officer as a nonresident."

It is important to stress at this point that Pharos House—like many other community centers—does not accept any resident into the program against his will. This is an important element in any form of treatment which places its reliance on other than compulsory programs. For example, some juvenile institutions permit youngsters who are about to be paroled, whose own homes are unsuitable to receive them, to be first taken to meet their prospective foster home parent before being assigned directly to them, sight unseen. If, for one reason or another, the child does not get on well with his prospective parents, he is then given an opportunity to visit another place. Once a person, whether young or old, is placed under compulsion in a community residence, this becomes a continuation of the institution itself. It is, therefore, important to permit a certain amount of choice to the individual before the step is taken to place him in the community.

Halfway houses and other community centers can become replicas of other institutions, and encourage the same kind of dependency that the prison or the training school engenders if residents are permitted to remain over-long. For this reason, the length of stay tends to be limited to a few short months, with a resultant rapid turnover of the population, and a sense of urgency in the program itself. There will always be a number—not very large, but some—who commit a crime and go back to the only society they know where they have friends, where they know the rules, and no new or unexpected problems confront them. The aim of the halfway house is to break that dependency by not allowing its residents to stay for two or five or ten years, but only for a period of months. The halfway house for released offenders can be seen as a temporary haven which takes care of them only for their first most difficult months, on a note of intensity and immediacy which would not be the case if they were permitted to stay longer. There is a further economic advantage in that such short programs make possible the use of the same bed several times a year.

Pharos House is by no means unique. In its latest directory, the International Halfway House Association now lists over 300 residences.[18] Hundreds more, not listed, are opening up all over the country, in a widely

ranging variety of programs in large and small communities.[19] Many are under private auspices; some are under religious sponsorship. Some are privately
run but publicly supported under contract with state or federal correction
agencies. How some of them manage to survive or what they do for money is
a continual mystery. Setting up a community residence is an area where private
enterprise can operate effectively in the field of corrections. Only the state
can run a jail or prison. During feudal times, bishops and nobles had their
private "keeps," but since then, prisons have become the monopoly of government. Today's community-based centers, whether residential or nonresidential,
whether for juveniles or adults, whether for parolees or in lieu of imprisonment, are, in the majority of instances, privately run.

At a conference called in the state of Maine in March 1973, for
the purpose of organizing the private agencies which were engaged in work
with children, some twenty-two agencies endorsed the principle of group
home placement and issued the following statement in support of it.

"The demands of close interpersonal relationships is reduced.
This provides the opportunity for the individual to reestablish ties to other
people gradually without pressure. Certain deviant behaviors are learned
in the group setting. Group homes provide the setting to use peer group pressures to learn and reinforce more acceptable patterns of behavior. Children
with needs requiring professional help can be grouped to make maximum use
of the professional. Juveniles who have accepted society's norms and have
incorporated them into their personal goals provide a strong influence on
incoming or newer residents. The group home can better provide a tactical
approach to the rehabilitation of each resident on an individual basis. Group
homes are forced to provide a larger staff than foster homes, thus the possibility of establishing a personal relationship is increased. Individual responsibility
can be a central aspect of group home living. The use of the peer group can be
an effective tool in maintaining the accountability of its members. The coordi-
nation of community services used by the residents can be provided more
efficiently in the group home. One visit to a public school can incorporate a
review of the progress of several residents. Group homes provide a relief for
overloaded case workers. The localization of several clients can increase the
efficiency and amount of services provided by social workers, probation officers, or Youth Aid Bureau counselors."[20]

The federal juvenile training school at Morgantown, West Virginia—
the Robert F. Kennedy Center—has as its stated purpose the prevention of
juvenile exposure to hardened criminals. Here the youths are separated into
groups according to their individual traits, whether gangs, vulnerable or com-
pliant, aggressive and assaultive, or childish and frightened. The main activities
are school-oriented, with consideration given to interests of the youth as well
as to their abilities. It has been described as a self-sufficient community whose
approach is based on "differential treatment;" that is, the treatment program

developed differs from individual to individual, and is based on the behavioral characteristics, maturity level, and psychological orientation of each young person. The classifications, in addition to the traits listed above, are "inade-quate-immature," "neurotic-conflicted," "unsocialized-aggressive," or "psy-chopathic," and "socialized or subcultural delinquency."[21]

Strong emphasis is placed on behavior modification, and a system of rewards has been devised whereby each youth regularly receives a check based on a system of "points." These are obtained by performance of accept-able behavior.

NEW YORK PROGRAMS FOR YOUTHS

The New York Division for Youth was given, in 1960, a legislative mandate to establish a program of residential facilities for 15-through 17-year-old pre-delinquents and delinquents, and began at once to provide an intensive and experimental program that would offer a diversification of facilities for such youths. Several approaches are worth recording: conservation groups in forestry settings, a short-term adolescent residential training program (START) patterned to some extent after the original Highfields program, wherein boys work together during the day and share their reactions—and interactions—in guided-group sessions in the evenings; a short-term aid to youth (STAY) program combining many of the START features, except that boys go back to their homes at night. Parent-youth group sessions under the leader-ship of the director are also conducted. Homes are set up with a capacity for twenty boys each and apartments for seven in urban communities. Here the young people go out to work or school during the day and return to the house at night.

One of the noteworthy features of this program is its clear con-ception of the kind of youths whom it regards as eligible—generally those who exhibit the following characteristics.

"Expressed unhappiness over his situation and desire to make a better life for himself (denial by the youth of any dissatisfaction was discount-ed, if it was recognized that he was hiding his true feelings); exhibited a will-ingness to admit, even reluctantly, that his troubles were at least partly of his own making; showed a capacity to relate to people—to exhibit some emotional response, even though it might be negative; could establish sufficient rapport with an adult to discuss his situation with him—though not necessarily from the standpoint of seeking or accepting help at first; gave some indications that he could recall his life experiences, even though he might have been reluc-tant to discuss them."[22]

The four basic program approaches were premised on six principles of treatment as follows: "Youths had to be helped to accept that they had worth and potential . . .; youth contact with the real world had to be maxi-

mized . . .; youth involvement in programs of service to others was important . . .; youth work experiences had to be realistically interpreted . . .; youth
acceptance of responsibility was paramount . . .; community acceptance was
needed and nurtured."[23]

Additional approaches modify and enrich the original program.
Under a "New Careers" slogan, the department set out to carefully select,
train and assign former offenders—graduates of the department's facilities—
as full-time staff to work with adolescent boys. Approximately 10 percent of
the personnel are currently working as supervisors in camps, as child-care
personnel in group homes for children, as maintenance men, and as intake
and after-care workers.

As an outgrowth of the forestry camps and in conjunction with
them, the youths construct facilities on the campsites to which disadvantaged
urban boys, ten to thirteen years old, are invited. A full program, including
recreation, nature study, cultural trips, and sports, is offered, the counselors
being in some instances their own "big brothers."

Finally, "youths from our facilities were programmed to enroll
in summer college institutes established to train teachers. Having the opportunity to participate in informal recreational and cultural activities with
teachers, as well as receiving tutorial instructions from them, modified the
stereotypes which our youths held about teachers. The teachers' attitudes
concerning delinquent adolescents were affected as well."[24]

The New York Division for Youth reports that about 6,000
young people have gone through these programs of short-term treatment in
the past ten years. The average stay was nine months, with an authorized period
of two years of followup. Thereafter, an evaluation of results shows a post-
treatment arrest rate ranging from 33 percent to 42 percent for youths discharged between 1966 and 1969, after a two-year followup. Recommitment
rates ranged from 7 percent to 16 percent, which includes commitment to
state and all local correctional institutions including narcotic commitments.[25]
By comparison, the average recidivism rates over the nation range from 30
percent to 80 percent, based on arrests.

OPEN INSTITUTIONS IN ASIA

In 1965, the United Nations published a report on open institutions, based
on material provided in a UNAFEI course during the preceding year. A very
brief summary for each country contributing to that report appears below.[26]
Only the most distinctive and salient characteristics are given, for it is assumed
that the other features are found in open institutions elsewhere described. The
roster is evidence of the widespread extent of the open institution movement.

Before listing the open institutions available for offenders in this
area, an early historical antecedent may be cited: Indonesia, as far back as

1917, while still under Dutch rule, passed a bill which, in addition to providing the usual three stages of security prisons, authorized "the establishment of an open institution that is not based on physical control but on a sense of responsibility."

Burma—This country reports four open institutions at Prome, Pyinmana, Monywa and Padung, as well as an open borstal for young offenders under age 19. These open institutions are apparently prerelease camps where the prisoner is assigned for a year or less prior to discharge. They are designed to provide the prisoner a period of training in self-control and responsibility in an atmosphere of greater freedom of activity than that provided by a walled institution.

Sri Lanka—An interesting feature of Ceylon's prisons is that 89 percent of the convicted population in 1962–63 served sentences of under twelve months, seemingly ideal for open institutions. The first open institution for adults was opened in 1951 at Pallekelle, and is called "the pioneer institution of its kind in Southeast Asia." In addition, three satellite prison farms have been established at Anuradhapura, Kopay, and Batticoloa, with populations of 201, 303, and 121, respectively. There is a borstal at Watupitiwela.

Taiwan—In 1965 there were no open institutions on Taiwan, but action was in progress to implement one, promulgated by a presidential decree which would feature: limited entry to prisoners between 20–50 years of age who are capable of physical labor and who have served at least one year of their sentence with good conduct and have more than a year left to serve. Barred from transfer to an open prison are habitual offenders or those who have been convicted of murder, robbery, or offenses against state security. Prisoners are expected to work eight-hour days at public construction or development projects away from the prison site. While no provisions for education, counseling or recreation are listed, payment for work was to be set at the rate of 40 percent of the wage paid by local enterprises for similar work. Prisoners who do well may be given supervisory positions in the institution, have deductions made from their sentences, and may be allowed to go home on Sundays or holidays.

Hong Kong—All adult prisoners serving sentences of three years and under are treated in open institutions, of which there are two; at Chi Ma Wan (with a capacity of 660) and Tai Lam for drug addicts (800 capacity). There is no parole system, but prisoners can earn remission of one-third of their sentence subject to good conduct and industry. In 1962–63, 60 percent of convicted prisoners were there for various drug offenses; hence the need for the drug treatment center at Tai Lam. This is a correctional institution with a medical program designed to restore the prisoners to a state of physical well-being, followed by an after-care rehabilitation program. Treatment follows a simple routine of denial of the drug for two to three weeks, during which the patients get tranquilizers and sleeping pills, followed by a health-building up period in which the prisoner gets a plentiful supply of plain, nutritious food, hard work in the open air, and adequate rest.

India—No single picture of the state of corrections covers all of India, because prisons are a state, rather than central government matter. Statistical gathering varies among the states, and no comparisons can therefore be made between them. However, the following open institutions do exist (as of 1959) although the list is not complete: Himachal Pradesh—one open prison for 50; Bihar—3 small camps for a total capacity of 90; Kerala—one open prison for 100; Andhra Pradesh—one camp for 50; Bombay—two open institutions for a total of 49 inmates and one semi-open camp for 900; Utter Pradesh—2 open institutions for a total of 2,600; Rajasthan—2 open institutions for a total of 55. The probation camp at Bihar is located within the confines of the town and is reported to have caused no concern to the townsfolk.

Malaysia—The Federation runs three open borstals for boys and one for girls. One prison camp for men at Pengkalan Chepa is called "open" but may be only marginally so. It has maximum, medium, and minimum security sections and a separate women's section, all under guard. The regime is reported to be liberal and relaxed, and the building arrangement gives the impression of openness. In addition, there is a prerelease discharge camp and a prison farm attached to the security prison at Changi. The most open institution, the Pulau Semang Settlement located on an island 15 miles from the mainland, was reported closed in 1963 after a bloody riot in which the superintendent and two attendants were murdered. The settlement was not for convicted prisoners, however, but for persons detained for activities in secret societies which are a problem in Hong Kong and Singapore as well.

Pakistan—This country has one open institution, the Reformatory Farms at Burewala, West Pakistan, with a capacity of 400–500 annually. Pakistan reports that steps have been taken in the last few years to turn certain security institutions into semisecurity ones.

The Philippines—This country has established three physically separate open institutions—Iwahig Penal Colony in 1904, Davao Penal Colony in 1932, and Sablayan Penal Colony in 1955. In addition, there are two penal farms attached to the prisons at San Ramon and at New Bilibid. The dates suggest an early tendency toward open institutions, and the rehabilitation advantages of open treatment are said to have the support of the public and of administrators. Inmates are transferable from the main prison to any of the prison colonies and farms after an eight-week diagnostic stay at the Reception-Guidance Center, regardless of offense.

Thailand—Thailand has two fully open institutions: at Hoi Pong, established in 1961, and, due to its success, a second open institution, Aranyik. Residents work seven to eight hours per day on agriculturally related projects, but no educational programs exist. The regime is permissive and liberal and families of prisoners may make visits. Inmates are permitted four days home leave. Admission to the open institutions is based on classification in at least class II of a six-class system: a good conduct record in a closed institution, and serving of usually one-half of the sentence in a closed institution.

An exception to the general pattern of drabness in penal institutions now and again appears, as at the Aranyik open institution, where the entrance has been turned into a park, complete with flower gardens and summer house, and the dormitories are scattered over the land area, each in its own garden. Also in Thailand, the Hoi Pong Open Institution has been made attractive despite a relatively flat, unimpressive site. The buildings, in traditional Thai style, resemble ordinary dwelling houses. The area has been carefully landscaped.

For those who may see little value in resolutions of international bodies, it is interesting to review one of these recommendations which appeared in the Report of the First Crime Congress in Geneva in 1955, convened by the United Nations: "While in the open institution the risk of escape and the danger that the inmate may make improper use of his contacts with the outside world are admittedly greater than in other types of penal institutions, these disadvantages are amply outweighed by the following advantages, which make the open institutions superior to the other types of institutions: (a) The open institution is more favourable to the social readjustment of the prisoners and at the same time more conducive to their physical and mental health; (b) the flexibility inherent in the open system is expressed in a liberalization of the regulations; the tensions of prison life are relieved and discipline consequently improves. Moreover, the absence of material and physical constraint and the relations of greater confidence between prisoners and staff, tend to create a genuine desire for social readjustment; (c) the conditions of life in open institutions resemble more closely those of normal life. Consequently, desirable contacts can more easily be arranged with the outside world and the inmate can thus be brought to realize that he has not severed all links with society; in this connection it might perhaps be possible to arrange, for instance, group walks, sporting competition with outside teams, and even individual leave of absence, particularly for the purpose of preserving family ties; (d) the same measure is less costly if applied in an open institution than in an institution of another type, in particular because of lower building costs, and, in the case of an agricultural institution, the higher income obtained from cultivation, if cultivation is organized in a rational manner." [27]

The second fully open institution established by Japan in 1970 appears to have followed these recommendations as if they were a prescription. [28] It is the Kitsuregawa Agricultural and Engineering Institution, attached to the main prison of Kurobane, and as its title suggests, is devoted to vocational training. Among the subjects taught are mathematics, auto mechanics and repair, and bookkeeping. After a two-month period of observation and classification in Tokyo Regional Correction Headquarters, selected nonserious first offenders between the ages of 20 and 45 receive a month of preparatory training at the main institution, and are then transferred to the open branch for a further 15 months of training, after which they are released.

The engineering course specializes in training inmates, many of them unskilled, to pass the examination required for being licensed as a heavy construction machine operator. Additional courses are given in civil engineering and in surveying. Agricultural courses include field and class work in gardening, farming, fruit and stock raising, and some forestry. The marketing aspects of these industries is covered in courses on the economics of florist and truck gardening operations, food processing and agronomy, so as to prepare graduates to enter these fields, for which there is great demand.

Capacity of the institution is 100; the staff totals 29, including five engineering and two agriculture teachers. The one-story prefabricated buildings were purposely kept simple and inexpensive. They are dispersed over the site to avoid the close or clustered feeling of the traditional institution, and are without any walls or bars. The inmates sleep in dormitories accommodating two groups of 20. Each man has a curtain around his bed for privacy.

Like the Borstals of England, the institution has close ties with the local community, and has their support.[29] A beginning has been made to have the agriculture students go out to help local farmers on weekends; the construction machinery operators do work for the local villages and towns. The inmates have access to a variety of publications, radio, and T.V. Recreation includes sports and entertainment, including two choral groups. A program of guided-group interaction, admittedly based on the Highfields model, is a prominent feature of the school.

In the three years since the opening of the institution in March of 1970, there has been one absconder. Dr. Bixby, who reported on Kitsuregawa in 1971, stated: "The school has not been in operation long enough to have any follow-up figures to publish." Of the 110 released from the institution since its inception, none has returned to any other prison in Japan. This fact has been confirmed by the Chief of Security at the institution between October 1971 and March of 1973, after consulting the central prisoner files kept at the security prison where he now serves.[30]

PRERELEASE

Prerelease from institutions and after-care was one of the four major items discussed at the second United Nations Crime Congress in London in 1960. [31] Part of the stimulation for that recommendation was the experience of the Federal Bureau of Prisons after World War II, based on a study of the reasons for parolee failure after release. This research discovered that the period immediately before, and the first ninety days after, release were the most critical for persons paroled from prison. Understandably, problems of jobs, of places to live, and of money were the main difficulties confronting these parolees. If these matters were not resolved within the first ninety days, the possibility of violating the terms of parole was found to be greatly increased. Some years after that original study, the Department of Justice secured passage of legislation to establish prerelease guidance centers at six federal correctional institutions.

Here, separate wings were set aside for persons to be prepared for release during the last three months of their stay. A special program was devised to prepare them to adjust to life on the outside: they became accustomed to wearing civilian clothes again in place of their prison uniforms, and were permitted personal choice in its selection. Gradually, they were allowed leave from the institution under supervision, and later on their own, to seek employment, to be interviewed, and to find housing.

Stress was laid on reorientation, in groups, and on gradual relaxation of strict custodial and other regulations. While the isolation of these prerelease units did not provide the interaction with the community which is the essence of the residential center, it was, nevertheless, a valuable pioneering effort. Experts in various fields come in to discuss such problems as how to handle money, how to budget earnings, how to buy on the installment plan, what to avoid in purchasing a used car. In most institutions, money is contraband, in order to assure that an escapee will be penniless when he absconds. A man who has been forbidden to carry money or to deal in it (except clandestinely) in prison is faced with a whole new monetary order of things when he hits the street again. A long-term prisoner recently released from prison after sentence had $150 in his pocket, which he had earned during his stay. He spent one-half of that taking a taxi to his home. Especially these days, with inflation increasing at so rapid a pace, if a man comes out with an idea of the economy which prevailed when he first went in, he will be completely at a loss as to how to cope with it.

The same thing is true with automobiles and traffic. A prisoner released from six years of confinement had earlier confided to a prison pal of his: "I have no worries. My girl friend has taken care of my clothes, my automobile is in storage, I have money tucked away, and when I get out, I have it made." His fantasy lasted exactly twenty-four hours, when he was killed on one of the new expressways which had been built during his absence in a speed of traffic to which he was completely unaccustomed. The pace of life had—in this regard as in others—altered.

Admittedly an extreme example, it illustrates the necessity of helping men to gradually adjust to conditions of freedom after they have been

confined. Many schemes for prerelease centers, halfway houses, and community
residences of one kind or another all have a parallel with a very different
kind of life—deep-sea diving. A diver who goes down below the level of the
ocean to a considerable depth has to adjust gradually to the increased pressure,
and after he has been down for any considerable length of time, he must be
returned by an even slower and more gradual process. If he comes up too
suddenly, a condition known as the bends sets in, and he may die in agony.
In order to prevent this from occurring, a returning diver is compelled to
spend a certain amount of time in a decompression chamber. Here the pressure upon him is reduced gradually until it is the equivalent of sea level, where
he can again resume his normal life. This is the physical equivalent of the
psychological "bends" experienced by men released from the pressures of
confinement in an institution who find themselves with few if any controls
or guidelines for adjusting to the conditions of freedom. At the prerelease
center, men are taught how to fill out an application for employment, not
an easy task for a man who has never secured a job this way before. Where to
hang his coat and hat while being interviewed or how to answer questions
about his criminal record, such questions that are not matters of concern
for persons in the free society can be for the ex-prisoner insuperable obstacles,
because they have had up to the point of release every major and minor decision made for them by someone else.

A man who has spent considerable time in prison finds that one
of the most difficult things to adjust to is the opening of a door. When for
many years he has had to stop before every door because someone else must
lift the latch or turn the key, for the first few weeks after he is released when
he comes to the door of an office, lavatory or private home, he is conditioned
to stop and wait for someone else to open it. So what is for persons in freedom
the easiest thing to do is for the ex-convict initially, one of the most difficult.
If that be true, in a matter as simple as opening a door, how much more difficult must it be to make a decision in the large areas of life?

During his period of confinement, the prisoner has not had the
power to decide when or what he would eat, when to bathe, when to go to
bed, when to get up, or what to wear. The philosophy behind the prerelease
center is to give a man training by slow stages under conditions of gradually
relaxed controls until he can take over the management and control of all the
details of his own living.

"Programs of 'graduated release' are designed to reduce the severity
of impact of an abrupt transition between two divergent and possibly antag-
onistic climates. Prisons tend to represent, in Erving Goffman's words 'total
institutions,' settings in which an inmate is forced into conformity and dependency, with the basic decisions made for him by others. His needs for food,
for medical care, for companionship and work, and for shelter, tend to be as
thoroughly scheduled and carefully supervised. He need not bear fully the

consequences of inept decisions that he may make. Nor will his failures or inadequacies produce the kinds of deprivations and distress likely to attend them in the outside community. Failure to work satisfactorily—by free market standards—will not result in the inmate being fired from the job nor in a failure to secure satisfactory food or lodging." [32]

Sweden has been cited before in these pages for its progressive and innovative penal programs. In April of 1970, they initiated a prerelease program, the objective of which was to give inmates, before they were released from the institution, an increased "chance of adaptation to society by giving them social training and psychological treatment, as a supplement to the usual help with housing, and job employment during the final phase of their institutionalization." [33]

This prerelease training takes place in the last few months of the institution stay and permits men long furloughs in the community (72 hours) initially accompanied by a guard and ultimately on their own. The probability of absconding is very slight at this stage for a man who is so near his release date and therefore does not want to jeopardize his chances of getting parole. This period also provides the best possible atmosphere and incentive for a man to do well on furlough. The men who received this prerelease training in a separate wing of a prison "were given psychological therapy mainly in groups, in which the emphasis was on sensitivity training, role playing, and social training in the form of visits to different public institutions, including employment agencies, industries, theatres, etc." [34]

The usual procedure in the granting or withholding of release on parole is to notify the inmate only of the results of his hearing. The Federal Parole Board, after a successful experience in five pilot institutions, expanded its new program to all federal prisons. From now on, inmates will be informed of the reasons why their parole is denied, and will be given two chances to appeal that decision. They will also be given an opportunity to appear at the hearing where their request for parole is being considered. [35]

MANDATORY PAROLE

The importance of prerelease training was emphasized in a 1973 report from a council in Canada which studied reform in the penal system of that country. They strongly recommended that "the sentencing provisions set out in Canadian criminal legislation be amended to make the last third of any fixed prison sentence a period of automatic mandatory supervision." [36] There are in all prisons everywhere some men who prefer to serve out their entire sentence in prison rather than to accept any control or supervision after they have been released. The rationale is understandable: such men do not intend when they are released to submit themselves for another minute to the surveillance or control of anyone else. This Canadian recommendation postulates that the fact

that a man does not want controls over him when he is released is the very
reason for not releasing him without some mandatory period of supervision.
This may well reduce the recidivism rate by making it possible for no man
to serve all of his sentence inside the institution: some portion of it must be
served in the community.

Jurisdictions vary with regard to the conditions under which a man
is returned to the institution for violation of parole. In some places there is
a hearing before a judge, or before a parole board. In others, the parole officer
reports the violation, and if it is a new offense, the parolee may be returned
without court or other administrative action. Increasingly, as the civil liberties
of offenders begin to receive belated attention, there is the requirement of
a hearing with representation by counsel before a parolee may be returned for
a violation. There is wide range of possible steps of an administrative or legal
nature which can be taken to intervene in behalf of a parolee, between his
alleged violation of the rules of parole and his return to prison custody.

One of the universal complaints of parole services is the heavy
caseloads under which parole officers attempt to supervise men under their
care. As a result, no matter how dedicated or how skilled the officer, most
supervision is superficial and routine, consisting mainly of periodic checkups
at home or place of employment, or at the parole office, to make sure the
man is living where he says he is, continues to be employed, and is not engaged
in any activity which flagrantly violates the conditions of his release.

Attempts are being made in some places to supplement this
superficial kind of oversight with the efforts of community-based agencies
which are in a position to give individual attention to parolees. The following gives the details of one such community program:

"The Community Corrections Project is a community-based,
service delivery system for released offenders. . . . Goals of the project are:
to facilitate the readjustment of paroled and released offenders to their community; and to reduce the probability that released offenders will commit
subsequent offenses.

"The number of persons (men and women) paroled or released
to these communities annually is 232. They suffer educational and vocational
handicaps (80 percent did not enter high school or dropped out before completion; 76 percent were unskilled or only semiskilled and had unstable job
histories) and lack social support (53 percent lived alone; 90 percent lacked
organizational affiliation). These conditions make it almost predictable that
the released offender will return to criminal activity unless there is intervention.

"This program seeks to intervene by providing the following services
to released offenders: employment counseling, job development and placement; housing services for the released offender and his family (if needed),
and 'foster home' arrangements for ex-inmates who have no family ties and
who have been assessed to need and want a family setting; personal and

family counseling and psychotherapy; a transitional reorientation program; legal counseling; and additional services through referral to health, educational or other specialized agencies.

"Services are provided through a one-to-one relationship established between the client and a program representative, the advocate. For the advocate/client relationship to be a trust-bond, the advocates are drawn from backgrounds common to their clients (e.g., black offenders familiar with the residents of the community served).

"Services begin in the prerelease stage when the client is informed of the services available; if he wishes to utilize the service, he is interviewed and his advocate develops a service plan suited to his particular needs. Housing is found, if needed, and other necessary arrangements are made for the client's release. Upon release, the advocate makes himself available to the client, as desired, to aid him in the transition from prison life to civilian status. Supportive contact and counseling continues through the client's adjustment period and decreases in frequency as the need decreases. Contact may continue for as much as two to three years. Periodic evaluation sessions are held by the staff for assessment."[37]

A grant proposal recently submitted by a private, nonprofit agency places its emphasis on serving not only parolees but ex-prisoners as well. It aims to employ them "within the system" to make changes, as well as serving as a resource of information to correctional and paroling authorities. The program plans to be based in a placement center located in the state reformatory, plus regional offices in each of the four main areas of the state. The objectives of the proposal are to provide a wide range of services for adult parolees:

"—a central administration and facility for the placement of up to 500 men or women returning to the community from state correctional institutions;
"—a site for communication between placement staff, the Department of Correction and the Parole Board;
"—a system for developing community resources for up to 1000 offenders per year including jobs, training, education, housing, and supportive services;
"—intensive statewide advocacy services for up to 350 inmates returning to all regions;
"—on-the-job training for inmate placement specialists and clerical workers;
"—employment for ex-offenders;
"—data on community resources which will assist the Parole Board in making decisions;
"—data on community resources to the Department of Correction which will assist in program evaluation and development"[38]

The above describes a program for adult parolees, but the same kind of approach can be utilized for juveniles as well. The practical economics of employing juveniles who are released back to their communities is described in some of the novel programs being carried on by a community group:

"The Community Aftercare Program works with parolees from Massachusetts reform schools, providing educational, recreational, individual and group counseling programs. Recently, it has expanded its operations to include job training and work experience. It has done this by opening up three food service establishments (two ice cream parlors and one pizza parlor). These businesses employ the delinquent youths, providing both wages and job training

"CAP hopes to expand its job training/work experience program in the following areas: (1) food service: opening of seven more businesses, each of which could employ 8–10 youths part-time or full-time; (2) photostat copy center: located in a college neighborhood where demand is high, delinquent youths in school could work on a part-time basis; (3) gas station-auto repair shop: designed to utilize juvenile offender's auto-mechanics skills and interest in cars: higher skill levels would be taught under close supervision; (4) manufacturing: development of a small manufacturing firm which utilizes a large amount of semiskilled labor to provide better-paying jobs at increasingly more complex skill levels (e.g. manufacture of black toys or greeting cards).

"The over-all goal is to develop skills and responsibility and to provide salaries, not profit. The juvenile offenders will be making money, learning skills, keeping busy, acquiring good work habits and a sense of responsibility, and developing, hopefully, a better self-image.

"CAP, thus far, has attracted a large number of volunteers from the college community. It is hoped that the business units would attract volunteers from the business community to offer expertise and experience and that voluntary legal aid could be obtained to negotiate leases and contracts." [39]

Nonresidential treatment centers have many programmatic features in common with places where residents live and interact with one another under a common roof. One of these is in the Dadefield County, Miami nonresidential treatment program for "hard-core" juvenile delinquents between the ages of 15 and 17, which opened in October 1969. [40] The youths assigned here have had a long record of offenses, have broken probation, and are given a choice by the judge between training school or participation in this program.

The program has three goals: to encourage the development of new attitudes and more socially accepted behavior; to provide group members with tools for living a better, more meaningful life; and to provide a third alternative to the court and the offender in addition to training schools and probation.

The group meets at the center each week day at 8 a.m. and is driven by bus to privately-owned groves. Here they do several kinds of paid work, such as fixing machinery, picking fruit, cleaning the groves. Lunch and supper is provided. After supper, four nights a week, the youths meet for guided-group interaction therapy in groups of ten, under the supervision of trained personnel. Their obligations end and they are free to go home at 7 each evening; week-ends are also free. If at the end of a four- to six-month involvement in the program, a boy has not shown sufficient improvement, he may be returned to the court for further action.

In the state of Washington, citizen involvement and concern have resulted in a new awareness of the need to reduce failure rates of juveniles and adults returning to society from state correctional institutions. In line with this commitment, several programs are currently underway in the state, aimed directly at decreasing the rate of juvenile commitment to institutions. Like California, where the idea started, Washington has undertaken a probation subsidy program on much the same lines, which has resulted in a 54 percent lower juvenile commitment rate in 1971 in the participating counties, and savings of more than $6 million in the past two years. The rate of juvenile re-peaters is reported to be running about 16 percent, compared to three to four times that rate in some other states.

"Juvenile Parole Services' Specialized Service Units have been established in each of five state regions. These units are fully staffed to aug-ment and supplement regular parole staffs and reduce the institutional popu-lation by increasing the number of diagnostic paroles, while reducing parole revocations. The staff in each unit includes a curriculum coordinator, family therapist, group therapist, coordinator of volunteer services and a resource specialist."[41]

"In the past few years the barriers between institutions and the community have been reduced further through the development of special programs which allow selected residents to attend public school in nearby communities, either for academic or vocational training. Other residents are released to work at jobs during the day, returning in the evening for partici-pation in the institution or camp programs. These special programs are designed to meet the individual needs of juvenile offenders.

"Another community-based program is the Juvenile Parole Ser-vices Learning Centers, located in the state's major metropolitan areas. They are designed to help those juveniles who have been released from institutions and are unable to integrate into regular school classes. These young people are able to complete class work begun in institutional schools and readjust to the community without the added pressures of the public school setting. The centers also help those youngsters who, for a variety of reasons, academic, social or emotional, are unable to handle a regular school program."[42]

Consistent with its enlightened juvenile reform program, the state of Washington has introduced four reforms which became effective in 1970, permitting long-distance telephoning by inmates to family or friends, abolishing mail censorship in all adult correctional institutions, doing away with the strip cell, and creating a resident government organization in each adult institution, which involves inmates, staff, and private citizens on a resident council.

PROBATION

Probation is the earliest and best-known community alternative to imprisonment. Whether with or without a suspended sentence of imprisonment as a condition, probation assures supervision in the community of those persons deemed suitable for this form of treatment. The intensity of care, of service to the needs of probationers to help them in maintaining the kind of conduct which will not result in new offenses, depends in large measure on the quality of the supervision they receive. This is not the place to go into the details of what true probation entails, considering the vast literature [43] which has grown up about probation from the time it was first introduced by John Augustus, the humble shoemaker of Boston in 1841.[44]

Since then probation has spread to all fifty states and to many countries. It has been pointed out that in the past decade the percentage of convicted federal offenders placed on probation instead of being imprisoned is now better than one-half. This is in "recognition of the necessity for adaptability to individual needs and pressures," as a recent commentator of the international criminological scene has described it.[45] This same commentator goes on to point out that the effective development of probation is necessarily dependent upon the acceptance and support of the public—as are all other measures of community treatment. The effectiveness of probation measures are in direct proportion to the hostility or lack of hostility in the social environment. He commends, too, the value of extending probation services to the family as well as to the individual probationer so as to influence in a positive fashion the relationships of the probationer with the significant persons in his life.

In the area of community dealing, California has long pioneered, as early exemplified in the Community Coordinating Council idea for crime prevention thirty years ago. A contemporary program in Los Angeles appears to continue this tradition. RODEO—(Reduction of Delinquency through Expansion of Opportunity) is a model probation program based on the concept of intensive supervision with caseloads no larger than fifteen, serving juveniles 13 to 18 years old instead of sending them to a camp or an institution.

The program seeks to identify deficits in the home, the community and in the individual development of each youth, and to direct probation services toward overcoming these. In many cases services have to be extended to include all those family members who are sufficiently concerned to be involved.

The program makes use of nonprofessionals as aides to the probation officer, persons at least 21 years old with "an ability to understand and communicate with delinquents and to provide a new and needed bridge of understanding between the middle-class professional and the disadvantaged client." Special training takes place during a six-week period provided for RODEO aides. Aides take a team approach to the services they render to their probationers in helping them to find jobs, providing transportation, serving as recreational supervisors and raising funds for support of the program. As probation aides gain sufficient experience to pass the civil service examination for community worker, they may be appointed to full-time, paid RODEO positions."[46]

In light of the movement to promote group teaching in education, it is not surprising to find the same idea being tried in the area of re-education or supervision of probationers. Such a team approach in probation means that professional probation officers, paraprofessionals and volunteers, each possessing different skills, work together as a team to more adequately deal with increased caseloads and the diversity of the problems presented by probationers. Research findings demonstrate that within the framework of teams, individuals have been meeting higher levels of personal needs and of productivity.

Three models are offered. The first, the Resource Coordinating Model, assigns specific roles; the interviewer-classifier is responsible for assigning the probationers to the appropriate team and familiarizing him with the program; the group counselor who works out personal problems through twice-weekly group meetings; the human services out-worker, who aids probationers to get jobs; a school liaison person who tries to locate available school resources; paraprofessionals or volunteers who visit the probationer, offer support, and in some cases help to locate probationers who lose contact with the team.

The Reintegration Team Model is concerned with attempting to effect change in the community's opportunity structure, power groups, and to strengthen crime preventive efforts.

The New Careers Model makes it possible for offenders to assume a major role in their own adjustment. Some probationers assist the team in group counseling sessions, or make helpful contacts in the community in areas where professionals might be barred. The individual may begin to develop an interest in making a career for himself in probation or in related areas, as a result of this experience.[47]

There has, perhaps, never been a time when so many people were willing to volunteer their time and energies as today—not only among college students and young people, but in the general population, including those euphemistically called the "golden agers." Retired people—grandparents—are finding useful lives as companions to retarded children, or, as in earlier time, as babysitters for the very young—as in China for thousands of years.

In Japan, here and now, an intensively organized network of citizen services makes nationally available some 50,000 probation officers who counsel and befriend probationers, under the supervision of paid full-time professionals. These are part of a nationwide network of volunteer programs in behalf of offenders. Legally viewed, these voluntary probation officers are part-time government officials appointed by the Minister of Justice. Except for reimbursement of their immediate expenses, they receive no further compensation. As volunteers, they seldom assume responsibility for more than two probationers, thus relieving the caseloads of the full-time probation officers whose case loads run upwards of 100. Volunteer probation officers are selected by a National Selection Council, which operates directly out of the office of the Rehabilitation Bureau in the National Ministry of Justice. There are 50 such selection councils, whose work is supplemented by over 100 volunteer rehabilitation aid societies, which extend the same kind of service to the discharged prisoner as is provided by volunteers to the probationer.[48]

Sri Lanka (Ceylon) since its independence—first from Great Britain and more recently from India—has continued a program which goes back to their late colonial years, the so called "Uncle and Aunt Service." Any couple a father and mother—who visits a hostel or training school and become acquainted with or attracted to a particular boy or girl may thereafter act as "uncle" or "aunt" to the youngster, particularly one who has otherwise no family. His foster aunt and uncle invite him to their home, take him on outings, let him play with their own children, and return him to the institution at the time appointed.[49]

In Sweden, "the country is divided into 40 districts for noninstitutional care according to the directives in the Penal Code concerning imprisonment, probation, youth imprisonment, and internment. Each district is headed by a protective consultant. The organization currently has a staff of 275 employees. Approximately 11,630 voluntary probation officers are working in the non-institutional sector, each of whom had an average case load of two persons.

"The work is based on the traditional concept of probation, namely, continuous contact with clients combined with advice from the social welfare authorities and individual counseling. However, one product of the recent increased importance of noninstitutional care, resulting from social developments and legislative changes, has been less conventional supportive and therapeutic measures."[50]

The conclusion is inescapable. When duties that were formerly considered the responsibility of the punitive side of government are, at least partially, entrusted to laymen and volunteers in the community, the results are inevitably "less conventional supportive and therapeutic measures"—that is, in effect, less punitive.

THE ROLE OF THE EX-OFFENDER

The extra-mural services described in this chapter can be provided by persons with a broad variety of skills, interests, and attitudes. Paraprofessionals and nonprofessionals increasingly find satisfying careers in corrections at both the juvenile and adult levels. The service of volunteers can give richness and variety to many programs. "The indigenous nonprofessional," a person from the same social class as the great majority of offenders, is coming to be regarded as a valuable resource in the correctional field:

"He is a peer of the client, and shares a common background, language, ethnic origin, style and group of interests. . . . He belongs, he is a 'significant other,' he is 'one of us.' . . ." The style of the nonprofessional is significantly related to his effectiveness, because it matches the client's.[51]

Their personal backgrounds as ex-offenders—as with ex-alcoholics and ex-drug addicts—can make them highly effective in dealing with offenders at all stages of the court-correctional process, especially if they are trained and supervised by full-time professionals.

California and New York have experimented successfully with the hiring of specially screened, selected and trained ex-youth offenders as staff members to work with youths. "Their participation and presence served as clear evidence that youths could aspire to the 'helping' professions. The experience also aided rehabilitation of the ex-offenders by providing them the opportunity to make a significant contribution to helping someone else."[52] In Massachusetts, ex-offenders with long prior records of serious delinquency who had themselves been helped during their stay at a youth serving center proved to be most effective in working with very seriously emotionally disturbed youngsters.[53] This program was undertaken by an organization of ex-offenders which had incorporated itself so it could negotiate and sign contracts to provide services to the state, such as the above. A nonprofit organization, its members consist also of community representatives, although the primary staff is composed of persons who have served time in prison. It furnishes services of job and home-finding for released prisoners, conducts a constant campaign of public education, and also runs programs.[54]

Parallel with this development, today sees the growth of many organizations of ex-convicts. Like the Fortune Society,[55] one of the best known, these groups are taking the lead in public programs for prison reform as well as offering direct services for after-care, counseling, halfway houses, drug-treatment centers and group therapy programs. At the 1971 Congress of Correction, representatives of several of these state-wide ex-prisoner organizations met to discuss the formation of a national federation. It has not yet taken place, but before too many years, with the tide turning in that direction, it may yet come to pass.

NOTES

1. Gerard O.W. Mueller, "Imprisonment and its Alternatives," in *A Program for Prison Reform* (Cambridge: Roscoe Pound American Trial Lawyers Foundation, 1973), p. 45.

2. Yushio Suzuki, Counsellor, Criminal Affairs Bureau, Ministry of Justice, Tokyo, in a lecture at UNAFEI on "Politics and Criminal Law in Japan," May 1, 1973.

3. John Robson, "Crime and Penal Policy in New Zealand," *New Zealand Journal of Public Administration,* March 1971, p. 36.

4. Ibid.

5. *Non-Institutional Treatment of Offenders in Japan* (Tokyo: Rehabilitation Bureau, Ministry of Justice, 1970), pp. 18–19.

6. Edwin Powers, "Halfway Houses: An Historical Perspective," *American Journal of Correction,* Vol. 21 (July–August, 1959), p. 35.

7. William Kresey, "Hoodlum Priest and Respectable Convicts," *Harper's,* (February 1961), pp. 57–62.

8. Lloyd W. McCorkle, Albert Elias, and F. Lovell Bixby, *The Highfield Story* (New York: Henry Holt, 1958).

9. H. Ashley Weeks, *Youthful Offenders at Highfield* (Ann Arbor: University of Michigan Press, 1958).

10. Newark, New Jersey. Albert Elias and Saul Pilnick, "The Essexfields Group Rehabilitation Project for Youthful Offenders," *Correction in the Community* (Sacramento: Youth and Corrections Agency, June 1964), pp. 51–57.

11. Louisville, Kentucky.

12. Red Wing, Minnesota.

13. Information available from International Halfway House Association, 2316 Auburncrest, Cincinnati, Ohio 45219.

14. John M. Flackett and Gail Flackett, "Criswell House: An Alternative to Institutional Commitment for the Juvenile Offender," *Federal Probation* (December 1970), pp. 30–37.

15. For detailed suggestions regarding planning and operation of residential community centers, including specific budgets, consult *The Residential Center: Corrections in the Community* (Washington: Bureau of Prisons, 1968). See also Oliver J. Keller, Jr., and Benedict S. Alper, *Halfway Houses: Community-Centered Correction and Treatment* (Lexington, Mass.. D.C. Heath, 1970), and Richard L. Rachin, "So You Want to Open a Halfway House," *Federal Probation* (March 1972), pp. 30–37.

16. "A Study of Florida's Halfway Houses—Part I," Tallahassee, Department of Health and Rehabilitative Services, Florida Division of Youth Services, 1972, from which the following table is taken.

Youths released from Florida Half-Way Houses, February 1968–December 1971.

Totals	Graduates	Transfers	Totals
Released	168	90	258
Successful	125	48	173
Unsuccessful*	43	42	85

(*Unsuccessful means youth transferred to another program.)

17. 196 Spring Street, Portland, Maine.
18. Available from the Association. See note 13, above.
19. See Benedict S. Alper, "Community Residential Treatment Centers," (New York: National Council on Crime and Delinquency, April 1966).
20. "Statement of Guiding Principles" (Augusta, Maine: Bureau of Corrections, March-9, 1973) (dup.).
21. Robert Coles, "Experiment in Rehabilitation," *New Republic* (October 4, 1969), pp. 12–15.
22. Milton Luger, "Innovations in the Treatment of Juvenile Offenders," *The Annals*, Vol. 39 (January 1969), pp. 60–70.
23. Ibid.
24. Ibid.
25. Roslyn G. McDonald, "Validity in Judging 'Success' in Programs for Juvenile Delinquency," in *Proceedings: Seventh Annual Interagency Workshop* (Huntsville: Institute of Contemporary Corrections and Behavioral Sciences, June 5–16, 1970, p. 223.
26. *The Open Correctional Institution in Asia and the Far East* (New York: United Nations Report No. TAO/AFE/14, January 28, 1965).
27. *Report of the First United Nations Crime Congress, Geneva, 1955* (New York: United Nations, 1966), pp. 27–28.
28. Based on F. Lowell Bixby, "Two Modern Correctional Facilities in Japan," *Federal Probation* (September 1971), pp. 14–15; and on information received from Tomiyoshe Kawahara of UNAFEI, who was the first Chief of Security of Kitsuregawa.
29. William Healy and Benedict S. Alper, *Criminal Youth and the Borstal System* (New York: Commonwealth Fund, 1941).
30. Mr. Teruo Miyauchi, of Fuchu Prison, Tokyo, May 1973.
31. *Report of the Second United Nations Crime Congress, London, 1960* (New York: United Nations, 1961). See also Daniel Glaser, *Effectiveness of a Prison and Parole System* (Indianapolis: Bobbs-Merrill, 1964), pp. 406–407. The fact cited by Glaser that prisons spend much more time and care orienting prisoners to the prison when they first come in than is ever spent thereafter orienting them for release cannot be denied.

32. National Institute of Mental Health, "Graduated Release" (Washington: U.S. Government Printing Office, Public Health Service Pub. No. 2128, 1971), p. 1.
33. *Kriminal Varden* [The Correctional System] (Stockholm: National Correctional Administration, 1970), p. 11.
34. Ibid.
35. *Washington Post,* August 25, 1973.
36. Recommendation number 7 of the "Parole System in Canada: A Brief by the Association to the Standing Senate Committee on Legal and Constitutional Affairs" (Ottawa: Canadian Criminology and Corrections Association, January 1973), p. 8.
37. Roxbury Multi-Service Center, "Community Corrections Proposal," Boston, January 10, 1972 (mimeo.).
38. Ibid.
39. From "CAP: Delinquent Youth Job-Creation and Work Skills Development Program" (Bedford, Mass.: Technical Development Corporation, 1972 (dup.).
40. "Report: A Special Probation Project, Dadefields—A Community-Based Non-Residential Treatment Project for Juvenile Delinquents," Miami, [800 N.W. 28th Street 33127]: State Division of Youth Services, December 1971 (dup.). No information is available on the results of the program to date.
41. Howard Shuman, "Juvenile Rehabilitation in Washington State," *American Journal of Correction* (January–February 1973), p. 32.
42. William R. Conte, "Modern-Day Reforms in Washington State Penal Programs," *American Journal of Correction,* Vol. 33, No. 3 (1971), p. 28.
43. *Probation Supervision and Training* (Sacramento: California Youth Authority, 1964. See also Robert M. Carter and Leslie T. Wilkins, eds., *Probation and Parole* (New York: John Wiley & Sons, 1970); and Don C. Gibbons, *Changing the Lawbreaker* (Englewood-Cliffs, New Jersey: Prentice-Hall, 1965).
44. *John Augustus: First Probation Office* (New York: National Probation Association, 1939. Reprinted from *John Augustus* (Boston: Wright and Hasty, 1852).
45. John Robson, *Criminology in Evolution–The Impact of International Congresses,* Wellington, February 1973 (dup.).
46. Jack Cocks, "From WHISP to RODEO," *California Youth Authority Quarterly,* Vol. 21, No. 4 (1968), pp. 7–11.
47. Dennis C. Sullivan, *Team Management in Probation* (Paramus, N.J.: National Council on Crime and Delinquency, 1972).
48. *Non-Institutional Treatment, op. cit.,* pp. 14–16.
49. From information furnished by Mrs. Viola DeSilva, Probation and Child Care Officer, Juvenile Court, Colombo.
50. *Kriminal Varden for 1970, loc. cit.*
51. Reiff and Reissman, *The Indigenous Non-Professional* (Cambridge, Mass.: Libra, Inc., 1964), p. 45 (dup.).

52. Milton Luger and Elias B. Saltman, "The Youthful Offender," in *The Task Force Report: Juvenile Delinquency and Youth Crime* (Washington: 1967). President's Commission Report on Law Enforcement and Administration of Justice.
53. The "Andros Project" of the Massachusetts Department of Youth Services, 450 Canterbury Street, Boston. See Chapter 10, below.
54. Libra, Inc., 1145 Massachusetts Avenue, Cambridge, Mass. 02138.
55. 29 East 22nd Street, New York, N.Y. 10010.

Chapter Eight

Alternatives to the
Traditional Institution

The earliest precedent for today's alternatives to the traditional institution is to be found in a school for boys which was built before the penitentiary itself came on the scene. This was the Hospice of San Michele, established in Rome in 1704, at the instigation of Pope Clemente XI.[1] In the places of detention of the time—where persons were held for trial—children and adults were locked up together. In its day and for its time, the Hospice was a radical departure, for it promulgated a principle to which a great deal of lip service has since been paid, but which in practice is still violated in many of our most enlightened juris-dictions—that children should not under any circumstances be confined with adults. It followed, as might be anticipated, the model of the monastery of that period, both in its architectural arrangements and in its reliance upon a program of silence, hard work and prayer.

A century later the first private institutions for children were estab-lished, first in New York state, followed soon thereafter by similar places under public auspices, the first in Massachusetts in 1846. The open work programs of some prisons in Spain and Italy during the second half of the nineteenth century, the beginnings of probation, parole and after-care at about that same time, all anticipated today's "new" emphasis on community alternatives to imprisonment.

Once a breach has been made in the solid practice of sentencing convicted offenders to closed institutions, by permitting certain persons for reasons of age, sex, mental condition, or likely response to conditions of limited freedom to serve their sentences in the community, the court-correctional system must seek additional and more effective forms of dealing with more and more offenders in this way. At the end, the only ones that should be left for whom incarceration is required is a hard core of persons whose degree of dangerousness to the community is so great and whose present inability to respond to rehabili-tative programs is so doubtful, that there is no safe way of permitting them abroad in the community.

129

For the implementation of a policy of placing in the community all those whose prognosis for response to it is good, all that is required is the necessary facilities and personnel, and the imagination and courage to bring them together in a community setting, under varying degrees of supervision and control.

As with traditional forms of release into the community under supervision—probation and parole—there is always available the last resort—imprisonment—the threat of being committed or returned to an institution as a punishment for failure to take advantage of modified conditions of control outside of it. This is the ultimate sanction. When viewed as such, rather than as first choice, the ground is prepared for its replacement by a host of alternatives.

FOSTER HOMES

Foster homes—the homes of persons willing to open their dwellings to care for boys and girls whose own families either reject them or are incapable of caring for them—are the first choice for young people, at least, among these many available alternatives. All authorities agree with the principle that a child's own home is the best place for him to be. It is there that he will in most instances ultimately return after a term in school or institution or whatever. But when the home is—if only temporarily—regarded as unfit to take in a son or daughter, the home of someone else is the next best place.

Over the years the foster home has maintained its place as one of the best alternatives to traditional institutional care. Originally designed to care for the neglected and dependent child, used in some places for the temporary detention of children awaiting trial who would otherwise be confined in jails, recent years have seen the extension of foster-home services to many other kinds of children,[2] and even to adults. The old idea of searching for homes of people who were at an economic level where a few dollars a week would make a sizeable difference to their budgets has been replaced by the attitude that foster parents should be amply recompensed for the actual extra expense of caring for a child, plus enough of an overage to provide an inducement to them to open their homes to children who are not their own.

Some states—notably in the Midwest—have developed the foster home idea to a very high point indeed. Special state departments with responsibility in this area of child care actively seek out foster homes. They also develop and impose high standards under which children are placed. By paying a monthly stipend for a bed in such homes, foster parents are assured of a regular source of income, whether the bed is occupied or not, and the authorities are assured of a place to which youngsters can be assigned. When a child is accepted for care in one of these homes, the rate is then increased to cover expenses in addition to such items as pocket money, clothing, and medical and dental care. As in so many other areas of dealing with people, once the economic factor has been resolved, there is then room for attention to the less impersonal aspects of life—the atmosphere, the attitudes, the kind of concern and involvement of foster-parents in the lives of their foster child which is the distinctive characteristic, and contribution, of this kind of care.

Many couples whose own children have grown up and moved away find themselves with living quarters larger than they require for their own needs. Such couples are sought out as prospective foster parents. Parents of large families have even been known to accept—and deal effectively with more than one child. The so-called group foster home has thus emerged as an excellent way of dealing with children who can be dealt with more effectively in a group than as an only child. Foster homes accommodating as many as twelve or fifteen children have been reported.[3]

The most recent innovation in foster-home care provides another example of a reversion to earlier familial patterns of caring for children who, for whatever reason, did not or could not make their homes with their natural parents. Based on the same custom of less highly developed tribal societies in Africa and Polynesia, this type of foster care seeks out blood relatives of the child in need of a home—aunt, uncle, grandparents, cousins—who might be willing to board and care for a young relative if their income were to be supplemented by funds from a private or public child- care source. Next to the child's own home, this would appear to offer the most desirable alternative.

BORSTAL

There are correctional systems which contain within themselves a variety of measures—from the freest conditions to tight security. One of the best known of these is the Borstal system of training in Great Britain.[4] Beginning in 1902 in the village of Borstal near Rochester in Kent, with one unit, the system by 1939 had grown to twelve, and in 1972 to a total of twenty-nine: twelve completely open schools for boys and one for girls; thirteen closed schools for boys and three for girls.[5] Like the Youth Authority Plan, which derived from the experience of Borstal, any youth who is deemed in need of institutional care is committed by the court to Borstal, and sent first to a reception and observation center for a determination of his or her needs and condition.

It is here that the decision is made about what available program is best suited for a particular boy or girl. One of the advantages of this initial observation period is to give the young persons the benefit of the doubt, that is, of sending them, as their initial commitment, to a place of greater rather than of less freedom. For there is available, always, the alternative of a tighter program should they find it difficult or impossible to adjust at the outset to conditions of greater freedom. This is of the essence of the system of Borstal training: provision of the widest possible range of facilities and programs all under one integrated administration, with latitude to transfer youngsters between them as their changing needs and development dictate.

The advantage of this approach is the more readily appreciated when compared with the lack of alternatives in many of our juvenile training schools. Here, if a young person fails to adjust or is a chronic threat to the security and program of the school, the ultimate alternative is usually transfer to an adult institution, where the advantages of tight security are more than outweighed by the baneful influence on a young person of being confined with adults. That this is not an isolated occurrence is seen in the large number of children—somewhere between 500 and 1000—who are transferred each year to adult prisons and reformatories, without court order or any review, simply by administrative decision and action on the part of the two agencies involved—the training school and the adult corrections department.[6]

Borstal offers a broad choice of locations and programs: forestry camps, a seaside camp where the main work is reclaiming land from the North Sea, farms, open cottage layouts, former jails and prisons remodelled to accommodate younger inmates, and a variety of educational and vocational programs. Initially the Borstals were all organized on the house plan, each with its own housemaster, deliberately patterned after the English "public school" system, from which in years past many Borstal housemasters and governors (superintendents or wardens) were drawn, under the influence of the founder of the Borstal idea, Sir Alec Paterson.

Closely related to the freedom to transfer among units in the system, another characteristic of Borstal training which was in its time unique is the interrelationship between institution and community. Boys and girls from these schools attend church in the neighboring communities, enroll in classes, clubs and choral groups with other children, are given an opportunity to work for pay, and to attend theatre in the nearby towns where the schools are located. Reciprocally, the community participates in the activities of the Borstals: volunteers with special talents or interests come out to teach classes or crafts or share their hobbies and skills with Borstal boys and girls. Many individuals become informal sponsors of children in these schools, and invite them to spend weekends or holidays with them—especially boys and girls who have no family of their own.

Parole is an integrated part of the Borstal system. The parole officer who is to supervise after release meets his young charge at the observation center after he has been assigned to his specific school, but before he is sent there. From the outset of the sentence, the details of job and residence are worked out between the officer and the boy or girl assigned to him. After release, the parole officer assumes full supervision of the parolee, aided by volunteers—men and women from all walks of life who serve as big brothers and big sisters to Borstal releasees.

The commission which administers the Borstals as a branch of the prison service admits that the schools are not so effective today as they were, seemingly, in earlier years. The recidivism rate, which stood at 36 percent in 1934, increased to 64 percent in 1960—almost an exact reciprocal after twenty-six years of operation of the Borstals.[7] Many reasons are brought forward to explain this rise, but perhaps the most telling is the same as that responsible for the rise in delinquency generally: the growing dissatisfaction of youth with contemporary life and their rejection of the values which were once accepted by a larger proportion of young people.

The Borstal scheme of training nevertheless remains one of the great seminal ideas in contemporary training for delinquents. Its spread, while limited to British Commonwealth countries—Canada, New Zealand, Hong Kong, Burma, Malaysia, and Sri Lanka (Ceylon)—is but one evidence of its strong and lasting influence.

DELINQUENTS AT SEA—FLORIDA AND JAPAN

A unique departure from the traditional school for delinquents is a privately run agency called the Florida Ocean Science Institute.[8] All of the students there are delinquents—either placed on probation, under suspended sentence, or on parole. Their ages range from sixteen to nineteen. Here they learn about the sea in many of the ways in which young people are interested: oceanography, navigation, deep-sea diving and seamanship; they study the tides, the erosion effects of the ocean, marine biology, fish and fishing, outboard motor repair and maintenance. The projects, which are carried out jointly by staff and "inmates," are by contract with the state government, the Army Corps of Engineers, and other bodies interested in oceanographic problems. These projects are serious and worthwhile, the kind which would otherwise be given to a research institute or carried out by government itself.

The staff of this "correctional institution," the faculty, are young men with a wide variety of experience in these matters who are also interested teachers of youth. They include sailors, men who have knocked around the world, some of them doctors of philosophy who chose not to teach in a university. Faculty and students do not "play" at being oceanographers, they work at serious adult problems which are useful to society, and to themselves as learning experiences. The Institute has received gifts of small boats and yachts; from time to time it sells one of the donated vessels, the proceeds going toward support for the program.

The posted class schedule gives no indication of what subject will be given during any specific morning or afternoon session during the week. The numbers designating the course to which they refer are changed weekly—navigation, mathematics, seamanship, motor mechanics, scuba diving, marine biology—together with the regular high school courses. Only the director of the school program knows which courses are being given at any specific time. In this way, not knowing in advance what subject will be given during what period, all the boys attend all the classes in order to make sure that they do not miss out on their favorite subjects.

The atmosphere can only be described as completely informal. The equipment is not fancy, and the quarters are a series of interconnecting shops off the main street. About sixty boys are accommodated in this program. Boys from Miami take public transportation to the county line, where they are picked up by an Institute car, as no housing accommodations are as yet available. At the end of their initial period of training, the boys are taken on cruises for several days at a time, which gives them an opportunity to practice at sea what they have learned in class.

This is a complete reversal of the way in which boys of this age are taught in the traditional public school. But the result is that some of these delinquent boys will travel eight hours a day between the Institute and their homes in order to enjoy school, what for almost all of them in their previous lives would have been anathema. It would be hard to find a more extreme example of an alternative to the traditional training school. It demonstrates clearly that by ingenuity, by setting out to appeal to young people on the basis of their real interests, rather than on the basis of what it is thought they *should* be interested in, largely because that is the way it has always been, it is possible to deal in positive and constructive fashion with the problems of young people.

The success of the first school organized by the Institute has led to the establishment, since, of three additional units in Florida, all with much the same program as the original project, with which they are affiliated in the Associated Marine Institutes.[9]

In 1947, the Japanese Ministry of Justice established an experimental "Juvenile Prison Without Walls" on the site of what had formerly been a marine training school and disciplinary barracks. Its innovator, currently at the Ministry's National Training Institute for Correctional Personnel, outfitted the first cadre of boys received from the courts in hand-me-downs from the Naval Academy. The experiment led to a change in 1964 to its present designation as the Shinko Maritime School, though its purpose remains the same: to prepare boys committed there by the juvenile court, for the merchant marine in a program of "seaman's training." Eligible applicants who plan to go to sea after their release are selected from among the inmates of the juvenile training schools throughout the country.

The school had inherited a small wooden ship, which has been replaced today by a vessel specially built and equipped for instruction and practical training. The school accommodates 320 boys with a staff of 75, including one full-time physician and a nurse. Located on the shores of the inland sea of Seto, it is equipped with cutters, guard boats, port derrick, floating dock, and electronic communication equipment. In addition to the regular academic courses, physics and mathematics, taught both by correspondence and classroom methods, the school places strong emphasis on gymnastics and physical training. The specially designed curriculum offers meteorology, seamanship, navigation, sea rescue, fishery and marine biology, maritime laws and regulations, small boat and engine operation and repair, as well as special courses in radio communication and steward services, leading to certification in these skills after taking national examinations. The school aims to keep its young charges busy, and provides craft and hobby opportunities, as well as a full program of athletics and sports.[10]

The sea is also the setting for a second training school—the OHI work camp—located on an island in the inland sea of Japan, which trains young men in shipbuilding. Begun as a matter of wartime necessity in 1942, under the leadership of a progressive correctional administrator, the program began with fifty specially selected adult prisoners from various prisons around Tokyo who were considered suitable for employment in an open setting.[11] They were promised a reduction of one-third of their sentence—each day would be calculated as three—for satisfactory performance. Inmates were permitted to wear ordinary clothes instead of prison uniforms, their guards worked with them instead of supervising them, and prisoners shared the same facilities as did the ordinary workers. "An honor system was applied to every aspect of the working process: no discrimination and no locking up." It is still today an open institution with 120 inmates and 12 staff members. Offenses represented by the prisoners range from various property crimes—theft, fraud and burglary—to injury of persons, including murder.[12]

The success of the initial project—the learning by prisoners of every step of shipbuilding and their contribution to the actual construction of ships—resulted in the development of a corps of skilled workers who were, at the same time, serving out their sentences. In the following year, six more such corps were taken from prisons to work in the shipyards, including two groups of older juveniles. Prisoners paroled from the shipbuilding corps went directly into employment in the dock, ship, and repair yards, thus obviating any problems of finding employment for them. In all, over 6000 men at one time or another have served their time in this enterprise. As in other penal institutions in Japan today, prisoners were paid only a very small allowance for working; the employer pays to the prison department the much larger amounts which the rate of inmate production earns; thus netting the institutions a sizeable sum each year.

A noteworthy feature of this institution is that it exemplifies the cooperation of government and private industry in preparing offenders for independence and a highly marketable skill when they are released. The shipbuilding company built, and thereafter turned over to the government, a three-story building to house this prison unit.

Learning how to build ships—and building them—is the main activity. The men, under their own elected leaders, go off each day in small groups to work at assigned jobs along with the regularly employed, skilled workers. After the day's work is done, they return to an evening of study of the theoretical aspects of the trade, in preparation for national examinations in whatever branch they have specialized. Regular evening meetings are also held to consider and decide questions of the camp as a whole, and there are also groups for athletics, hobbies and sports.

The administration encourages visits, which are permitted on non-working days, but may be held at other times as well. During the summer months, inmates and their visitors may be boated to one of the nearby islands for picnics and swimming, in completely open and unsupervised fashion.

The surrounding community is the recipient of the inmates' efforts in their off-hours in cleaning, painting, gardening, and generally sprucing up their public areas. Of the 664 inmates released from the camp in the eight years between September 1961 and December 1969, 74 were re-arrested for new crimes; a very respectable recidivism rate of 11.2 percent.

What began as an experiment has been continued to this day. A man who completes his sentence by working in the shipyards, and is released on parole, finds his co-workers—fellow prisoners and staff as well as the regular employees—lined up outside the administration office to applaud him and wave goodbye, as he is driven away.

OUTWARD BOUND [13]

In Great Britain during World War II, the government was concerned that large numbers of their seamen literally gave up their lives with little struggle when forced to abandon ship in the cold waters of the North Atlantic—while many more experienced sailors, although older and in poorer physical condition, managed to survive the same ordeal.

As a result, the first Outward Bound school was established in Aberdovey, Wales. Dr. Hahn, the initiator, was interested in developing more than muscle in young merchant seamen, for, in addition to physical conditioning, he stressed the importance of group pride, personal contribution, and trust in one's self and in others. This school, as in other Outward Bound schools to follow, recognized the value of structuring stressful situations to unify groups toward a common goal, as well as the merit of repeated and hard-won successes in establishing confidence and a more positive self-image.

Following Hahn's model, the Colorado Outward Bound Program School was opened in 1962 in the Rocky Mountains. The program involves mountaineering, backpacking, high-altitude camping, solo survival, rappelling and rock climbing. In 1964, five adjudicated delinquents from Massachusetts entered the Colorado program. A year later, twenty-five more entered similar programs in Minnesota and Maine. The success of this program led to the opening of a series of pilot programs for adjudicated delinquents in Massachusetts.

Homeward Bound, as this program was called, has evolved into a two-phase program lasting six weeks.

Prior to his coming into the Homeward Bound program, the youth is told that it is very rugged, has limited openings, is voluntary, that once begun it must be completed, and that once completed it would allow the graduate to be paroled directly home. The first phase is devoted to orientations and basic skill-building in survival. Phase II involves cross-country hiking, land and/or sea expeditions, rock climbing, and navigation and is climaxed by a three-day, three-night solo experience of survival in the wilderness. The program involves severe physical challenge, excitement, danger, and periods of calm where the participants can absorb, and reflect on, their accomplishments.

The thrust of the program is to accept the offender, emphasize his worthiness, build up his self-esteem and confidence and, through personal achievement, help him to find an identity which will not dissolve or diminish once he leaves the program. Through activity-with-purpose, the debilitating effects of a correctional regime are held to a minimum. Results of a followup study seven to fourteen months after parole from the program found that 20.8 percent of the Homeward Bound group recidivated, in contrast to 42.7 percent of the control group. There was an increased chance of success through the Homeward Bound program as the age of the participants increased. Of the total number of boys who entered the program, 70.3 percent successfully completed it; 29.7 percent failed. Two new Homeward Bound programs are currently being planned: a thirty-day program for girls, and a thirty-day program for boys aged 11-13. High school youngsters who are not delinquent are being accepted, with parental permission, in order to provide a variety in each group.[14]

This program can be seen as closely related to the forestry camps for boys, first established in California in the 1930s, themselves patterned after the Civilian Conservation Corps programs begun during the first years of the New Deal. The CCC camps took unemployed youth off the streets and utilized their energies in the national forests to cut fire lanes and do conservation work, and to help build and maintain facilities for campers and tourists in the national parks.

Halfway houses have been described in the preceding chapter, as they originated to serve persons paroled from institutions who could not be released because they could not meet the requirements of a job and a place to live. These are what might be called "halfway-out houses" to distinguish them from those residences in the community which may receive persons *in lieu of* imprisonment. While program, location, and purpose hardly differ from those places which serve persons who have spent time in an institution, they are recognized here as distinct alternatives to institutional commitment. One of the most extensive uses of this type of facility is found in England, which uses the term "hostel"—familiar to any young person who has hiked, biked or camped almost anywhere in the United States or abroad as "youth hostels."

Noting that "perhaps as many as half the men discharged from prison each year are homeless," the National Association for the Care and Resettlement of Offenders (NACRO) goes on to describe many of these men as having, "in the course of lives interspersed with institutional experiences, lost all contact with family and friends, and become rootless individuals with no ties in a local community." Such hostels are now coming to be used as an alternative to imprisonment for men who are referred by the courts. Between one-half and one-third of the persons received in the hostels are referred in this way.

NACRO describes the following types of hostel programs:

"Family Model—This type of hostel regime is based on the assumption that a simulated family situation can repair damage created by the deprivation and unsatisfactory early relationships experienced by many offenders. This approach was popular in the early days of hostels for offenders, but it has since been recognized that this type of regime can easily become too paternalistic and protective, undermining offenders and increasing their dependency.

"Supportive Boarding House Model—The majority of hostels can best be seen as akin to commercial boarding houses where the residents pay a set rent in return for board and lodgings. In addition the staff give support to the residents, ranging from advice on practical matters like jobs and finance, to help on a one-to-one basis with personal problems. .

"Democratic Community Model—In this type of hostel the residents are expected to play a major part in the running of the hostel. Relationships between the staff and resident groups are of prime importance. For a considerable number of residents, active participation in decisions enables them to achieve a degree of independence and to realize their full potential."[15]

In addition to these three types, NACRO suggests the use of apartments as short-term accommodations for persons for whom some kind of confinement might be the only possible solution. This type of living arrangement is not unknown in the mental health field, especially for persons released on a trial basis from institutions for psychotics.

The possibilities of adapting "adult" facilities and "grown up" programs for the care and training of young people who come before the juvenile court cannot be more dramatically demonstrated than in the following story written by a sergeant at McCoy Air Force Base in Florida. It is reprinted here as it was published, with minor deletions.[16]

"For 25 boys now residing at McCoy AFB, Florida, reveille at 5:30 each morning signals another step in a new way of life as well as a new day. And for them, reveille is a happy symbol of their opportunity.

"For them, the newly opened door is called *Boys' Base*, a dramatic new halfway house program operated since June 1971 by the State of Florida—Division of Youth Services.

"The unique aspect is that the state program is operated on a federal installation—namely, McCoy AFB.

"The 25 boys are involved directly in the McCoy community. They attend public schools, and enjoy the privileges of the youth center, base gym, library, ceramics shop, chapel, theater and bowling lanes. They have their own basketball team that competes with the other base teams in the Orlando area.

"The boys also eat at the dining hall with the airmen (meals are paid for) and some have reported a 35-pound increase in weight.

"Of course they aren't 'hardened criminals,' and the idea of the program is to see that they never will be. Ranging in age from 15 to 17, all have been adjudicated by the Florida Juvenile Court in their home counties. The offenses are varied. Some are 'in' for drug abuse, others for breaking and entering or armed robbery. Some are only guilty of chronic truancy.

"A quick walk around the 'house' proves that Boys Base is not a correctional institution in the usual sense of the term. There are no bars and no weapons. In fact, if a resident decided to leave, he would have no problem in doing so.

"But the boys don't leave. They stay because they feel they belong, and by leaving they would be copping out on the family. After all, the group voted each boy into the house, and ultimately, it will be the group that will award him his freedom.

"The resident director and his wife and five children live in the same dormitory as the boys. The director has a strong background in education, psychology and sociology, backed by several years of experience in rehabilitation.

"He believes that first-term offenders do not belong in conventional confinement facilities. He feels they need a way to get at the root of their problems, to find their own solutions, and to learn to function as productive members of society.

"The foundation of the program is, simply, peer group pressure.

"The boys get up at 5:30 a.m. and are ready to depart by county bus or state station wagon for school at 6:45. They return at 2:30 for the most important part of their rehabilitative process.

"For one and a half hours they hold their 'group meeting.'

"Emphasis is on helping to find solutions to problems various members have. Free time before and after these sessions is used for informal rap sessions.

"After supper, there is a quiet evening time and a study period. Everyone spends about an hour each night on housekeeping chores.

"During a normal week, several special meetings are called to discuss evaluations, home visits, reassignment of groups, housekeeping duties and other necessities.

"Sunday is visiting day when parents also get a chance to learn the philosophy of the program and talk about their son's progress.

"On weekends, the boys can pursue recreational activities at any of McCoy's facilities. On a recent Sunday, the whole house was 'turned loose' at a base open-house and got to see the USAF thunderbirds.

"The important thing is that at McCoy's Boy's Base, juvenile offenders are not stuck in the corner of a cell. They are living and working together for a common goal. They attend school with kids from the local community, work, play, and attend church at McCoy with the men in blue.

"New members must be 'voted in' by a peer group just as they are released by the group if it's felt they are ready to make it on the outside. But the process doesn't end with release.

"The youth becomes the responsibility of an after-care counselor, and is usually required to attend two after-care meetings per week in his own home community.

"Moreover, job placement procedure has been developed through the State Vocational Rehabilitation Office at Orlando, the McCoy AFB personnel office, and community businesses."

BUCKEYE RANCH

In the state of Ohio, two residential units, both under the same management, exemplify the possibility of varying the locus and the program, and even the kind of young people accepted for care, as long as the principles and the leadership, under which they operate, are largely the same.[17] The first is Buckeye Ranch, an 80-acre residential treatment center for about twenty-five boys between the ages of fourteen and sixteen. The school was designed from the outset to provide a setting which would allow for a high degree of freedom. Rooms are without bars, locks, or a traditionally custodial appearance. This openness is a reflection of the director's basic assumption that people who live together can together work out the problems of their living, while respecting one's own rights as well as those of others. The director's simple and direct approach reads refreshingly, as in the brief extracts from a statement of his philosophy.

"Our experience has shown that the little dependent kid stays dependent; and when you turn him out of the institution because he has reached a maximum age, he probably will fall right on his face because no one has taught him how to make decisions. . . .

"The aura of delinquency that comes with a lot of these kids charged with gross delinquent behavior, is not in and of itself a factor that should screen kids out from places like this. We should not cream the top of the crop and take only those kids who are going to make it anyway. We must go beyond that and take kids into these places who are on their way toward a hardened life of rough behavior and becoming misfits in society. In my view, delinquents probably have more capacity to make a good show and to do well in life than many who come under the banner of being 'emotionally disturbed but nondelinquent.' It is nice in an institution to have a little guy running around who wants you to put your hand on his shoulder, and who pulls at the apron strings of the house mother in the kitchen, and does little errands. He likes all this; he is just a polite little kid. People can enjoy that much more than they can the kid who is busting out the windows, and fighting, and cursing, and kicking you in the shins.

"Our whole focus at Buckeye Boys Ranch is to have the time with a kid, one or two years in the program, so that opportunities for relationship formation can take place. This is not to say that even though we are well trained, and we have skilled people, we do not make mistakes. We make a lot of mistakes. But we try to let the kids know that we are human beings who are going to make some wrong decisions, and when we get angry, we are going to show it. We would rather show it, even though we may make the wrong decision, than to cover it with a false smile and walk off into the office and curse the kids.

"I think conflict is the greatest thing we have going for us. Conflict has to be there; it is only through successful resolution of conflict that change can occur. Nice, peaceful, happy, superficial relationships do not pay off; they lead nowhere. But when a kid is conflicted and angry, because he may see you as a rejecting parent of years past, and after he at some point can handle that with you and understands that you are a different kind of person—that you are human and have some hangups like people he has known, but you also have different kinds of attitudes—then this is where the payoff takes place."

A few years after the establishment of the Ranch, the director opened, in Columbus near the campus of Ohio State University, a halfway house for a dozen older teen-age boys. Here is how he describes its purpose and approach.

"Most of the kids we deal with are going back to the cities, so we are not going to teach them how to be farmers. We must somehow help them deal with the realities of the community life. There are times when these kids are going to have to be on their own at an early age, and so we must help them move toward an emancipated youth structure—to get them into the community as emancipated minors of age 17, and to be in a potential work situation, or to be living in some type of boarding house, and to make it. That's all they have.

"In this halfway house, we tried to help them demonstrate for themselves what living in the community is all about for a 17-year-old who will have to make his own decisions. They sign in and out of the house and are able to go into the community. If they get in a bar and have some beer, that is part of life, and we don't kick them in their shins for it. If they get involved with drug use in the community, we try to deal with it. Simply because that is where he is going to be living six months from now and he must learn how to deal with it. . . . Delinquent kids make decisions all the time; they are decision-makers. Their choice of decisions is what gets them into trouble."[18]

A more traditional, but still nonpunitive setting for dealing with
emotionally disturbed children, is found in a private agency setting in Maine
with a capacity of seventy-two boys and girls between the ages of six and nineteen. Three types of children are accepted for treatment, described by the school
as follows:

"Behavior disorders (the largest group)—withdrawing reactions,
overanxious reactions, unsocialized aggressive reactions, group delinquent reactions; psycho-physiologic disorders—musculoskeletal, cardiovascular, gastro-
intestinal; special symptom defects—feeding disturbances, enuresis, speech
disturbances, specific learning disturbances."[19]

The prime goal of the program here is to help the child recognize
and resolve problems caused by social and emotional stress so as to be able to
return to society as a productive and satisfied member. The total living experience approximates as far as possible a "normal family situation which sets firm,
fair and consistent limits." Cottages accommodate 12-16 children of both sexes
and all age ranges (each child shares a room with another). The cottage staff
consists of cottage parents (a married couple), an associate cottage mother, and
a cook. Each cottage, designed like a home, has a large kitchen, livingroom,
diningroom and sleeping quarters.

Children with learning difficulties are served by an on-campus school
which employs a remedial reading specialist and eight special education teachers.
The treatment staff (two psychiatrists, three clinical psychologists, seven psychiatric social caseworkers, three registered nurses, and one speech therapist) use a
multiple approach based on their preference as to which approach is best suited
for each individual child. The basic approach is derived from milieu therapy.

THE "CORRIDOR" IN HOLLAND

This experimental unit, north of Amsterdam, combines two interesting features—
the Outward Bound program plus guided-group interaction. The regime at this
institution revolves around an obstacle course which the young men are put
through—climbing poles, crossing trestles, scaling ropes, scrambling up ramps—the
kind of activities found in basic training courses in the armed forces. The
experiences which these young men have had during the day in the obstacle
course forms the basis for their group discussion in the evening.

After they have completed the obstacle course as individuals, they
then divide into groups of three. Each group is given a block of wood, almost as
long and heavy as a railroad tie, and the three young men together have to carry
this log with them as they go through the various steps of the obstacle course.
In the process they learn the value—and necessity—of cooperation in order
to accomplish a common goal.

The stay at this institution is short—from six to twelve weeks, and is
planned to provide an intensive experience for the young men, aged 17 to 23,

sentenced here. The program is limited to first offenders, which does not mean that many of them have not had prior criminal experiences. Work and physical fitness are emphasized. The program aims to combine what is described as "the influence process"—in which the leader plays the role model for his group, and a "self-awareness process" which aims "through group activities and discussions to [give] each member a more realistic image of his social relationship to the group."[20]

The Corridor "does not provide an exhibit of the criminal life as a status experience as ordinary prisons do; it is not a deeply stigmatizing experience for the persons going through it; it minimizes the opportunities for the young offender to develop hostilities to justice and life and society as a result of the experience; and, finally, it provides a situation in which harmfully unrealistic masks and images of the inmates can be removed voluntarily by life together with the group."[21] Of the first 1,000 young men who served time here, only 19 (2 percent) have escaped.

What has been described above is by no means a complete or comprehensive review of the variety of imaginative experiments being carried out in the world today as alternatives to what we know as the traditional prison, reformatory and training school. Many of these schemes are new and lacking in scientific evaluation of results. The totality of what has been presented aims to give the reader some idea that in many widely separated places, much thought, energy, and ingenuity is being applied to the search for replacements for the fixed institutions which have dominated penal thought and practice for the past 200 years.

NOTES

1. Harry E. Barnes and Negley K. Teeters, *New Horizons in Criminology* (Englewood Cliffs, N.J.: Prentice-Hall, 1945), p. 474.
2. Oliver J. Keller, Jr. and Benedict S. Alper, *Halfway Houses* (Lexington, Mass.: D.C. Heath, 1970), Chapter 6.
3. Ibid. All that is needed for the extension of this excellent mode of treatment is the commitment on the part of correction authorities to the foster home idea, and energy and determination to extend it—at a cost in dollars and a benefit in more humane treatment that makes it a prime alternative to the fixed institution.
4. Hermann Mannheim and Leslie T. Wilkins, *Prediction Methods in Relation to Borstal Training* (London: HMSO, 1955), Roger Hood, *Borstal Re-Assessed* (London: Heinemann, 1965).
5. *Report on the Work of the Prison Department, 1971* (London: HMSO 1972), pp. 80–84.
6. *Delinquent Children in Penal Institutions,* (Washington: Children's Bureau Publication, No. 415, 1964).
7. Roger Hood, *op. cit.,* p. 208.

8. Florida Ocean Sciences Institute, Inc., 1605 Deerfield Beach, Florida 334410.
9. The Tampa Marine Institute at 1310 Shoreline Drive, Hookers Point, Tampa 33605; the Pinellas Marine Institute, 111 108th Avenue, Treasure Island 33706; the Jacksonville Marine Institute, 725 South Main Street, Jacksonville 32207.
10. From information furnished by the Correction Bureau, Ministry of Justice, Tokyo.
11. Akira Masaki, "Reminiscences of a Japanese Penologist," Tokyo, 1964 (English edition), p. 11.
12. F. Lovell Bixby, "Two Modern Correctional Facilities in Japan," *Federal Probation* (September 1971), pp. 13–15.
13. Francis J. Kelly and Daniel J. Baer, *Outward Bound Schools as an Alternative to Institutionalization for Adolescent Delinquent Boys* (Boston: Fandel Press, 1968).
14. Herb C. Willman, Jr. and Ron Y.F. Chun, "Homeward Bound: An Alternative to the Institutionalization of Adjudicated Juvenile Offenders," *Federal Probation* (September 1973), pp. 52–58.
15. *Establishing Hostels and Lodging Schemes for Offenders* (London: National Association for the Care and Resettlement of Offenders, 1972), pp. 2, 3.
16. Sgt. Keith Johnson, "Boy's Base," *The Airman* (November 1972), pp. 29, 30.
17. *Proceedings: Seventh Annual Interagency Workshop* (Huntsville: Institute of Contemporary Corrections and Behavioral Sciences, 1970), pp. 198–200.
18. Ibid., p. 203.
19. "What is Sweetser Children's Home?" (Saco, Maine: Sweetser Children's Home, March 1973 [dup.]).
20. *Tussen Nu en Straks* [Between Now and Tomorrow] (Amsterdam: Prison Department, Ministry of Justice, 1971).
21. *After Conviction, op. cit.*, p. 121.

Chapter Nine

Five Modes of Treatment of Convicted Offenders

Before any program of effective corrective action for the convicted offender can be undertaken, there must be a clear understanding of its purpose and some consistency sought in the concept itself, and its implications both for the offender and for society. From time to time, corrections has been seen to aim at punishment, restraint, deterrence, correction, reformation, rehabilitation—or that most recent term—reintegration. Changes in correctional administrators coincidental with changes in the politics of a particular state are inevitably accompanied by superficial shifts in emphasis among these various aims, without any basic reformulation of correctional purpose or program design resulting.

A recently appointed commissioner of corrections, in a speech shortly after he assumed office, stated that the easiest thing for him to do would be to "preach reformation and practice punishment." The reality is that after several centuries of trial and error, no single policy consistently guides the institutions which receive sentenced prisoners from the courts. Wide mood swings on the part of the public are partially responsible for this continuing inconsistency, in response to real or created crime waves.

An interesting attempt was made recently to bring the entire area under some kind of critical review by a task force on delinquency which undertook to state succinctly some possible alternative approaches to delinquency within the range of a developmental sequence. The five models described below start with the prevailing concept of punishment and proceed outward in successive, less stringent, but more radical stages. Each model begins with defining the content and assumptions of the approach, including identification of the concept of delinquency implicit in it, followed by programmatic implications. What follows is but little changed from the original version as developed by the task force.[1] While its emphasis is on the juvenile, this should not detract from its value for application to dealing with the adult offender as well.

145

PUNITIVE MODEL

The first model is easily recognized as embodying the prevailing notions of delinquency and measures for dealing with it.

"This model begins with the assumption that young people who engage in delinquent acts are guilty of having committed illegal, immoral and antisocial acts. It tends to assume that such behavior is abnormal, that it is engaged in by only a very small percentage of young people. These few tend to be thought of as possessing character defects; they are rotten kids.

"This approach assumes that the most effective response to such antisocial behavior is to punish the offender, as by confining him in an institution. Such punishment is thought to be appropriate because it provides retribution for the offender's antisocial acts, because the punishment is expected to deter him and others who might engage in such behavior from committing such acts, and because incarceration and/or the deterrent effects of punishment are expected to reduce the incidence of such behavior and, therefore, protect society.

"Delinquent behavior is thought to reflect a character defect which can be corrected through punishment. Therefore, this model is concerned with neither non-punitive approaches to individual remediation, nor with attempts to change social or institutional conditions (which are not seen as having a causal role). In implementing this approach, one is not concerned about the possible negative impact of punishment on the individual offender, because punishment is thought to have beneficial consequences for the offender and, in any case, he has it coming.

"This model suggests programs designed to increase the effectiveness of the criminal and juvenile justice systems, so that individual offenders can be apprehended and punished with greater speed, efficiency, and certainly by such measures as improvement in police communication and court management, mandatory minimum sentencing, and the establishment of more institutions."

Judgements as to who are the criminals and what are their characteristics based on this model, results in a very selective sample. If statistics are derived from persons who have been found guilty, this represents a larger sample than if derived from persons committed to institutions. But compared to all cases of crimes actually committed, it is infinitesimal. Yet most studies of the characteristics of criminals are based on those inaccurate, highly selective data.

A young, successful scientist describes his adolescence as having been spent in a gang area in Brooklyn; he still carries in his legs shrapnel from bullets received from the police.[2] The other members of his former gang are either dead or in prison. He describes himself as always having been a rapid talker and a fast runner. One of the favorite sports of his gang, in an area where there was little opportunity for any kind of constructive recreational activity, was to provoke the police. The gang would make a fire in a vacant lot or break windows or start a fight with another group in the neighborhood. The police would come with lights blazing and guns drawn, jump out of their cars, leaving the motors running, and the kids would take off in the police cars—great sport! He was a hurdler, and the police could never catch him. And if they did, he out-talked them. So today he is a PhD teaching in a university, and those of his young friends who are not dead are in Sing Sing. He was characterially no better and no worse than they; he came from a broken home; he was not morally defective; he just avoided being caught.

But our statistics are based on those who don't talk or run fast enough. We treat the "character defects"—of those who are caught—by punish ment, because it is thought to be appropriate, because it provides retribution, all of which is expected to reduce the incidence of this kind of behavior, and in this way to protect society. Delinquent behavior is commonly thought to reflect family deficiencies or individual defects which cannot be corrected in any other way, as exemplified in the work of the Gluecks.[3] The argument throughout their work is that poverty and social conditions cannot be a cause of crime because there are fewer poor people who engage in delinquent acts than there are those who do not—Q.E.D. After studying the likely effects of 60 charac- teristics in the lives of a thousand offenders, they came to the conclusion that three factors are most directly related to proneness to delinquency: supervision of boy by his mother; discipline of the boy by his mother; and the degree of the cohesiveness of the family.[4]

Interestingly enough, these are three areas in which society cannot intervene. Society may not enter the home of the family where there is no discipline, affection or supervision—and compel the mother to love her child, the father to discipline his son, the parents to supervise the activity of their children. The enormous work done by these two researchers during a lifetime of profes- sional devotion leaves untouched the social and institutional conditions which appear as constant concomitants of most early offenders.

In implementing this punitive model, no concern is expressed for the possible bad effects of punishment on the individual delinquent, because it views punishment as beneficial in its consequences, and in any case the offender committed his act knowing that he would be punished if he were caught. So, in a sense, he was asking for it.

This model suggests programs designed to increase the effectiveness of the criminal justice system, as applied to both juveniles and adults, in order to make more efficient their apprehension and punishment and to increase the certainty of dealing with them. Improvement in existing methods of police communications and court management, mandatory increases in sentencing, expansion of the number of institutions, are the avenues suggested. In other words, we are unsuccessful not because the basic approach is wrong, but because the punitive efforts are too scant and scattered.

This first model starts with the basic assumption that young people who engage in delinquent acts are guilty of having done so in response to character defects, or willfulness. It assumes that such conduct is abnormal, in the sense of being out of the ordinary, or of not being expected. In other words, only a very small percentage of young people engage in crime in the same way that we tend to view only a small fraction of the total population as possessing character defects.

Persons caught up in the system premised on this model are the same groups which compose our statistics on causation: those who have been apprehended, brought before a criminal court, convicted and sentenced. These represent only a very small percentage of the population of all those persons who commit crimes, however. For of all the crimes actually committed, the fact is that far less than one-half ever get reported. Of the nearly 3 million index crimes reported in 1965, slightly less than one-fourth were cleared by the arrest of a suspect. Of 727,000 such arrests, approximately one-fifth were sentenced; less than one-half of those sentenced went to prison.[5] If, then, less than 10 percent of all persons arrested for the commission of an offence ever land in an institution, how much reliability can be placed on statistics based on this group? How much credibility should be attached to conclusions drawn from the characteristics of such persons? Yet most of our delinquent and criminal stereotypes are derived from persons in this category. In the same way and to the same degree, we tend to accept the traditional ways of treating such persons—punishment—as not only the normal, but also as the most effective way of ridding society of them if only for a limited period of time—the length of their sentence—in the full realization that 98 percent of all of them will ultimately be released back into the community.

CORRECTIONAL MODEL

Most readers will probably find that this model is one that they can deal with comfortably, for it is somewhat a departure from the first, purely punitive. It does not so harshly label delinquents as "bad," and at the same time that it emphasizes the salvageable features of young offenders, it takes the prevailing correctional system pretty much for granted, as largely satisfactory in approach, wanting only, perhaps, some liberalization of procedures, professionalization of personnel, and larger appropriations to reduce correctional caseloads.

"This model assumes that delinquency is antisocial behavior which indicates the existence of deficiencies in the individual which must be 'corrected.' It assumes that the juvenile justice system has a legitimate role to play and that correctional programming can work, that is, that a significant portion of the offender population can be rehabilitated. The focus is on the individual client, not upon social or institutional conditions which might be causally related to his antisocial behavior."

This model does not necessarily deny the existence or possible importance of such causal factors, but at the same time, they are not of significant concern because of the individual focus of the model. The model tends to assume that the offender population is a relatively small percentage of the total population, and that the offender group has been selected as the focus of correctional efforts through legitimate, socially necessary and just procedures.

"The correctional model is open to a wide range of approaches to and settings for individual remediation, including institutionalization, community-based alternatives, group therapy, individual psychotherapy and educational and motivational programs. Choices among these options are made on the basis of their relative effectiveness in achieving rehabilitation. Concern about the well-being and human development of the offender is consistent with this model. However, the basic assumption remains that the individual is guilty of behavior which has been properly proscribed by society."

This approach may be described as embodying the progressive, liberal approach—the one which motivates most prison reform organizations, and that portion of the citizenry who regard themselves as enlightened, concerned about the problem of crime, and even desirous of doing something about it.

At the same time it is based on an assumption identical to that of the first model: it equates crime with the activities of persons who are in some way deficient—though not necessarily immoral or basically destructive. It is also an "individualized" approach. Social workers, counsellors, psychologists and psychiatrists would tend to agree with its basic tenet—as the professions they represent are looked to for treating more effectively the individual inadequacies which are the focus of this approach.

Yet it disregards, to the same extent as does the first model, the fact that persons who are caught up in delinquent patterns are only a small proportion of all those who actually commit offenses. We have seen the effect of the funneling process, which produces a smaller and smaller number—more and more finely screened—as the criminal process moves from the persons arrested for crime to those who are finally convicted and imprisoned.

This model likewise assumes that those who come out of the small end of that funnel are indeed the worst of all the offenders who have committed offenses, whereas all the studies that we know establish clearly that a majority of the population engages in one way or another in antisocial acts and that, again, what we are measuring and what we are correcting here is a very small percentage of all those who have committed such acts.

This approach guides those who urge the importance of followup researches into the results of treatment, of continued evaluative studies between various correctional programs in order to sift out those which are truly effective. Lost sight of in this search for effective measures of correction is the fact that followup studies into the results of treatment, research into recidivism, confront the difficulty of isolating the influence of a correctional experience out from the multitude of other influences in an offender's life. The fact that the research may hypothesize that a term in an institution can constitute an effective correctional experience does not mean that in the life of the offender under review, this same experience is in reality the most significant one in his life—compared, for example, with his inability to get a job, a physical difficulty, a serious lack in his education, or a personal tragedy in the life of a member of his family.

Basic to this approach, above all, is the assumption that the offender, however individualized the treatment he receives, is guilty of behavior which has been forbidden, or proscribed by society. It is this characteristic which brackets this model with the first model described.

DIVERSIONARY MODEL

The basic assumption of this model begins to question some of the two earlier positions. Here, for the first time, is found reference to a fact which has been earlier stated: the criminal justice system is involved with only a very small portion of the totality of criminal behavior. Much of that behavior among the young is of a transitory nature, the kind of acts which have always been characteristic of young people growing up in Western society. If such behavior is dealt with understandingly, the young person may be helped through the difficult years of adolescence. Reaching adulthood, the consequent involvement in activities which express and satisfy a newly found identity may carry him out of the "delinquency-prone" period, leaving behind, at the same time, any great possibility that delinquent behavior will become a fixed mode of expression for him.

Considering that 80 percent of adults and children questioned in various studies freely admit to having committed acts for which they could have been arrested had there been a policeman present,[6] use of the term "tip of the iceberg" to describe those who get caught in the toils of the law is not extreme. The findings of a recent study in Japan confirm a fact well recognized in our country: the amount of "dark" or unreported crime approximates one-half the number of criminal acts which come to official attention.[7]

"This model begins with the assumption that delinquent behavior is a universally prevalent, or at least widely dispersed, phenomenon. Delinquency defined in terms of legal standards or contact with the juvenile justice system represents only the tip of the iceberg.

"Some advocates of this approach argue that patterns of delinquent behavior are nearly identical among various communities, socioeconomic groups, ethnic groups, and other populations. It implies acceptance of the idea that most of the adult population have engaged in acts which could have resulted in an adjudication of delinquency, and tends to view delinquency as 'mischief.' It emphasizes the fact that most of the behavior which is identified as delinquent does not have serious social consequences. It considers the concepts of moral and legal guilt to be an inappropriate way to characterize such behavior.

"This model considers the great bulk of such behavior to be the result of environmental conditions or spontaneous occurrences not related to the character of the individual participant. Among the environmental factors which are seen as causally significant, the law enforcement and juvenile justice systems themselves are given particular emphasis. Advocates of this model point out that individuals who eventually engage in the most serious delinquent and criminal behavior tend to be those who have been exposed earliest and most often to the juvenile justice system. It is felt that not only is it clear that juvenile corrections do not and cannot correct, but that the justice system itself is a principal cause of criminality. This is thought to be so because the system brutalizes and dehumanizes individuals, labels them as social deviants, and at the same time provides opportunities for training for criminal careers.

"It is argued that, while this dehumanizing criminalization process is applied selectively, variations do exist in enforcement patterns and political leverage among different communities, resulting in the system's focusing upon some groups but not upon others. In particular, the poor and the minority group members are thought to be subjects of such discriminatory enforcement activities.

"The principal policy implication which derives from this analysis relates to the desirability of diverting young people from the juvenile justice system at every possible point: throughout the schools or social service agencies prior to contact with the system, at the point of first police contact or arrest, at the point of court intake or disposition, or upon institutionalization.

"This model is compatible with either diversion to traditional agencies and programs, diversion to new alternative programs, or simple release to the community. The model may be consistent with diverting all young people or some part of the population presently handled by the system. The approach requires consideration of whether a residual population will be handled by the system (or some new system), and consideration of the nature of this residual population."

While the model points out that much of what may be termed mischief winds up in the court as adjudicated delinquency, it is a fact that much of this kind of conduct is not socially serious in its long-run consequences, especially if contrasted with the felonies committed by individuals in high positions of trust in government and business.

This approach in contradistinction to the earlier ones—begins to emphasize the necessity of paying attention to the basic social conditions which mark, if they do not directly cause, delinquent behavior. Delinquent young people are not *always* delinquent, nor constantly engaged in that kind of behavior to the exclusion of other activities. In most boys and girls, it is an occasional thing. But once apprehended, they are thereafter characterized or labeled delinquent with resulting effects on their images of themselves as this mirrors what they see as society's attitude toward them.

The earlier the label *delinquent* is applied to a young person, the more certain it is that he will continue to break the law and to be the object of police attention. The period just before, but especially during and after, puberty, is marked by the potential onset of delinquent behavior. This becomes learned behavior when the young person is detained in or committed to places where he mingles with other delinquents, thus enlarging his criminal knowledge, and acquiring what are, in such acts as burglary and auto theft, detailed professional training.

The laws of most states prohibit the detention of young persons with adults in jails or other places of confinement. The efforts of progressive correctional administrators, backed by concerned citizens are required in order to see that this provision of the law is adhered to.

In Philadelphia, in 1968, the Pennsylvania Prison Society exposed the fact that young men who were transported in police vans between jail and court were forced to subject themselves to brutal homosexual attacks by older and stronger men.[8] It was only after the scandal had been aired in the press that the police consented to replace their old vans with vehicles which had glass. Some of these young victims were innocent, or at least presumed to be, in that they had not yet had their day in court, yet they were the helpless victims of this most vicious and traumatic kind of attack. If, in addition to being young, the defendant is also both poor and black, he is trebly disadvantaged by what is here referred to as selective and discriminatory action by law enforcement agencies.

A serious question is raised here—directly rather than by implication: what kind of a criminal justice system do we have that many of its practitioners, in addition to its critics, join in urging diversion from its current procedures? It is difficult to think of any other area of social concern which is characterized by a move to keep the beneficiaries—or patients, or clients—*out* of it. This model, in arguing for the correctness of its assumptions, points squarely to the deficiencies in a system which has been created to deal with the problem of crime which does not only fail to deal effectively with it, but may actually be "causally significant" as one of the environmental factors conducive to, or related to, criminal behavior.

We do not usually think of medical or public health services as causing or spreading disease, and therefore as places to steer clear of. Yet this diversionary model asks us to consider the possibility that the criminal justice system itself creates crime.

Is this an over-statement? Every large city in recent years has been witness to provocation and harassment by the police, especially of young people. The police are very much on the defensive these days and gatherings of young people or insults by them are frequently met by over-reaction. In this sense, the police, as do other elements of the process, become causative instead of curative or ameliorative.

When the police of Washington, D.C., acting on direct orders from the Department of Justice, rounded up some 13,000 demonstrators (and innocent bystanders) in a dragnet arrest, and placed them for hours in an open stadium without any provision for the amenities or the necessities, only to release all but a few score of them later with no charges leveled, could the police and the courts be said to have acted in a manner calculated to create a respect for law?[9] Or did this action constitute a repudiation of the "law and order" slogans which guide much of law enforcement in many large cities? Similar examples could be given for the other steps in the criminal justice process. Together, such findings emphasize the importance of diverting from the system as many persons as can be dealt with in nonpolice, noncourt, and noninstitutional ways, for reasons which are set out more strongly in the next model.

INSTITUTIONAL CHANGE MODEL

By "institutions," this model does not mean prisons, jails, and reform schools, but instead the larger systems which compose society. Rather than regarding criminal behavior as the expression of the pathology of an individual, it views the totality of criminal behavior as indicative of the "deviance" of the entire social system and its components: the schools, the economics of production and distribution, the ameliorative social services, and, finally, the agencies which compose law enforcement. In this latter area is found a reference to the preceding diversionary model, wherein police, courts and institutions are regarded as in themselves causative of much of what is called crime.

"This model by deliberate choice focuses upon causal factors, not upon a specific target population or problematic behavior. It sees delinquency as a response to the oppressive character of various social institutions. These institutions include the educational system, the work system, the social service system and the law enforcement system, all of which taken together compose the political system.

"The political system is thought to have an oppressive character which inhibits the healthy development of individual human beings. This can be described in several ways. One formulation talks in terms of institutional practices which systematically foreclose access to legitimate roles. Another formulation speaks of three dimensions of human development—development of a concept of self, development of an acceptable social role (relationship to the community), and development of a concept of the meaning of human existence (relationship to life).

"The oppressive character of social institutions is thought to affect everyone in society. Delinquency is seen as but one of many responses to oppression. The particular reaction of an individual will depend upon the individual and his environment. Examples other than delinquency include: alcoholism, drug addiction, divorce, dropping out of school, excessive preoccupation with acquiring material goods, prison riots, student unrest, and political assassinations.

"The oppressive character of the various institutional systems relates to traditional, liberal American values, which emphasize competition: among products, among ideas, among political candidates, and among individuals. A competitive model has by definition both winners and losers. Losers are identified early in life, notably by the educational and social service systems. Various institutions other than the law enforcement system begin the labeling process, by identifying individuals as 'poor', 'dumb', or 'rotten'. The labeling process within various institutions tends to overlap and reinforce itself, so that those caught up consistently come out as losers and get into a cycle of stigmatization. These individuals eventually come to be viewed by society and by themselves as having no worth; they become stereotyped and dehumanized; they are seen as objects.

"Typically, this process is likely to be far advanced before the juvenile justice system intervenes, reinforcing the labeling process and adding the further connotation that the individual is not only worthless, but also wicked or evil.

"This process can—in theory—capture anyone, but it is thought to focus in particular upon those who start the race at its outset from an uncompetitive position, who are the objects of discrimination, such as the poor and the members of minorities.

"A principal policy implication of this model in its purest form is the conclusion that resources should be devoted to efforts to achieve fundamental institutional change, even at the cost of sacrificing efforts directed toward individual remediation. Programs concerned with individual remediation are thought of as 'bandaids' which may help individuals, but which divert the resources which are critically needed to address the basic causal factors, which if not so addressed, will continue to produce further delinquency and more individuals requiring help.

"The types of changes suggested by this model are those which may alter the excessively competitive, inequitably competitive, or labeling character of existing institutions. They are changes which will create alternative channels for self-development—new and additional ways to allow individuals to recognize and fulfill their human potential. In this sense, the institutional change model is affirmative, in contrast to the diversionary model, which is thought of as negative, because its principal thrust is to limit exposure to one among many sources of labeling and inhibited personal development. Problems in adopting this approach include questions about the feasibility of altering the fundamental character of society, given limited resources; questions concerning the effectiveness of demonstration or model programs as an approach to social change; and questions concerning the linkages, in a pragmatic setting, between this theoretical framework which applies to all of society and the specific problems of crime and delinquency."

This model says essentially that if the agencies and institutions of society were differently organized or oriented, criminal activity would not be the mass phenomenon it is today.

Parallels with public health are the first to come to mind: as if epidemics were to be dealt with by treating one after the other of the victims of a disease, rather than by isolating and eliminating the source of the infection. Eradication of the malarial mosquito, and of purifying contaminated water supplies are well known ways of ridding us of malaria and typhoid, respectively.

This approach is a far cry from the reference in earlier models to character defect, immorality or abnormality as precipitating causes of crime. It goes further and states that the institutions of society are to be regarded as oppressive and therefore causative of delinquency: education, the economic system, social services and law enforcement, which together are described as "the political system," are included among these.

Inherent in this approach is the view that individuals in present-day society are not only "re-ified," that is, regarded as "things" by specific institutions, but that they are also the objects or even the victims of many special interest groups. To the politician, people are voters; to industry they are consumers; to the military, draftees, to government bureaucracy, taxpayers. The total effect of these separate approaches is that people are fragmented and alienated. Far from feeling themselves appreciated, they react by regarding society as an impersonal, exploitive institution which they feel justified in "ripping off."

Is it possible that our schools contribute to delinquency? Many students of this area of crime causation would answer in the affirmative: "School problems, failure in school work and misbehavior in school are often judged to be a common source of the frustration and alienation which motivate delinquent conduct. The school is frequently the setting within which children and youth first come to think of themselves as consistently inadequate or dumb, and especially, as bad or troublesome. . . . Some authorities report that delinquent adolescents' sense of injustice and unfairness centers much more on how they were handled by the school system than by police or court authorities."[10]

In some cities marked by high rates of juvenile delinquency, the proportion of children within compulsory school age range who are not enrolled in school or do not attend regularly runs very high. Between 1.5 and 2 million children, according to 1970 census data, are not in school: "In county after county across the United States, the census showed from 10 to 30 percent non-enrollment of children between 7 and 15."[11] In that same census year, a study in a large eastern city discovered that up to 15,000 children were out of school: non-English-speaking, pregnant girls; behaviorally or otherwise disturbed; mentally, perceptually or physically handicapped.[12] This figure represents one-sixth of the total presently enrolled public school population in that city.

No profile of any prison inmate sample population reveals a level of schooling much above the eighth or ninth grade. Does the school have a responsibility for dealing with these kinds of kids, or is its responsibility limited to those who are sufficiently motivated—children and their parents—to see to it that they attend school regularly?

The economic system comes in for its share of examination under this model, with national levels of unemployment standing currently near 6 percent and reaching as high as 16 percent for minority groups in certain areas. For 1969, the Census Bureau reports that while 1.5 million people over the age of fourteen received incomes of $25,000 and over, 20 million people (13 times as many) received less than $1,000.[13] The top tenth of family units in the United States, based on income rank, received close to 30 percent of the total national income.[14]

A United States Department of Commerce study, "Poverty and Jobs," in Denver, found that 20 percent of that city's population accounted for 46 percent of the city's juvenile delinquency, 67 percent of other than traffic misdemeanors, and 65 percent of felony arrests.[15] "Recent developments in the criminal law in the United States can be understood best in the context of the much broader movement to combat the great problem of poverty. The root cause of much criminal conduct is unquestionably poverty, and all that this term connotes: hopelessness, disease, ignorance, and hostility toward established norms of behavior." These are the opening sentences of a publication issued by our Department of Justice and distributed to participants at the Third United Nations Crime Congress in Stockholm in 1965.[16]

One of the most highly respected of our federal judges has recently declared that "our first priority in distributing justice to children ought to be distributing income to their families. It is simply not right that children in this country grow up in poverty. . . . Commission after commission on crime, race, violence, or children has recommended some form of income redistribution as the only way to begin to solve our toughest social problems."[17]

Sociologists explain delinquency as resulting from the conflict between the goals of society as embodied in the value system and the opportunities realistically available to attain those goals. This model holds that one who is poor and black, and lives in a slum area, and suffers from inadequate housing, poor education and few vocational opportunities, is being held responsible by society for situations which are literally beyond his control, and which are, as far as he is concerned, oppressive. William Ryan has documented how such persons are condemned for the results of institutionalized discrimination against them over a long period of years.[18]

No description of the problem of crime in the United States is complete without some reference to the role played by black people. In some jurisdictions they make up one-third of all prisoners. In the Federal system of prisons they constitute close to 40 percent of the inmate population. In Attica, blacks and Puerto Ricans composed 63 percent of the total inmates. The fact that there was not a single black or Puerto Rican on the correctional staff gives added emphasis to the singularly unrepresentative and disproportionate racial nature of many prison populations in America today. The institutional change model implies that only by the removal of such discrimination, by making the good things of society generally available, will harmony be achieved between stated goals and available means, with consequent reduction in crime.

The model points out, finally, that delinquency is but one reaction to the oppression and fruitlessness felt in the lives of persons condemned to live under these conditions. It lists other ways of reacting, touching on involvement in drugs only in passing. Yet narcotics as an offense, or as a factor in the lives of persons who commit other kinds of offenses, has been reported as running as high as 65 percent among persons awaiting trial in two large metropolitan jails.[19] Alcohol is an "out" not only for the poor; neuroticism and the luxury of individual psychotherapy represent additional ways in which middle- and upper-class persons react to purposelessness or frustration at their level of living. In this sense, the model ranges beyond what are generally seen as delinquents and criminals—members of the lower socioeconomic classes—and reaches out to include other nonpoor victims of the competitive and inequitable features of society, including the emphasis on materialism which results when the *summum bonum* is seen in the acquisition, possession and ostentation of money and all it can buy. By inference, steps in the direction of the redistribution of wealth, and making it possible for individuals and communities to exert a greater degree of self-direction, are suggested as ways of reducing tension and thereby providing opportunities for higher levels of personal achievement and individual self-development.

RADICAL MODEL

This last model is also the shortest. Perhaps this is fitting, because the implications inherent in it go further than any of the preceding, yet enough is left to the imagination or inclination of the reader to obviate the necessity for a longer presentation of what is a relatively simple idea.

Such a viewpoint, not so many years ago, would have emanated only from the most militant segment of society. It is in its way a political manifesto, yet what it says comes hardly as a shock to many young people, or to others in our society who have been made increasingly critical and impatient by recent events in this country, and in the world beyond.

One is reminded by this model of Merton's typology of the five modes of reaction to the contradictions between socially approved goals and values and the means available for their attainment.[20] Among the five possible responses is the one he labeled "rebellion." It may be a matter of logic, rather than of coincidence, that this model is also the last of the five here presented.

"This model challenges the assumption that delinquency or antisocial behavior is a legitimate object of concern and governmental action. It views delinquency as a legitimate expression in response to intolerable oppression. It considers the existing political system to be so unworkable and immoral as to justify delinquent behavior as a matter of individual choice or political expression.

"One variation of this approach sees delinquency as a legitimate career option, or a way of supporting one's self in a society which provides inequitable patterns of opportunity or access of material goods and personal fulfillment. Another variation interprets delinquency as a political expression, as an attack on a system with which the individual is at war. This model suggests policies either of nonintervention in the lives of individuals or of support for delinquent behavior."

Those who profess this view are suggesting that the behavior of delinquents is not dysfunctional, but is, in fact, a highly adaptive response to an oppressive society which they are, by this means, forcing to face up to its inequities and injustices. From this point of view, criminal activity is a kind of guerilla warfare between those who see themselves embattled and desirous of ushering in a "new world in birth." Recent news stories of sky-jackings, kidnappings of wealthy men and politicians for ransom, can from this point of view be seen as noncriminal, praiseworthy, in fact, if one is in sympathy with the ultimate objectives of those who commit such acts, who see themselves, in such acts, as agents of social change. They regard the inequities imposed upon the so-called enemies of society by the criminal court and correctional process as far outweighing the harm which they themselves inflict or may inflict on that society.

Coming closer to home, the model looks upon persons in institutions as prisoners in a war which they are waging against society. There is in fact hardly a form of punishment imposed upon "prisoners of peace" which at one time or another has not been, or is not now being, used against prisoners of war. Exile, imprisonment, torture, maiming, death, hard labor, are things to which prisoners of war have been and are being subjected. This model says in effect: "You treat us as prisoners of war, and you should, because in fact we are at war with society." In many places, especially in some communities where blacks predominate, there have indeed been political battles between them and the agents of the established society.

The essence of this final model is contained in the last sentence which advocates "policies either of nonintervention or of support for delinquent behavior."

NOTES

1. "Task Force on Delinquency, Governor's Committee on Law Enforcement and Administration of Justice," Boston, December, 1972, unpaginated. The unnoted quotations in this chapter are all from this document.

2. In a communication to the author.
3. Sheldon Glueck and Eleanor Glueck, *500 Criminal Careers* (New York: Knopf, 1930); see also *500 Delinquent Women* (New York: Knopf, 1934); and *1,000 Juvenile Delinquents: Their Treatment by Court and Clinic* (Cambridge, Massachusetts: Harvard University Press, 1934).
4. Ibid., *1,000 Juvenile Delinquents,* pp. 302–321.
5. *Task Force Report: Science and Technology* (Washington: President's Commission Report on Law Enforcement and Administration of Justice, 1967), p. 61, Fig. 18
6. Sophia M. Robison and Gene N. Levine, *Career Patterns Project: A Study of the Youthful Delinquent Behavior of Men Who Are Responsible Members of Society* (Garden City: Adelphi University, 1965).
7. Unpublished study by the National Police Agency, Tokyo, 1971.
8. Alan J. Davis, "Sexual Assaults in the Philadelphia Prison System and Sheriff's Vans," *Transaction* (December 1968), p. 8.
9. *New York Times,* May 4 & 5, 1971.
10. Stanton Wheeler and Leonard S. Cottrell, Jr., *Juvenile Delinquency: Its Prevention and Control* (New York: Russell Sage Foundation, 1966), pp. 17–18.
11. From information provided by the Children's Defense Fund of the Washington Research Project, Inc., 1763 R Street, N.W., Washington, D.C. 20009. The nonenrollment study is expected to be completed by the winter of 1974.
12. "The Way We Go to School: The Exclusion of Children in Boston" (Boston: Task Force on Children out of School, 889 Harrison Avenue 02118, 1970).
13. *Census of Population, 1970* (Washington: U.S. Bureau of the Census, 1971), Table 244.
14. *Statistical Abstracts of the United States, 1972* (Washington: U.S. Bureau of the Census, 1972), Table 529.
15. Cited in "Correctional Processes," report of the Standing Committee on Classification and Treatment, American Correctional Association, Leonard J. Hippchen, Chairman, State College, Glassboro, New Jersey, p. 1.
16. *Trends in the Administration of Justice and Correctional Programs in the United States* (Lompoc, California: Federal Correctional Institution, 1973).
17. David L. Bazelon, Chief Judge, U.S. Court of Appeals for the District of Columbia, "Juvenile Justice: A Love-Hate Story," a speech delivered at N.Y. University School of Law, March 15, 1973, p. 9.
18. William Ryan, *Blaming the Victim* (New York: Pantheon Press, 1971).
19. Jane H. Stein, et al., *Metropolitan Boston Detention Study* (Boston: Center for Corrections and the Law, Boston College Law School, 1972), p. 78.
20. Robert K. Merton, "Social Structure and Anomie," in *Social Theory and Social Structure* (Glencoe, Illinois: The Free Press, 1964), pp. 139–155.

Chapter Ten

Abolishing the Traditional Institution

MASSACHUSETTS CLOSES ITS TRAINING SCHOOLS

The state of Massachusetts pioneered with the establishment of the first public reform school for boys in 1846. That day was expected to usher in a new and enlightened era in the handling of juvenile offenders. No longer would they be confined with adult felons, nor would cruel and unusual punishments be inflicted on them. In subsequent years more and more states, following this lead, developed "reform" or "industrial" schools in which regimentation was the cardinal purpose. "To conform to rules and regulations was to be rehabilitated. Days leading into weeks, then into months were spent walking in line, two abreast, with hands in trouser pockets, lining up for 'headcounts,' and sleeping in large impersonal dormitories."[1]

It is an historically interesting fact that this same state should, 125 years later, close down that school, and all others under public auspices which received delinquent boys and girls from the courts. The man responsible for that drastic step, Dr. Jerome Miller, State Commissioner of Youth Services, took formal note of this change in public and official attitudes toward delinquency when he first launched what he called his "Crusade for Children."[2] Up until three years ago, there were in the commonwealth, four institutions for confining boys and girls committed by the courts as juvenile delinquents with an average total population of more than 1,000. In addition, there were three so-called county training schools in the state, all that remained of the original ten which had been established some years after the first compulsory education law passed in the state in 1852. These were to hold habitual truants and school offenders.

Commissioner Miller took steps which led to the ultimate abolition of the three county schools, and the transfer of their few remaining boys to community-based programs. He then turned his attention to the state juvenile institutions which, in his words, "seemed designed more to provide society with scapegoats than to deal with the causes of public offending. This system, characterized by political patronage, was filled with staff whose talents lay more in running political campaigns than in rehabilitating youthful offenders. More often than not, their purpose was blatantly punitive, instilling in young inmates a growing hatred of all authority and preparing them for the subculture of adult offenders."[3] Of the children received each year into the Department of Youth Services from the courts, 90 percent came from families receiving some form of welfare and approximately 60 percent of these families had histories of parental alcoholism, drug abuse, mental instability or child abuse.[4]

Closing down such an extended, traditional system is the most radical step in deinstitutionalizing the treatment of offenders that has yet taken place. It is not only without precedent in this country, it was accomplished without direct legislative authorization. While aware that much of what he was attempting to do flew in the face of authority, Dr. Miller was determined to make the changes and to leave it to the state legislature later to codify those changes into law after he was gone. The move would not have been possible had he not had the support of the Governor who appointed him and of the Governor's wife who, after a tour of the juvenile institutions in the state, was equally convinced that the time had arrived for them to be closed.

The Governor spared no effort to make his views, not always popular, known in a variety of public forums. On one occasion, two years after the program had received its new commissioner, the Governor stated: "As we have begun to move toward a community-based program, we have discovered an interesting fact. We can provide better services at lower costs through community programs. Under the old system, we found ourselves supporting an entire system at a level that only a small minority of the population needed. We spent approximately $10,000 a year to keep a child in an institution.

"For this money, we could buy each child a complete wardrobe at Brooks Brothers, give him a $20 a week allowance, send him to a private school and, in the summer, send him to Europe with all expenses paid. We could do all that and still save the taxpayer over $1,300 per year. This is the kind of money we have been investing in our institutions . . . and all of you know the results.

"If, on the other hand, we invest in a community treatment program, we can provide individual services, personal counseling, job training, specialized education, and healthy group home settings for about *half* the cost. Even more important, we can begin to help a child understand his behavior and motivation in an atmosphere of trust and support.

"For the child who needs an intensive parole counseling program, the cost is a little over $2,600 per year, per child. A foster home . . . which provides needed parental guidance . . . costs $1,200 per year, per child. And for those children who need a group home, the cost is approximately $7,500 per year, per child.

"The community-based treatment concept can eventually apply not only to juvenile offenders, but to adults as well. In my opinion, it is a new and needed direction for correction in general."[5]

As might be expected, all of this did not go off without many difficulties and tremendous opposition—the price to be paid for bold new approaches to social problems, whether in delinquency or any other field. Opposition came from the police, juvenile court judges, probation officers—and the public. The police asked why they should bother to arrest juveniles; the judges complained that two days after a hearing, in most cases, the same kids were back on the street. The community, glad to be rid of their troublesome youngsters, resented that after they had reported them to the police, the same youngsters were back in the neighborhood. They put pressure on the legislators to halt Commissioner Miller and his mad ideas.

But the greatest opposition came from the traditional civil service guards in the schools. When the sanction of confinement is removed, when the possibility of imprisonment, of placing youths in solitary, of restricting their diet or meting out corporal punishment are all proscribed, other nonpunitive ways of handling them must be provided. That is a very much more difficult thing to accomplish.

By the summer of 1972, a conference was held on the topic: "The Closing Down of Institutions and New Strategies in Youth Services" which attracted over 300 attendants from across the country.[6] The opening statement of the preliminary report on the conference sums up its purpose and prospect: "We who have organized this conference regard it as a possible turning point in youth services—away from big institutions, toward the development of new alternatives. The time of institutions has clearly passed. . . . Now the responsibility to think in new ways and to find new solutions lies at our doorstep. Closing our familiar institutions eliminates the easy answer, the easy solution of putting children in institutions. It forces us to search for new and dynamic · solutions, not to fall back on the old routines.

"These new solutions will range from court diversion programs to community-based homes for committed youths. They will be comprehensive and systematic, not piecemeal. They will require radical restructuring of youth services networks, and new types of professionals: administrators who are change agents rather than defenders of the status quo; middle managers who can move aggressively out into the community to mobilize resources for youth in trouble; youth workers who know how to work with youngsters in the community. Indeed, we may be at the threshold of a new social movement, of tremendous significance not only to youth services but to the whole realm of human services. We are moving closer to the source, closer to the community, to help people cope more effectively with an increasingly complex and difficult society."[7]

The courts of Massachusetts committed or recommitted 1,000

youths to the Department of Youth Services in 1971, of whom almost 90 percent
were placed in institutions. A year later those institutions were closed, a swift
and massive deinstitutionalization which was without precedent in any penal system in the world.

The mandate for change arose from several sources, including critical
studies of the old department which had been carried out by various groups. The
most intensive one was conducted by the Children's Bureau of the United States
Department of Health, Education, and Welfare. Other committees were appointed
by the Governor or the state legislature after allegations of brutality and mishandling of children were made public.

The legal mandate of the acts of 1969 transformed the old Division
of Youth and the Youth Service Board into a single Department of Youth
Services (DYS).[8] Employees and their positions remained as before, and land-
holdings of the former division were maintained, though the new departmental
administrative chain of command was significantly altered to meet its new
responsibilities.

The department's spending flexibility was significantly increased, and
it was now permitted to allocate funds out of its grants-in-aid program to cities
and towns in support of delinquency prevention and treatment programs, and to
purchase services from outside sources. For purposes of acquiring land and other
holdings in trust, the department was enabled to act as a corporation, and, in
addition, was given full management and control over the juvenile institutions
which had formerly maintained a somewhat autonomous status.

The powers of the department to act as a guardian for children was
enlarged upon when it was granted authority to place children in any home or
program of which it approved, to make use of both public and private placement
alternatives, or freely to transfer children among all available resources. The new
commissioner was appointed in October 1969, but it was almost a year before
funds were allocated to appoint assistant commissioners for the four newly
created bureaus. During his first year, the commissioner had to continue to operate within the context of the system he had inherited.

The process of change began with widespread dissatisfaction and a
demand for a new approach from professional groups, members of the legislature, and some segments of the public, no less than from the DYS staff itself.
This impetus was augmented by continuing public allegations that the juvenile
institutions were mishandling children, and that brutality and corruption were
commonplace. Recidivism was high and annual per capita costs were rising
above $10,000. The new commissioner's mandate was to improve the quality and
cost-effectiveness of youth services, not specifically to close down the institutions. Supported by a small reform wing within the staff of his department, Dr.
Miller first introduced the concept of the therapeutic community, when in 1970
he invited Dr. Maxwell Hones, a British expert on the subject, to undertake a
pilot training program at the industrial school for older boys.

This experiment essentially polarized the department, because it exposed fundamental differences in points of view and treatment philosophies. Some veteran staff tended to regard children as "culprits" who required supervision, discipline, and occasionally, direct punishment. They saw their role as strictly custodial rather than therapeutic, though as custodians many had worked hard to provide the children with decent amenities and facilities. The newer, and generally younger, staff members, tended to see delinquents as "victims," requiring support, interaction, and trust from professionals.

Because this experimental approach demanded that they learn and apply non-punitive measures of control, and probably because they feared for the security of their jobs if the institutions were all to be closed and replaced by community programs, many guards had organized early opposition. This was expressed through union grievances, and by persons not opposed to using political influence with the legislature, who also triggered a series of crises and runaways from the institutions. Shortly after the new program was initiated, the staff in one school posted a map on the bulletin board showing a suggested escape route: a high absconding rate would reveal to the world that the new program was a disaster. It now became evident that there was a political campaign to be waged to expose the old system and defend the new, at the same time that there arose a strong impetus for an alternative structure to the traditional schools.

In March 1971, the operation of the department was decentralized into seven regions, each with its own director, staff, and office. Further decentralization took place with the opening of group homes on the grounds of the training schools. The aim was to make each of these "cottages" a genuinely supportive residential unit.

The phasing out of all institutions in favor of community-based alternatives was now begun in earnest, but found very difficult for several reasons. Many established community group homes and centers were in disagreement with the plan and reluctant to accept youngsters referred to them directly from the institutions, citing lack of space and facilities as their reasons, despite the fact that the youngsters referred to them were, in fact, residents of the areas which such centers were established to serve. So long as the training schools remained open, community groups were slow to organize and come forward with proposals for caring for their young residents. Community agencies which traditionally had held the threat of commitment to an institution over the heads of their charges in order to insure conformity were especially loath to act in a direct-treatment capacity. Training school staff expressed open opposition to the new approaches, became demoralized, restive, and feared loss of their jobs. The youngsters themselves were caught in the middle between institutions which were being phased out and alternatives yet unborn.

The gradual approach to the closing down of the institutions allowed political opposition to mobilize in the state legislature. As a result of this mounting opposition, the Department decided now to abolish gradualism, and during the January 1972 legislative recess, the commissioner decisively exercised the discretionary powers of his office to close down the institutions under his control. All the youngsters who could possibly be immediately paroled, placed in, or referred to community programs were sent away from the institutions. Some 300 youths were placed in halfway houses or group homes; 150 were placed in foster homes. A small residuum, less than 100, were temporarily housed on the campus of the University of Massachusetts.

This campus operation, called JOE (after one of the boys involved) in Amherst was planned and executed by a group of university student volunteers and the regional DYS staff. The operation made the closing down of the school for younger boys easy on its residents and was accomplished with little staff opposition or sabotage. Each youngster who stayed in the JOE Program for a month on the university campus was matched on an individual basis with a student advocate. Each advocate was paid to supervise and befriend the youth while arrangements were made for placement in community-based programs, and he and his young charge spent three nights and one full weekend day together, if the boy had been returned to his home.

Meanwhile, the maximum-security unit at the Bridgewater Correctional Center, an ancient multipurpose state institution caring for the criminally insane, sex offenders, and some terminal mental patients, which had been used to house more than sixty children, had been closed in September 1970. Since this had been the first facility to be closed, at a time when the department was not ready with alternatives, most of the children from this unit had been either paroled or transferred to the remaining institutions.

The Shirley Industrial School was phased out in early January 1972, after sixty-four years as a training school for older boys, with a stated emphasis on vocational education. In the last year before its closing, it had been used as a training and testing ground for the new group homes. Several cottages were transformed into group homes which functioned independently and apart from the rest of the school.

The Lyman School, the oldest public training school in the country, formerly accommodated 450 younger boys between the ages of thirteen and sixteen. It was closed to new intake on January 16, 1972, by which time most of the 150 boys still there were placed in community programs, released on parole to Project JOE, or treated in small groups in the intensive programs at the department's Worcester and Roslindale detention facilities.

The Industrial School at Lancaster, the first public training school for girls when it was established in 1854, was closed at the end of 1972. At that time only a few girls remained to be placed. The rest of the facility was being used to house private groups caring for children and to accommodate a coeducational cottage run as a group home by the department. The John Augustus Hall Youth Center in Oakdale, the most modern—and secure—unit in the department, had formerly served boys between the ages of seven and eleven. It was now turned into a new reception diagnostic center, where children are medically and psychologically evaluated for placement. The score of children who were the last at Oakdale have been placed in a variety of residential and home settings.

Two former juvenile detention centers were reorganized to meet the needs of youth requiring intensive psychiatric treatment in a secure setting. Each facility accommodates about fifteen, including boys committed under court order as well as disturbed boys in a detention status.

Six months after the drastic step of closing down all the Massachusetts juvenile training schools, the new approach is reported to be functioning well in all its three major approaches: nonresidential alternatives to replace former residential institutions; small, community-based residential homes instead of the large institutions; and purchase of contracted services from private community groups rather than state operation of all programs.

The result is a network of privately operated projects publicly supported and supervised and coordinated through the department's regional offices. Projects underway or planned by the department are illustrative of the range of programs which could be available to other jurisdictions interested in doing away with institutions for delinquent boys and girls, and include the following:

Court Liaison Program: In large measure, the success of deinstitutionalization is dependent upon good communication between the juvenile courts and the agency. The department has placed liaison personnel in most of the juvenile courts of the state to help develop community-based programs for children who come before it.

Services for Children Referred by Courts: The department is placing an increasing emphasis on working with juveniles who are first and second offenders. To avoid the stigmatization of an adjudication of "delinquent" (labeling), the department is providing the courts with alternatives to adjudication on a referral basis to such programs as Forestry, which is modeled on the Outward Bound Program.

Detained Youth Advocate Program: Social Service agencies under contract to DYS provide spaces to house fifty to one hundred children in detention homes throughout the state with the supervision, and assistance, of the department, which will have responsibility for recruitment, study, selection, and supportive services to the designated homes.

Parole Volunteer Program: This program began a year ago with carefully selected and trained volunteers assigned initially to positions as friendly supportive counselors or tutor-advocates in academic, occupational, vocational or social skills. The goal of this program is to implement an effective service plan for every youth paroled from the department, through the use of volunteer services.

Youth Advocate Program: This program, funded by the President's Emergency Employment Act [9] and channeled through the Department of Manpower/Office of Human Services, currently employs youth advocate workers from major urban areas who provide intensive counseling and referral for up to three youths in the home of a youth advocate worker. To date this program is said to have had only limited success.

Expanded Use of Existing State-Funded Private Group Homes: As an alternative program for those children who do not require secure intensive care, the department plans to double its purchase of private group home care.

New Federally-Funded Group Homes: Through Law Enforcement Assistance Administration (LEAA) funding, the department is contracting for a minimum of seventeen group homes which will house 200 youths at any one time and a total of some 600 youths on an annual basis.

Secure and Intensive Care Units: A special, psychiatrically oriented unit at Roslindale treats violent-aggressive and highly disturbed youngsters who require therapy in a secure setting. The Worcester Detention Center also has provision for treatment of youth not permitted on the street awaiting trial. A similar program is under development in another part of Roslindale and a very small unit is planned for the Westfield area. These units combine carefully selected department personnel with private psychiatric and social work resources.

Administration Planning and Information: This program provides assistance to improve the department's fiscal and administrative function in support of its community-based direction. A permanent planning unit within the department will make—and periodically update and revise—a multiyear plan for implementing a regionalized community-based network of prevention and rehabilitation programs. The department is also developing information-management capabilities in the areas of planning, research and evaluation.

While it is too early to evaluate with any precision the results of the drastic changes in policies and programs made when the juvenile training schools of Massachusetts were closed, some generalizations can nevertheless be made at this point:

1. The department has moved from operating the traditional one-dimensional program of institutions to a multidimensional approach which relies on community-based programs, both residential and nonresidential.
2. This shift makes administration and operation more complex, requiring more sophistication in management and organization.
3. Reliance on purchased services under contract between private agencies and the department necessitates evaluation and monitoring, requiring a broadening and expansion of its research and evaluation components to meet present needs, insure quality control, and provide planning for the future. The department's role as monitor and evaluator of contracted services alters its role from that of "defender" of the system to that of "advocate" for children and "promoter" of social change in the community.[10]

The population of the state-operated schools for delinquent boys and girls now dropped from 1,000 to 38. Most of them went back to the homes they came from, that is, to where they would return after release from their term in confinement. A significant statistic was cited before this plan went into operation: when the term of confinement had been reduced from 9 to 4.5 months, the rate of recidivism dropped from 70 to 45 percent.

An even more striking finding was that the recidivism rate from the most restrictively secure institution—for young, troublesome boys—had run over 90 percent. Children sent back to their community were placed under the supervision of counselors and advocates who helped them to adjust to their home situations and to some of the problems which had resulted in their getting into trouble in the first place—problems with family, with police, and with the school.

Schools play a decisive role in the creation of juvenile delinquency when they turn away boys and girls who do not conform. In one school system in an economically depressed area, where the school-leaving age is sixteen, it is reported that when a troublesome boy of fourteen or fifteen applies for a work permit, the school is only too glad to issue it in order to get rid of him.

The school is expected to cope with all kinds of special problems of children. If a child is found to be deaf, if he has problems in reading or arithmetic, tutoring and special aid are provided. The state supplies materials in Braille and special allowances for the blind. The mentally retarded receive special educational help at home or in classes specifically designed to deal with them. It provides transportation, and special programs for children with physical handicaps. The state is further authorized to place certain emotionally difficult children in expensive private facilities, including places in another state.[11] But when it comes to the kind of emotional maladjustment to which children react by various forms of defiance or delinquency, they are suddenly considered no longer educational problems—or even educable—but as correctional problems.

It is difficult to justify why the institution for delinquents is not under the Department of Education, instead of within a department of corrections or social welfare, or even as in some countries, of the Ministry of Justice. The needs of such children are for education or re-education because of their special problems—not of a physical nature, but of an emotional, social, or psychological nature. If all children were viewed as in need of education, some of whom require special handling by reason of individual difficulties, responsibility for dealing with delinquents would be placed squarely under the Department of Education. This is where they belong.[12]

There are forty-five colleges and universities in Massachusetts, and it has been estimated that if each of these were to take in twenty children, there would be no problem of institutionalizing juvenile delinquents in the state. Some of the boys who lived at colleges under the JOE program shared the dormitory space of the student-advocates with whom they stayed. These advocates were paid $40 or $50 a week. The boys went to classes with the students, to football games, played ball, and went swimming, camping, hiking or on picnics together. They sat around the rooms with other college students and "rapped" with them. They were not regarded as naughty boys who were not fit to associate with, but were treated rather as if they were a couple of years older than what they really were—like college students. They went from the college to a school in the neighborhood, while students in the School of Education who were training to be teachers gave them special tutoring and remedial reading.

A few of these children with special psychological and learning problems were sent to private boarding schools, along with some of the same kind of children from families whose financial and social position saved them from commitment to the public training schools. In places of this sort it costs the state a third to a half of what it would to keep these delinquents in training schools. In these ways, the problem of institutionalizing the juvenile delinquents has been resolved in Massachusetts. At the end, some forty boys were diagnosed as too psychologically disturbed or difficult to be trusted outside an institution. They were therefore placed in a special therapeutic program in a wing of what had been a detention home for children, under the intensive care of a staff composed of a psychiatrist, a psychologist, a caseworker, and a group of young counselors, some of whom had themselves served time in institutions before they were rehabilitated, others of whom were young women interested in working with disturbed youngsters.

Through intensive group-therapy sessions, through guided-group interaction, and through a variety of other approaches, this hard core of difficult boys, this 4 or 5 percent of the institution's population who were most troublesome, were retained in custody and placed in a special therapeutic setting. Everybody else—96 percent of the total juvenile institution population—was placed in the community in one setting or another.

Some of the boys so placed have continued to pursue delinquent ways—they have run away, stolen automobiles, committed thefts, even murder. But training schools—and prisons—have housed persons who escaped from them or were paroled from them who later committed auto theft and murder: those institutions were not as a result condemned and torn down. On the contrary, more of them were built, and made even more repressive.

If the recidivism rate from these new community placements does not exceed that of the institutions they have replaced, much of the heat will have been taken out of the process, and public costs greatly reduced. At the same time the state will have stopped labeling delinquents as exiles, to be sent away from their communities. It will have proven that the best way to socialize young people is not by isolating them as if in quarantine, but in assisting them to cope with the problems which led them to commit their delinquent acts in the first place, and ultimately to confinement. Massachusetts is not alone in this respect except that it is the only state in which the problem of delinquency has to date been completely deinstitutionalized at the juvenile level.[13]

When this step was first taken, dire forebodings of increased criminality were seen—by those who had supported the traditional institution—as the inevitable outcome. Some juvenile court officials were reported to be ready to transfer jurisdiction over the cases of children to the adult criminal court to prevent their commitment to the state Division of Youth Services. One year later, a study of the trend in prison commitments of those seventeen years old and younger indicated "that there has not been an upsurge in the percentage of young offenders sentenced to the adult correctional system in the year following the closing of the major facilities of the Department of Youth Services."[14]

THE IDEA SPREADS

The man responsible for abolishing the juvenile institutions of Massachusetts has been appointed to do the same thing for Illinois—though in a different manner and at a different rate, assuredly. Word also comes from Hawaii of a proposal approved by the state law enforcement and juvenile delinquency planning agency to do away with the state prison in favor of community-based corrections. In its place, if it is adopted, the new system will consist of three parts: an intake center in each county to provide pre-trial screening for pre-sentence investigation and alternatives to incarceration; a community correctional center to replace each county jail, with minimum to moderate security (the Hawaii State Prison would be converted to the Community Correctional Center for Oahu, the largest island); and one maximum-security jail facility, the Halawa Jail, for inmates who must be incarcerated.[15]

Dotted across the continental United States, other progressive state departments of correction are moving in the same direction, though at varying rates of speed. Maine, for example, previously cited in these pages for its leadership in penal affairs, is currently undertaking to apply to the male prisoner the same community approach which has marked the past decade of dealing with the female offender. In 1961, when the new regime began, more women with prior sentences were in prison than in any previous period. The average length of stay of thirty-four months for maximum sentences of thirty-six months has been gradually reduced—with parole board cooperation—to an average of nine months for a three-year indeterminate sentence. Of 1,500 furloughs for home and employment visits, the failure rate is reported to be only 1 percent.[16]

The maximum-security facility—the Women's Correctional Center— now houses no more than 10 percent of all women sentenced from the courts. The remaining 90 percent, classified as "tractable" are assigned to a former juvenile institution for treatment and training. The program here is operated on the basis of the school year, and emphasizes instruction leading to the high school diploma. Vocational training is provided, leading to certificates of competence—in retailing, business machines, office skills, nursing aide, home and child care, and appropriate factory training. Community halfway houses—some of them coeducational—are available for women who are considered not to require institutional supervision.

Great effort has been expended in the Maine system to train and

redirect old-line staff members to accept the newer approaches which replace
security and custody with counseling and advocacy. The success attained to date
with the program for women is beginning now to be extended to men prisoners.
Pre-release programs, work and educational release, furloughs, and minimal supervision during the last six months of sentence have been instituted.

The Maine Commissioner of the Bureau of Corrections has recently
declared that "within a framework of honest respect for the safety of the community, all treatment of the offender will be geared as much as possible to take
place in the community, and any rehabilitation, resocialization and/or reintegration program developed with and for the individual shall offer flexible alternatives. The least restricting alternative possible will be selected which offers the
best means of treatment for the individual. Care will also be taken to insure the
full protection of society during any phase of treatment when the individual is
considered to be still capable of harming society. . . . No persons should be
institutionalized if they can stabilize in their own community." This leads her
to conclude that "institutions as we have known them in the past will become
nonexistent."[17]

THE UNIVERSITY-TRAINING SCHOOL

Much has been made of the potential role of the college student and the
university campus in helping to handle individual delinquents who may have to
be temporarily removed from their homes. If the special education or re-education of disturbed youngsters is accepted by institutions of higher learning as an
appropriate function for them—as much to provide a teaching and learning
experience for their own student bodies—we shall have moved a long way toward
casting the "delinquency" problem in a new light. The following description of a
recent Florida program would seem to offer one way in which universities which
accept some share of responsibility in this area, can discharge that responsibility.

The Okeechobee Florida State School accommodates some 500
delinquent boys, black and white. On the grounds of that institution, a branch of
Florida Atlantic University, with 50 students in all, has been founded.[18]
These students live in mobile homes. They are juniors and seniors, young men
and women interested in careers in education, psychology, psychotherapy, counseling, and other areas of child care and training. Their campus away from the
university is the grounds of the state school. Their day is divided into morning,
afternoon, and evening programs. In the morning, they supplement the regular
school staff, as teachers of various academic subjects, including remedial reading.
They also serve as recreational aides and as substitute house parents when the
regular parents are on holiday or off duty. In these and other ways, they enrich
the regular program of the institution at minimal cost to the state. Their meals
are taken with the boys in the main dining room.

In the afternoon, their professors drive a distance of over a hundred miles to conduct seminars in their regular college work. These afternoon sessions are the equivalent of three regular meetings during the week in a college course, and include a variety of subjects—psychology, special education, sociology—depending upon the student's field of interest. In the evenings, the students on the grounds of the institution do what they would do elsewhere. They drink beer, study, read, dance, go to the movies, and play with kids.

Their work is marked by a high degree of dedication to, and interest in, these boys. Just before Christmas one year, a group of them spent an evening together making jewelry of polished stones into rings, pendants, and pins, which they were going to give to those boys who would be on campus during the holidays, because they had no homes to go to and were unlikely to receive Christmas presents from anyone else. This was entirely the idea of the students, done on their own time, a spontaneous offering to boys with whom they had become deeply involved after three months of playing, working, and living among them.

On a Saturday afternoon of that same pre-Christmas week, the college students worked to fix up as a coffee house in a loft which was not being used, where the boys could play, sing, dance, give concerts, and in general use it like the kind of coffee house where young people spend evenings on the outside. The college students did the work, with help from the boys, and raised the funds to pay for the materials.

The total program serves many purposes, as may be gathered from this brief description. It gives the boys the companionship of persons close to their own age whom they can look up to as role models; it gives the college students field experience in serving in those areas in which they plan later to concern themselves professionally; it helps to provide, for the correctional services, much-needed staff to diversify the offerings it can make to the children committed to state care.

The program is not, strictly speaking, an alternative to a juvenile institution. But it does bring a university campus and a truly educational atmosphere onto the grounds of a training school for delinquents. In this regard it serves as an example of what can be accomplished when traditional ways are replaced by fresh and courageous approaches which regard delinquents as children who need specialized attention, rather than as young criminals asking to be punished.

THE DEMISE OF THE PRISON

The trend toward deinstitutionalizing the custody and care of persons who are found guilty of crimes is not limited to youths. Professional bodies and commissions specially created to examine—once more—into the reasons for the failure of the fixed penal station are extending the notion of community care to the adult offender as well.

The President appointed a special fifteen-member Task Force on Prisoner Rehabilitation in 1969, charged with a mission "to review what the public and private sectors are now doing in the area of prisoner rehabilitation and to recommend what be done in the future." Its major recommendations included one which urged that "the federal government should undertake a demonstration project to test the effectiveness of noninstitutional therapeutic family-oriented programs for treating offenders from multiproblem families."[19]

Two years after this recommendation was announced, the board of trustees of the leading organization in the crime-prevention and treatment field issued the most far-reaching call yet made for a turn-around in American corrections. "No new detention or penal institution should be built before alternatives to incarceration are fully achieved. Specifically, the National Council on Crime and Delinquency (NCCD) calls for a halt on the construction of all prisons, jails, juvenile training schools, and detention homes until the maximum funding, staffing, and utilization of noninstitutional correction have been attained." Their rationale was that "institutions are necessary for only the dangerous offender. On that basis we have vastly more institutional space than we need. This is why NCCD calls for a halt in institutional construction until the potential of community treatment is fully achieved."[20]

The growing ferment which has characterized the peno-correctional field in recent years is starting now to take its effect. The pressure from men in prison, politicized and made vocal by their degrading experiences, the findings of researchers in public and private agencies and in our universities, the outrage of the public sickened by the increasing waves of prison killings and riots, no less than the soaring financial costs of incarceration, has brought us to this point. The years immediately ahead will return us, finally, to the point we were before the idea of the penitentiary was first launched a short two centuries ago—community dealing with those who break the law.

NOTES

1. Herb C. Willman, Jr. and Ron Y.F. Chun, "Homeward Bound: An Alternative to the Institutionalization of Adjudicated Juvenile Offenders," *Federal Probation* (September 1973), pp. 52–58.
2. "Closing Down of Institutions and New Strategies in Youth Services," Boston College, Newton, Mass., 1972.
3. From a speech by Dr. Jerome Miller at Boston College, May 8, 1972.
4. Ibid.
5. In a speech delivered before the Fouth National Symposium on Law Enforcement, Science and Technology, Washington, D.C., May 3, 1972.
6. The conference was convened under the joint sponsorship of the Massachusetts Department of Youth Services, the Institute for Social Research

of Fordham University, and the Department of Sociology, Boston
College, Newton, Mass., June 26–28, 1972.
7. "Closing Down of Institutions and New Strategies in Youth Services," *op.
cit.*, p. 1. What follows in the next several pages is abstracted from
that report.
8. Massachusetts General Laws, Chapter 83 of 1969.
9. P.L. 50–42, p. 15.
10. "Closing Down of Institutions and New Strategies in Youth Services," *op.
cit.*, esp Part 7.
11 Massachusetts General Laws, Chapter 71, Section 46, I.
12. Benedict S. Alper, "The Training School: Stepchild of Public Education,"
Federal Probation (December 1969), pp. 24–28.
13. Yitzhak Bakal, ed., *Closing Correctional Institutions* (Lexington, Mass.: D.C.
Heath, 1973).
14. "Information Bulletin," Boston, Mass. Department of Correction, May 30,
1973, p. 3.
15. *NCCD News*, March–April, 1972.
16. From information furnished by the Maine Bureau of Corrections.
17. Ms. Ward E. Murphy, Commissioner, "A Statement of Philosophy," Augusta,
October 1973, (dup.).
18. Under the direct supervision of the College of Education, Department of
Curriculum and Instruction, Boca Raton, Florida 33432.
19. "The Criminal Offender—What Should be Done?" A *Report of the President's
Task Force on Prisoner Rehabilitation* (Washington: Government
Printing Office, 1970), pp. vi and 23.
20. "Institutional Construction: A Policy Statement," *Crime and Delinquency*
(October 1972), pp. 331–2.

Chapter Eleven

Diversion

Some basic underlying considerations determine and give meaning to the choice of alternatives to police, criminal courts and institutions, and to their place in the total criminal justice system. These influence the alteration not only of modes of operation but of attitudes as well. Whatever is done with offenders, juvenile or adult, depends on society's disposition towards them, how they are regarded, as well as the reactions of citizens.

The concept of diversion is very much to the fore these days. For one thing, there now exists almost universal dissatisfaction with traditional and established ways of dealing with offenders at every stage in the court and correctional processes. We have recorded a growing realization that the criminal justice system may itself contribute to the spread of crime, however unpleasant this may be to admit. Along with this general awareness goes the realization that by bringing offenders into the criminal justice system, they are thereby set apart from other people by reason of having been branded or labeled. In this sense, official intervention in their lives fixes them in criminal patterns of attitudes and behavior in a manner little different—psychologically or socially (rather than physically)—from the time when the penitentiary and the reformatory replaced branding and maiming as the chief reliance of punishment.

If, therefore, as many offenders as possible can be diverted from and kept out of the criminal justice system—as many as do not absolutely need to be dealt with within it—a system will have been created which contributes to the decriminalizing of many of those whom the system today makes into criminals. Difficult as it may be to establish precisely the rates of recidivism, whether for closed or open establishments, so is it difficult to measure the professional training in crime which offenders, who may be young or unsophisticated, receive in the institutions which are supposed to rehabilitate them. The result is that they go out better trained, more proficient criminals than they were when they came in.

177

A leading theoretician in the causation of crime, Edwin Sutherland, in his theory of differential association, holds that criminal behavior, like other forms of behavior, is learned within the subculture of those socioeconomic classes which are disadvantaged [1] —much as reading and writing are learned in more approved institutions—like schools. A criminal group, such as a street gang, provides a way of teaching young people the techniques of committing crime. Jails, training schools and reformatories, especially for the young, do precisely what Sutherland warned against: they turn young people into hardened criminals. For this reason, among a variety of others, there is increasing interest in diverting young people from every step in the criminal justice system, whether it be from the hands of the police, from the court process itself, or the end of that process—reform school or prison.

DIVERSION FROM ARREST

During 1970, it is estimated, almost four million youngsters had some kind of police contact, of which one-half—two million—resulted in arrest. Half of these—1,052,000, or one-fourth of all young people who came to the attention of the police—ultimately appeared in court. Judging by the rate of increase between 1965 and 1970, it is conservatively estimated that by 1977 our juvenile courts will be confronted with 1.5 million juveniles, unless a strategy is evolved "for the establishment, nation-wide, of youth service systems which will divert youth, insofar as possible, from the juvenile justice system by providing comprehensive, integrated community-based programs designed to meet the needs of all youth, regardless of who they are or what their individual problem may be."[2] This strategy has been followed by beginning pilot projects in more than a score of communities across the land.

Many good projects—like many marriages—never advance beyond the proposal stage, but nevertheless contain many worthwhile features. One such proposal aims "to provide psychological and social services to delinquents, pre-delinquents, and their families. Under this project, every first-offender truant, runaway, or 'stubborn child' who comes before the juvenile court is diverted out of the court system at arraignment and sent for evaluation and treatment to an agency of the court. This group of children is one of the sectors of the court population most in need of channeling into the mental health field. The connection between family conflict and the offenses of truancy, runaway and stubbornness is especially strong and clear. Because of the psychological nature of the roots of these offenses, the children who commit them are particularly amenable to benefiting from intervention from a mental health agency. In the case of the offenses of runaway, and especially stubborn child, the parent taking out the complaint is nearly always asking for some form of intervention for herself or himself, too. The diversion program is an excellent model for delivering services to these parents, since the treatment plan developed for a child always includes attention to the needs of the parents and the program equipped to offer services to the whole family."[3]

In its resolve to divert youths from the criminal justice process at the initial level of arrest, the Quebec legislature, late in 1972, introduced a bill modifying the Youth Probation Act, to "provide for transfer of some youth protection services from the Social Affairs Department to a new Youth Protection Service within the Department of Justice. This new service would act as an intake and diagnostic service for youth under eighteen who would come to the attention of police and other services. The principal services affected are the Juvenile Probation Service and the youth detention centers."[4]

In California, nine youth service bureaus, locally administered, coordinate already-existing services for young persons referred by law enforcement, the courts, schools, and individual families, with the expressed objective of meeting the needs of young people for counseling and employment before it becomes necessary for them to enter the criminal justice system.

Cities and counties of this state have been developing such programs since 1968.[5] The first step in developing programs was the retraining of a number of parole officers who serve youthful offenders, to provide to the peers and neighbors of such parolees delinquency prevention and youth services in the community. A Volunteer Model Project begun in 1972 helps to recruit and train community volunteers. In addition, young lawyers in three counties work as volunteer parole officers with youthful offenders on a one-to-one basis.

Another unique diversion program, serving the needs of both juveniles and adults, has been developed in the Chicago suburbs of Wheaton and Niles.[6] It is based on the premise that a correctional approach should be introduced at the earliest point in the criminal justice system, to prevent the stigmatization and labeling which can lead to alienation from society. Each community has instituted a social service unit within its police department, consisting of two professional social workers to supervise four graduate social work students who work a minimum of twenty-four hours per week. These units provide four basic services: social assessments to law enforcement and to the client; a continuous twenty-four-hour-a-day crisis intervention service; short-term and some long-term individual counseling, marital counseling, family group therapy, group service, and referral to community agencies.

By speedy social assessment and early intervention, the project aims to demonstrate that continued overloading of the criminal justice system can be alleviated, and rehabilitation initiated immediately. Following a period of services by community agencies and nonviolative behavior on the part of the client, the case is closed without court action. Some casual misdemeanants are thus diverted into more effective and appropriate social resources within the community or the services of a worker in the police department. Individuals referred to the project include runaways, truants, incorrigibles, emergency cases of mental illness, persons with alcoholic, family or marital problems who come to the attention of the police, and those charged with minor theft, drug abuse and vandalism.

Preliminary research results indicate that a police-social work team model can succeed in relieving the problem of overloaded law enforcement agencies, courts, and probation services. People with social and personal problems can be diverted from official entry into the criminal justice system at an early point by referral to services appropriate to their needs.

Such police responsiveness to the preventive aspects of their work is relatively new, and a hopeful portent of what can be done to improve police-community relations. One of the most serious situations—especially in the core areas of our large cities—is the low esteem, for a variety of reasons, in which the police force is held, particularly among the young. The following description of a program which has been operating for the past two years is an example of what can be done—effectively—when a community determines to cope with its youth problems.

The Juvenile Division of this police force derives its support in part from federal funds. Directed by a police lieutenant, it is staffed by five juvenile officers and a secretary. "The juvenile officers have had training in the area of juvenile delinquency; three of them are bilingual—one in Spanish, and two in French. The division has two patrol cars and a station wagon. Its initial goal was to divert youthful offenders from the criminal justice system, i.e., to make every feasible attempt to keep the youths out of the courts. As a result, about 650 of the City's 'youth have avoided court, roughly 75 percent of those who would have been drawn into it."[7]

The alternatives at the disposal of the Juvenile Division are: to find a complaint unfounded and release the suspect; to counsel and release arrested persons; to refer youngsters to the Office of Youth Services; and finally, to refer them to court.

The Office of Youth Services is a new agency in the community, staffed with a director, a social worker, program organizer and secretary. It works directly with the Juvenile Division of the Police. Its board of directors consists of community people, lawyers, youth, representatives of other sectors of the community, a doctor, a judge, and the Chief of Police. Once a youth has been referred to the Office of Youth Services, an interview is set up with concerned persons and, if necessary, referral is made to the services of other agencies in the community for assistance.

The following are some factors considered when a juvenile officer is making his decision: the seriousness of the offense; the repetitiveness of the youth's encounters with the police; the family setting and peer-group influences; attitude of the youth and his parents; his maturity; the ability of the family to cope with the situation; vocational status; physical and mental status; and educational situation.

Officers in the division deliver talks to organizations, are members of youth councils, and are in other ways actively involved in youth programs in the community. They are at the same time full-fledged police officers, and as a result are also involved with adult arrests. Their time is also devoted to court appearances and assistance to schools and other officials.

In some places recently, drunkenness has been declared by court decision a treatable disease—a condition and not an offense. The magnitude of the implications of this new approach may be seen in just one state—Massachusetts, where there were, between 1950 and 1969, a total of 1.1. million arrests for drunkenness out of a population of close to 5 million. Drunkenness is only a crime when it is committed in public. Half the people arrested were convicted: in twenty years, 500,000 convicted of public drunkenness, with 122,000 of them incarcerated—better than 10 percent of all those arrested for that offense. The total cost of dealing with drunkenness over that period in that ineffective fashion was $116 million. Massachusetts has the fourth highest rate of alcoholism in the United States. The United States leads the world, having just recently surpassed France.[8]

On July 1, 1973, the crime of public drunkenness was removed from the criminal statute books of Massachusetts. This one legislative act will result in relieving the police of one-half of their duties, will clear the courts of one-half of their cases, and will have cleared the jails of one-quarter of their population. It takes a little ingenuity. The act which declared alcoholism no longer a crime went further to establish a comprehensive program for the treatment and rehabilitation of intoxicated persons and alcoholics.[9]

The province of Ontario in Canada, in a program to eliminate "drunk tanks," has recently designated, by an order-in-council, two hospitals as responsible for detoxication centers—one in Toronto and the other in Kenora. The Toronto unit is situated in an unused firehall, and the Kenora unit in an old warehouse. Four other centers are planned; in three years it is expected that sixteen will be established in each of eleven Ontario cities where drunkenness arrests exceed 1,000 per year. The Ontario Liquor Act now specifically authorizes the police to deliver a drunkenness offender to a designated detoxication center rather than to jail.[10] Similarly, the Prince Edward Island government plans to change the Liquor Control Act to make it possible for the courts to divert offenders convicted under this statute to treatment centers instead of to jails.[11]

Freeing the police in this way from the routine necessity for picking up and transporting alcoholics between street and station, court and jail, can lead to their being relieved of responsibility for the other so-called victimless crimes—gambling, narcotics, traffic offenses, prostitution and other sex offenses, all of which may be diverted to other than criminal justice agencies. When this has been done, the police can then be expected to turn their attention to the really serious crimes which are the greatest menace to persons and property. This should bring about a greater professionalization of the police and skill in using technical equipment. By this is not meant the latest sophisticated electronic devices for invading privacy of home and telephone, nor a stepping up of the use of riot equipment, weaponry and gas, nor the use of the "national identifier" for computerizing information on private citizens; but rather the use, for example, of radar in flagging down speeders, the more intensive use of the fingerprint for identification, time to work out—through the *modus operandi* and other methods of identification—the propensities and even the identities of professional thieves and burglars.

Samuel Butler, in the nineteenth century, wrote at a time when the world was seen as a very much more hopeful place than it seems today.[12] Butler describes a conversation between two men. The wife of one had just been released from the hospital by court order because she was now cured. In Butler's view, by the year 2000 disease would be considered a crime caused by negligence or bad intent, while crime would be considered a disease to be cured by medical science. The moral obloquy which today attaches to crime, would by this view be attached to sickness.

Butler implies that by 2000 there would be sufficient education in the world so that people would know how to take care of their health and, if not, they would be punished; whereas a person who committed a crime would be so obviously sick that the doctors would submit him to a process of cure. This entertaining notion is by no means extreme in the light of today's trend.

Some crimes, like alcoholism, are being considered a disease, a condition to be treated like other medical illnesses. This same attitude is now being taken toward persons who are addicted to narcotics. We are beginning to learn that to lock people up because they are addicted does not cure their habit unless and until the basic condition which brought about their involvement in or dependence upon drugs—as a way of dealing with life—has somehow been dealt with.

We lock people up for drug-related offenses, and they go out and get involved all over again, because the process has failed to cope with the fundamental problems which results in their responding by the taking of drugs. The dealing with alcoholics and various addicts in noncriminal ways is one of the first steps which can be taken in diverting from the criminal justice process at the initial level of arrest.

DIVERSION FROM COURT

The Quebec Legislature, late in 1972, introduced a bill modifying the Youth Protection Act, which "provides for transfer of some youth protections services from the Social Affairs Department to a new Youth Protection Service within the Department of Justice. This new service would act as an intake and diagnostic service for youth under eighteen who would come to the attention of police and other services. The principal services affected are the Juvenile Probation Service and the youth detention centers."[13]

"There are alternate ways of dealing with [delinquency] problems, but they are all solutions which are basically outside of the juvenile justice system. We can no longer believe in the myth of the omnipotence of the juvenile court to solve all the problems of troubled youth in a community—and God should not be in our repertory of roles. We simply must stop playing God on these various levels and admit that we just cannot deal with these children."[14]

Ingenuity and flexibility in programs for modifying the severity of the criminal process for youths, in effect diverting them from prosecution, saving them from a criminal record, and at the same time providing more effective measures for dealing with their basic condition, are illustrated in the following accounts.

In Baltimore, a special probation procedure takes place after a court hearing on the original charges against a young person, and a preliminary finding of fact. When the defendant has satisfactorily completed his probation period, a formal hearing then confirms the preliminary finding of fact, but no verdict is entered against him. Violation of probation during the interim period results in formal trial, as would have occurred if the intermediary process had not taken place.

Federal courts also utilize a system of deferred prosecution in criminal cases involving juveniles. Under this plan, formal proceedings against them in the federal courts may be postponed, pending satisfactory adjustments through the use of informal probation, special placement, or treatment. The consent of both the defendant and his counsel to any alternative plan is secured in advance, and on the reaching of a satisfactory solution, the court may then dismiss the complaint.

In the Detroit Recorder's Court, youths between the ages of fifteen and twenty-two are granted probation after conviction. Conditions of probation may include placement in the state probation camp for up to one year. Upon successful completion of his terms of probation, the youthful offender may apply for a new trial, usually under the claim of newly discovered evidence. His adjustment of probation may then be made the basis for his acquittal.

Recent years have seen many beginnings of these alternate ways to handle the problems of young people before their situation becomes so serious, or an arrest is made, that involvement in the court process becomes inevitable. One of the best-known of these schemes is the Youth Service Bureau, an organization outside the courts, which has the authority to take juveniles out of the juvenile court system and assign them to public or private agencies for help and treatment.

An experimental pretrial project, begun in the juvenile and general sessions courts of Washington, D.C. in 1968, provided a ninety-day community-based program of services, including counseling, job and training placements, and remedial education. The Project was designed for young men and women in the pretrial stage of court proceedings who were between sixteen and twenty-six, had no prior convictions, were not charged with crimes against the person, were unemployed, underemployed, in danger of losing their jobs due to arrest, were school drop-outs, or only tenuously enrolled in school. Upon their voluntary agreement to participate in the program, they then had to be approved for participation in the program by the court.

Four types of services are offered. At the outset, each participant is assigned a counselor who provides supportive services, and submits reports on his performance to the court. The counselor deals with such immediate needs as employment, financial assistance, and personal or family problems. Most work is done with young people on a one-to-one basis, but group sessions are held with some participants. The employment and training placement staff arranges job interviews for youths in areas of their interest, and continues until a suitable placement is made.

Remedial education provides individual tutoring four nights a week, and specialized programs, such as preparation for high school equivalency and armed forces examinations, remedial reading and job-test preparation. Help is given those who wish to re-enroll in school or to seek admission to college. Referral services provide liaison with local social agencies to provide medical and dental care, legal assistance, and emergency food, shelter and clothing for participants and their families.

After the successful completion of the three-month program, the youth's performance is reported to the court, with the recommendation that the charges against him be dismissed. The project enrolled 347 youths in its first year. Of these, approximately 60 percent had their charges dismissed because of satisfactory project participation.[15]

Another program for diverting juveniles from court—first offenders, truants, runaways and "stubborn children"—refers them to an unofficial agency which would furnish the services indicated as lacking in the life of the child. Particular emphasis is laid on providing services to the child in and with his family, because of the court's experience that the great majority of these cases stem from family inadequacies, discord and conflict. This is an excellent model for delivering delinquency preventive services, for it is directed toward serving the needs of parents and siblings as well as of the child who is in trouble.[16]

So-called "wayward minor" proceedings in several jurisdictions extend the protective quality of the juvenile court—definitions of misbehavior such as disobedience or incorrigibility—to older minors (usually sixteen to twenty-one). The condition of waywardness is more a civil status than a criminal offense. Conduct that is subject to complaint can include "truancy, habitual running away from home, failure to obey lawful commands of parents or guardians, habitual association with thieves, being found in a house of prostitution, or deporting oneself as to wilfully injure or endanger personal morals or health; being morally depraved or in danger of becoming so."[17]

While useful as an alternative to a criminal action in the adult court, wayward minor proceedings seldom help the offender, because the grounds for adjudication are more often designed to reenforce parental control over minors who are beyond juvenile court age than to prevent crime, in the sense of dealing with the basic needs or condition of the young offender.

The use of a "wayward minor" charge is one of the approaches of the New York City Youth Council Bureau, which interviews youths between the ages of sixteen and twenty-one after arrest but before arraignment. The bureau's findings aid the district attorney and the judges in determining whether proceedings and disposition other than prosecution under a penal statute should be brought. These may include substitution of wayward minor procedure, deferment of official action during good behavior and subsequent request for dismissal of the charges, release on bail or recognizance, transfer to an adolescent court for youthful offender proceedings, or vacating the charge.

After a year and a half of experimentation without explicit statutory authority by judges in six lower courts in metropolitan Boston, an innovative pretrial program sought, through enactment of legislation, to authorize it as a permanent part of the state-wide system of district courts.[18] Anyone between the ages of seventeen and twenty-six, accused of a misdemeanor or minor felony, was potentially eligible for the program; ideally, but not necessarily, he was a first offender in the sense of a person beginning criminal involvement, who was unemployed or underemployed, who was recommended as a person who could benefit from a program of community supervision.

Individuals excluded are those charged with serious felonies or crimes of violence, juveniles (as it is difficult to find jobs for them), and heavy drug offenders who require a different complex of resources to deal with their problems.

The program begins after arrest and arraignment but before trial. An accused individual considered for selection is released on fourteen-day "continuance" to the project if he, as well as the judge, probation officer, lawyer, and arresting officer, and the program screener who works in the court, agree on his potential for the project. During a two-week period of assessment, staff teams evaluate his suitability for the program. If the defendant prefers, and if he considers himself innocent, or if he believes that he does not need rehabilitation or will not submit to it, then he has his regular trial or hearing before the court.

Emphasis on the validity of the presumption of innocence does not obscure the fact that the majority of those who appear in court may not in fact be innocent. It is the responsibility of society to hold them for trial, meanwhile presuming them innocent until they are found guilty. But if the defendant is sufficiently aware of his involvement in the offense charged and is willing to cooperate with the rehabilitative process, he obviously has nothing to lose by this process. For it spares him going through a trial, and, most important, assures him that if he succeeds in the program to which he has given his consent, the charges against him will be dropped and he will be saved a criminal record. (Juvenile court laws universally provide that no record on any child who appears before it may be made public. But not every delinquency record in the juvenile court can be concealed forever, if an employer, the civil service, or the armed forces are determined to uncover it).

Acceptance into the program begins with a ninety-day continuance by the court, and the client's commitment to goals mutually set by him and the staff team. After ninety days, if the client successfully completes the diversion program, involvement in productive activity—work, school, or training—the judge may then dismiss the criminal charges against him. In both failure and success, final disposition remains with the court. Upon dismissal of charges after successful completion of the program, all official records relating to the arrest, arraignment, continuance and dismissal, except nonpublic probation records, would be sealed and closed to public access.

Under the bill proposed to incorporate the experimental procedure into legislation,[19] an advisory board has been recommended which would furnish general guidance and policy. This board, it is suggested, should be composed of the attorney general of the state, the state commissioners of mental health and education, a district court judge, the director of the state division of employment security, and seven experts in the area of delivery of services to disadvantaged persons through community-based programs. An ex-offender is specified to serve on the board as well. It has been recommended that the office of the state commissioner of probation grant licenses to pre-trial diversion programs, with the assistance of the advisory board, in the promulgation of rules and regulations to govern its procedures, as well as by helping to fund the program itself.

Among the better known diversionary programs are the Manhattan Court Employment Project, Project Crossroads, and similar projects in Atlanta, Cleveland, Minneapolis, San Antonio and San Francisco. All of these have in common the goal of identifying and referring young defendants in need of treatment as early as possible in the court process in order to start them on the path to rehabilitation. Not the least of their advantages is that they help to reduce court congestion. The Manhattan Project reports an arrest rate among participants of 0.04 percent, as compared to 12 percent before the project began. Almost three-fifths of the cases who passed through the program were dismissed by the court after successfully completing it.[20]

Programs like these would seem to be especially suited for the drug-dependent defendant. Diversion of such persons after arrest but before trial would make available a many-sided treatment program, and referral to a broad range of services to meet their social, medical, vocational, economic, and educational needs.

As the role of women is extended in many areas of private and public life as a result of their challenges to traditional practices which discriminate against them, so does their role expand in the area of criminal activity. The arrest rates for females have more than doubled in the past decade compared with the rates for males. Overall, arrests of women for violent crimes increased 69 percent from 1960 to 1970, while the total crime rate for women rose 74 percent during the decade. The increase in the total crime rate for men was one-third of that: 25 percent.[21]

It is not surprising, therefore, that proposals should now seek to extend the advantages of pre-trial diversionary services to women. One such recent proposal would offer the services of specially trained women "advocates"—a relatively new term in the criminal justice field, implying a combination of counselor, social worker, and spokesman—to all female first offenders (those with one to three previous court appearances) who are between the ages of seventeen and twenty-three.[22] Advocate services would be extended to such defendants in the areas of employment and training, legal assistance, health care, day care for their young children, temporary residences and subsidized housing for those with low income. Top priority for the availability of such services would be to women at the point of arraignment, through an office, specially staffed, situated at the court house.

The judge would then be petitioned to grant a continuance of from seven to fourteen days, during which time the defendant's needs would be assessed and a plan designed to meet her needs. If the woman is accepted into the program, and agrees to enter it, the judge would then be petitioned to continue the hearing of her case until ninety days of participation in the program had elapsed. Three options would then be open at this point: dropping of charges against the defendant; continuation in the program; or bringing her to trial.

Perhaps the most far-reaching of these court diversionary schemes is one contained in a bill filed in the United States Senate in February 1971.[23] While it excluded from its benefits persons charged with crimes of violence, a provision of the bill would permit even this type of offender to be included, with the permission of the authority which filed the original charges. This would, in effect, make the act, if passed, potentially applicable to all but the most serious types of offenses and offenders. The bill was also unusual in that it specified in its introductory declaration of policy that "it is the policy of the Congress that new and innovative means of disposing of charges of violating criminal laws by certain individuals will serve to protect society and benefit the individual, by creating added alternatives for rehabilitative treatment within the community. Innovative treatment will protect society by lessening the hardening process that may be a product of delay and institutionalization, and it will benefit the individual by giving him the opportunity to acquire those elements he needs to lead a lawful and useful life-style."[24]

The act also provides a two-year period for programs of community supervision and services, well beyond the usual three months specified in other plans, with the possibility of extending it for a third year. The offense, the charges, and the fact that the offender may have committed a crime have in this process disappeared. In effect, his need for rehabilitation and his ability to readjust to the community provides the basis for the court *not* to take jurisdiction.

Until recently, few fundamental changes have come about in the criminal justice system as a result of efforts of judges, lawyers, or prosecutors. Such pressure has come largely from the outside: The history of penology over the past 200 years includes but few judges or district attorneys who have taken the lead in reform. Change has come rather from impatient citizens, from reformers, from the universities, and most recently, from pressure by prisoners and ex-convicts.

It was only in the past few years that the American Bar Association, organized in 1878, appointed a committee specifically for corrections. Many people in our society are conservative and traditional, but judges and lawyers tend to be the most conservative and traditional. This is not purely a personal or psychological condition, it derives rather from the fact that their entire professional outlook is geared not to today but to yesterday. Points of law and court decisions are argued on the basis of precedents. The Common Law looks to the past for examples to guide the decisions of today. There is no other field of human endeavor (except history) where this is so. Developing countries look around the world to discover not what was well done yesterday, but what is best and most effectively done today. This makes all the more noteworthy the changes that are taking place in the criminal justice field—the new winds that are blowing because of the rapidly growing volume of crime and our present incapacity to deal effectively with it.

THE SCANDINAVIAN CHILD WELFARE BOARD

The juvenile court has spread in 75 years from Cook County, Illinois to every part of the United States and to most of the world.[25] Yet there are countries which have never had a juvenile court. The prime example is to be found in Scandinavia.[26] There, the so-called child welfare board is not a substitute for juvenile courts, since they never had them, but takes an entirely different approach to the problem of juvenile delinquency. It originated in Sweden under a statute passed around 1780 for the protection of children under the Crown, and has since been adopted in Denmark and Norway, as well.

The child welfare board is based on much the same kind of concept, which in the Common Law is known as *parens patriae*, one of the fundamentals of the juvenile court which views the state as the parent of all its children. The child welfare board is not a professional body, but instead is composed of citizens in the community. The only qualification they must have is that they be registered to vote, although it is recommended in the basic act that a lawyer be included in the membership of that board, which usually totals five.

Each of the 1,000 communes in Sweden, as well as those within the city of Stockholm itself, is empowered to create such a board and to elect members to it. The aim of these boards, as defined in the law, is "to protect children and young people from a harmful milieu . . . or to correct children who are misbehaving."[27] This provision is a legal recognition of the kind of attitude toward children which views much of what is termed "delinquency" rather as mischief or misbehavior on the part of children in need of protection or correction—not of punishment. The upper age limit of board jurisdiction is 21.

The measures available for disposition of cases range from dismissal of a complaint to commitment to an institution. The child's rights are safeguarded, including that of representation by counsel. Appeal from a decision of a board may be made to the county administration, and thereafter to the district court, ultimately to the Crown. The child welfare board idea was first brought to the attention of the world by the League of Nations in the mid-thirties.[28] It has not been extended beyond Scandinavia until very recently, when the effectiveness of juvenile courts has begun to be called into question and the movement for diversion from them began.

For example, in Great Britain a recommendation was made, in a government White Paper issued in 1966, for a radical reorganization of services for delinquent children and youth. Scotland has recently all but abolished the juvenile court and established in its place a child welfare board very much like that of Scandinavia.

"In England, raising of the school leaving age to sixteen is the starting point for the recommendation that children and young persons under twenty-one be divided into two categories: those under sixteen and those between ages sixteen and twenty-one. Children under sixteen who commit an act which would be a criminal offense in the case of an adult, would be brought before a local family council, consisting of at least one man and one woman. The council's endeavor will be to 'reach agreement with the parents of the child on the treatment to be applied. If the facts are in dispute or agreement cannot be reached on treatment, the issue will be referred to a court for determination'."[29]

The report further recommends that special magistrate's courts be created to hear disputed issues of fact and decide treatment in matters referred to it by the family council. Such magistrate's courts will also have jurisdiction over adoption and other matters affecting young persons under twenty-one. Sitting as young offender's courts, these special tribunals are also empowered to exercise criminal jurisdiction over persons between the ages of sixteen and twenty-one. The White Paper has been the subject of much debate and discussion in England, some forty organizations having made comments on it.

"Meanwhile in Scotland the Social Work Act of 1968 takes the drastic step of substituting for the juvenile court, so-called Children's Panels to be formed for every local authority. The panel is required to observe the requirements of notice, statement of the grounds for the referral of cases, right of legal representation and of appeal. In other respects, the procedure and philosophy of the panels follow that of the Child Welfare Boards of the Scandinavian countries. 'On the coming into operation (of the Children's Panel scheme) the jurisdiction of a juvenile court in relation to the care and protection of children shall cease . . . .'[30]

"The substitution of Children's Panels for juvenile courts is based on the finding that the latter have failed to resolve the basic conflict in juvenile court philosophy which both *Kent* and *Gault* have emphasized. The report which preceded the drafting of the legislation just cited states: 'The shortcomings inherent in the juvenile court system can, it seems to us, be traced essentially to the fact that they are required to combine the characteristics of a court of criminal law with those of a specialized agency for the treatment of children in need of care or protection.'

"The results of Scotland's attempt to incorporate into the common law procedure a device which began in the Scandinavian countries will be watched with interest. Surely it has relevance for the juvenile procedures in the United States, especially since the President's Commission Report has advocated a parallel procedure, though in nonspecific and most general terms. And for several of the new nations—the so-called developing countries—which have no tradition of their own in the legislative field and tend to look for a pattern to serve as a model for their own youth welfare services, it could be of value to compare the different systems and the experience gained in the Western world in dealing with children and youth suffering from problems of adjustment."[31]

What are the advantages of this noncourt procedure? In the first place, it decriminalizes the court process for young people. Most important, instead of the concept that the state or the crown is the ultimate father of all children, it says to the community, "You are the father of your own children in your own neighborhood." Who knows better the situation of young people in the community than those who live with them? Inherent in the idea of the community panel is the notion of decentralization of authority, and the debureaucratization of official procedures for dealing with youthful misconduct. Government structures are almost everywhere overloaded with civil servants, bogged down by paper, confined in too many boxes on organizational charts. In the process, people become dossiers, lives become statistics, and human problems become cases. Just as there has been overreliance on the criminal law for the solution of problems, so has there been overreliance on government as the ultimate arbiter for dealing with the problems of young people.

Nonjudicial handling of the cases of children has not been without its proponents in the United States. In the President's Commission Report on Crime in 1967 there is a brief suggestion that communities should involve themselves in the creation of nonlegal juvenile tribunals.[32] This tentative and vague reference is made specific by the Supreme Court of New Jersey, which in July 1966 adopted a rule authorizing the appointment of one or more juvenile conference committees for any county. Each committee is empowered to "serve as an arm of the court in hearing and deciding such matters involving alleged juvenile offenders as are specially referred to it by the court." Encouraged to "help forestall more serious future misconduct by the juvenile offender ... by obtaining the voluntary cooperation of the juvenile, it is empowered to supervise and follow up its recommendations."[33] The essential characteristic of the committee is its voluntary nature. No person can be compelled to appear before it or to comply with its recommendations, but the sanction of referral to the court may be the price of noncompliance.

Not all jurisdictions throughout the world are seeking less restrictive ways of dealing with delinquents, however. In Japan, for example, where the upper age limit of the family court in juvenile cases has been at age twenty, there is consideration within the Ministry of Justice to lower this age to eighteen, and to permit the family court to hear cases of those between eighteen and twenty in criminal proceedings, at the same time leaving it to that court to impose a criminal sentence on convicted offenders or to "make an order of protective measures." This proposal, which is seen as "killing the benevolent spirit of the present Juvenile court Law" is a reaction to the recent wave of student demonstrators and other young people in political opposition to policies of a government which evidently does not view them "benevolently."[34]

THE PANCHAYAT COURTS OF INDIA

Community—or communal—courts have been the reliance of some areas since ancient days, especially in Asia where the court system is still in local hands. In the tribal areas of northwestern Pakistan, there are frontier regions "which have never seen the Police, the Courts or the Revenue collecting agencies since man occupied this globe. There is no Penal Code or Procedure Code, Evidence Act or any special law in the area. One drives a car without acquiring a license— can keep a gun or any explosive without permit. People are brave, very well built, frank and outspoken and live a very simple life.

"Twice the government of Pakistan decided to extend the Law and Court system in this region, but the tribesmen revolted. The only liaison officer between them and the government is five or six political agents stationed at various places.

"These people govern themselves by electing their Tribal Jirga. Members of Jirga are normally Tribal chiefs. Each and every case is decided within a week or so. Modes of justice in almost all cases is compensation to the victim. Their code is the customary Law, which has more force and effect than the secular laws.

"Crime is almost nil. There are cases of clashes between one tribe or another or murder because of hot temper. Sex crimes and juvenile delinquency are not known to these people. The population is approximately two million." [35]

An account from another source adds a pertinent detailed description of the same community in action:

"In certain northern parts of Pakistan there is a custom that after a murder, the villagers gather around the house of the murderer. The idea is that should the relatives of the murdered person come to take revenge, the villagers may be able to persuade them not to take law in their own hands. This custom often saves further loss of life." [36]

In India, as well, long before the British thought of making it a colony, village councils called "Gram Panchayat" had been in existence since earliest times.[37] These bodies administered most of the affairs of the village, including the dispensation of justice. "Gram Panchayat" means, literally, village council. Its five members are elected by majority vote of the villagers. Generally they are elderly persons having status, respect, and influence, in whom their neighbors generally have faith and trust.

Up to about 1870, the system of common law which had been introduced under British rule, prevailed. But at about that time a movement for some local degree of self-government developed, and with it the revival of the Panchayat village courts, and their ultimate authorization by legislative acts in different provinces of India. The villages of India are where the people live, Mahatma Ghandi has said, and since earliest times the village has been the pivot of government administration, as it is still the keystone of the economy.

After independence, India's new Constitution specified the Panchayat system, leaving it to each of the component states to work out its own distinctive form. Generally speaking, the Gram Panchayat—there are said to be more than 8,000 of them in the state of Uttar Pradesh alone—is an elected body consisting of twenty-five members, divided into "benches" of five, each of which in turn elects its own chairman. At least three members of the Panchayat must participate in the hearing and disposition of disputes of all kinds, including minor offenses which may occur in the village. Lawyers are not allowed to appear before them in behalf of clients. These courts have power to hear both civil and criminal cases of a minor nature. Civil suits may be heard up to a value of 500 rupees (approximately $40)—like small claims courts in the United States. Cases which come before them entail such matters as recovery of property, damages caused by trespassing cattle, or debts. Criminal jurisdiction of these same courts includes cases of theft, "causing hurt," creating a public nuisance, criminal trespass or intimidation. The Panchayat calls the parties concerned before it, hears the evidence and then makes its decision, generally in the form of a compromise, compensation, and/or limited fines. After a finding of guilt, the courts may only impose a fine up to a maximum of 100 rupees, but not imprisonment. From this fine, compensation may be awarded by the court to the aggrieved person. Appeals from an order of the court may be taken to the regular magistrate's courts, and even up to the Supreme Court. It is reported that such appeals are fewer in recent years, as the village court is seen to be "working satisfactorily, as the justice is quick, sure, and available at negligible cost, and given by people intimately known to both parties and who work for the welfare of the village as a whole."[38]

PEOPLES' COURTS IN RUSSIA AND CHINA

In view of the détente in relations between the United States and the governments of the Soviet Union and the Peoples' Republic of China, at least a passing reference should be made to the criminal court systems of those two socialist countries. In the Soviet Union, where the inquisitorial rather than the adversary accusatory system prevails, the People's Courts have for some years dealt with the minor offenses and squabbles which take place in the community. The members of these courts are elected by and from the community, and are usually not trained in the law. Much the same kind of simple justice seems to be dispensed by the citizenry.[39]

"Even though street and resident's committees usually have certain members designated to look after public order, all members of the official and semiofficial local network may play a role in settling disputes and disposing of minor cases of antisocial behavior.

"For example, a dispute between tenants over sharing a bathroom or kitchen may be mediated by any residents' committee member, the small group leader, or the group itself. A serious dispute, such as a divorce complaint, will be dealt with in a series of long discussions and 'study' sessions that involve not only street committee officials, residents' committee members, family, friends, and the spouses themselves, but representatives of the factories or other units where the spouses are employed."

In China "a petty thief may in the first instance simply receive some private 'persuasion education' or criticism from his small group. But if he fails to reform, he may be censured by a meeting of the entire neighborhood convened by the resident's committee. An especially recalcitrant offender may be stigmatized as a 'bad element' and given one of several possible forms of compulsory labor by the public security apparatus. The situation is similar in the rural communes."[40]

It is easy to hear, in the last few sentences of that description of modern-day China, the echoes of a simpler time in our own country, when offenders could be punished by being exposed to shame before their fellow townspeople.

DIVERSION FROM INSTITUTIONS

Alternatives to traditional ways of dealing with young and old offenders, in extra-mural programs as well as alternatives to institution custody itself have already been described in earlier chapters. Going one step further, a program initiated in California in 1966 takes the major step forward from this point, by designing a program which is not only an alternative, but which gives a premium—financial inducement—to those courts which assign delinquents to a community program instead of sending them to institutions.

California's institutional commitment rates were climbing so rapidly—from 2,500 in 1952 to over 6,000 in 1965—that the state was confronted with the necessity of constructing new buildings to house them if no drastic alternatives were discovered. There is the added fact that here, as in many other states, probation is a county function, while juvenile institutions are a charge on the state budget.

To accommodate these two realities, the legislature was persuaded in 1965 to pass the so-called Probation Subsidy Law. This law, in effect, gave a financial credit to any county which in any succeeding year sent less than the average number of children to state training schools, based on previous years. The county was empowered to utilize the credits thus earned for community-based programs for these same kinds of children. During 1968–69, thirty-one counties took advantage of the program—almost 95 percent of the state's population—and earned in that period $9.6 million from the state treasury. This sum was used for intensive supervision of 26,650 probationers. Case loads of probation officers declined substantially below 50, in contrast to the usual 100 or 200. "Results since 1966 have exceeded expectations: . . . better protection to the general public and better supervision than ever before in California's 65 years of probation history."[41]

Since July 1, 1966, almost 4,000 people who would otherwise have come into the state correctional system have been diverted from it. At an estimated cost of $20,000 per bed, approximately $78 million in construction costs was thus saved to the taxpayers of the forty-seven counties of the state which now cooperate in the program. The result has been a drop of more than one-quarter in the commitment rate to institutions after two years of operation. Especially notable is the finding that the decrease in commitments is almost twice as great for counties participating in the plan. The number of persons granted probation rose 22 percent, and the number of probationers subsequently sentenced to institutions because of the violation of terms of probation—and therefore revocation—decreased by 2 percent. In the one year 1971–72, counties earned $22 million by reducing their expected commitments of what would have been at least 5,260 persons—100 a week—for a total decline of expected commitments to state institutions of more than 20,000. During that same year, a school for delinquent boys was closed, and a second is to follow suit shortly.

The success achieved by the program has led to the suggestion that enabling legislation "be broadened to include juveniles with delinquent tendencies, and misdemeanor offenders. Probation officers argue, and with merit, that they are dealing with only the serious offenders under the present legislation, and that timely work with lesser offenders might ultimately have a greater effect on reducing commitments to state institutions. Youth Authority staff working with the program tend to agree that good services to early problem cases may contribute to further reduction in commitments."[42]

The promising nature of diversion as an innovation in the criminal justice system may be seen in the very recent establishment of the National Pre-trial intervention Service Center in Washington, which aims to expand pre-trial diversion alternatives in ten to fifteen major cities. It will also serve as a clearing house of information to induce prosecution, courts, and social agencies in these cities to consider the possibility of—and to establish—pre-trial intervention units to serve both the juvenile and adult offender.[43]

The general concept of pre-trial intervention is thus being given increased recognition and endorsement as a community-based rehabilitation alternative for deferred prosecution cases. This concept is distinguished from informal diversion practices (e.g., police referrals, juvenile intake and adjustments) in that prosecutor-initiated pre-trial intervention referrals are based on formalized eligibility criteria. Helping services by staff will coordinate vocational training, counseling, job placement, educational assistance, and the like. It is expected that the introduction of this concept of pre-trial intervention will offer a real alternative to official court processing by encouraging the dismissal of formal charges against participants in the program who successfully fulfill their commitments under it.

The extent of interest in the Intervention Service Center may be seen in the endorsement and support it has received from such bodies as the American Bar Association and the National Association of District Attorneys, and the liaison already established with the National League of Cities, the U.S. Conference of Mayors, the Vera Institute, the American Correctional Association, and other interested public service groups.

NOTES

1. Edwin H. Sutherland, *Sociology* (Philadelphia: J.B. Lippincott, 1924).
2. Robert J. Gemignani, "Youth Services Systems, Diverting Youth from the Juvenile Justice System," *Federal Probation* (December 1972), p. 48.
3. Project Proposal to the Massachusetts Governor's Committee on Law Enforcement, Boston, Spring 1973.
4. *Bulletin of the Canadian Correctional Association,* Vol. II, No. 4 (March 1973), p. 3.

5. Allen F. Breed, "The Youth Authority in 1972," *Youth Authority Quarterly*, Vol. 25, No. 3, (1972), p. 9.
6. Harvey Treger, "Breakthrough in Preventive Corrections: A Police-Social Work Team Model," *Federal Probation*, Vol. 36 (1972), pp. 53–58.
7. *New England Correctional Digest* [Boston: New England Correctional Coordinating Council, Inc.] (Fall 1972), p. 18.
8. Figures furnished by the Massachusetts Council on Crime and Correction, 3 Joy Street, Boston 02108.
9. Chapter 1076 of the Acts of 1972.
10. *Bulletin of the Canadian Correctional Association*, Vol. 2, No. 4 (March 1973), p. 4.
11. Ibid.
12. Samuel Butler, *Erehwon and Erewohn Revisited* (New York: Random House, 1927), pp. 88–101.
13. *Bulletin of the Canadian Correctional Association, op. cit.*, p. 8.
14. *Proceedings: Seventh Annual Interagency Workshop* (Huntsville: Institute of Contemporary Corrections and Behavioral Sciences, 1970), p. 140.
15. *Final Report: Project Crossroads–Phase I* (Washington: The National Committee for Children and Youth, 1970).
16. Blue Hills Program, c/o Boston Juvenile Court, Court House, Pemberton Square, Boston, Mass. 02108.
17. Ibid.
18. Under leadership of the Boston Court Resources Project, 14 Somerset St., Boston, Mass. 02108.
19. Senate Bill 1135 of 1973.
20. "Bail and Parole Jumping in Manhattan in 1967" (New York: Vera Institute, 1970).
21. *Uniform Crime Reports, 1970* (Washington: U.S. Government Printing Office, 1970).
22. Donna Turek, "Office of Advocacy for Female Offenders: The Women's Pre-trial Diversion Project," Governor's Committee on Law Enforcement and Administration of Justice, Little Building, 80 Boylston Street, Boston, Mass., Jan. 15, 1973.
23. Titled "The Community Supervision and Services Act," introduced by Senator Quentin N. Burdick, Subcommittee on Penitentiaries.
24. Ibid., Section 2.
25. H. H. Lou, *Juvenile Court in the United States* (Chapel Hill: University of North Carolina Press 1927). See also Anthony M. Platt, *The Child-savers* (Chicago: University of Chicago Press, 1969).
26. Benedict S. Alper, "The Children's Court at Three Score and Ten: Will It Survive *Gault*?" *Albany Law Review*, Vol. 34, No. 1 (Fall 1969), pp. 62–63.
27. "The Child Welfare Act of Sweden" (Stockholm: Ministry of Justice, 1965).
28. See "Organization of Juvenile Courts and Results Attained Hitherto–Child Welfare Commission," Geneva, 1932; and "Enquiry into the Question of Children in Moral and Social Danger," 1934.
29. "The Child, the Family, and the Young Offender" (London, HMSO, 1966).

30. Social Work (Scotland) Act, Chapter 49 (London, HMSO, 1968).
31. *Albany Law Review,* Benedict S. Alper, op. cit., p. 64.
32. *Task Force Report: Juvenile Delinquency and Youth Crime* (Washington: President's Commission on Law Enforcement and Administration of Justice, 1967), p. 83.
33. Soney & Sage, "Rules Governing the New Jersey Courts," Part VI, "Rules Governing the Juvenile and Domestic Relations Court," pp. 537-8, 1968.
34. Yushio Suzuki, Counselor, Criminal Affairs Bureau, Ministry of Justice, Tokyo, in a lecture at UNAFEI on "Politics and Criminal Law in Japan," May 1, 1973.
35. Habib-Ur-Rahman Khan, participant from Pakistan at the 33rd Course at UNAFEI, to the author.
36. Ibid.
37. "Report of 1970 and Resource Material Series No. 1" (Fuchu: UNAFEI, March 1971), p. 156.
38. Udai Saroji Sah, "Gram Panchayats and Nyaya Panchayats," Durgakund India, Feb. 1973, unpublished.
39. M. Cherif Bassiouni, "The Criminal Justice System of the USSR and the People's Republic of China," in *Revista de Derecho Puerto Riqueno,* Vol. XI, No. 42 (October–December 1971), pp. 175-193. See also Vladimir Terebilov, *The Soviet Court* (Moscow: Progress Publishers, 1973).
40. Jerome Alan Cohen, "Chinese Law: At the Crossroads," *American Bar Association Journal,* Vol. 59 (January 1973), p. 43.
41. What follows is drawn from two issues of *Youth Authority Quarterly* [California Youth Authority, Sacramento] Vol. 21, No. 4, (1968), and Vol. 25, No. 3, (1972).
42. Ibid., Vol. 21, No. 4, pp. 3-5. See also R. Baron, F. Feeney and Warren Thornton, "Preventing Delinquency Through Diversion: The Sacramento County 601 Diversion Project," *Federal Probation,* (March 1973), pp. 13-18.
43. Under the financial sponsorship of the United States Department of Labor, Washington, D.C.

Chapter Twelve

Conclusion

The range of materials presented here testifies that traditional ways of dealing with lawbreakers are daily proving their inability to stop the reported increase in crime, and that newer and more effective ways must and are being found and implemented.

Reference was made in the introductory chapter to the concern of the Secretary-General of the United Nations, in his speech to the General Assembly, regarding the universality of the problem: "Cumulatively, these emanations from so many different countries represent disquieting signs of a very serious problem affecting an increasingly sophisticated world."[1] These "signs" included evidence, drawn from many sources, of the failure of the traditional institution to either deter crime or correct criminals.

Penologists who have urged, since the first penitentiary was established, that institutions be abolished, have been looked upon as dreamers, crackpots and sentimentalists more touched by the plight of the criminal than by the economic or personal harm done by him to his victim. Of hardly any other institution in society can it be said that such high hopes were held out for it when it was first ushered in, nor that it has—in recent years—so utterly failed to fulfill that promise.

"Prison punishment is a strange thing. Nations got along without it for centuries, introduced it suddenly as the great hope of society, suffered repeated disappointments at its failings—but cannot yet find the means to free themselves from it.

"It was less than 200 years ago, as America was entering the modern industrialized age, that her communities began to incarcerate the criminal—and the insane—in institutions. A new doctrine had emerged of society's obligation toward the criminal, the insane, and the destitute, which created three institutions in a new mold—the prison, the asylum, and the almshouse. Each was intended to serve both society and the affected individual by removing him from his fellow-citizens and ministering to him behind closed gates.

"Today the almshouse has virtually disappeared and the asylum is no longer expected to 'cure' the mentally ill. And, although the prison system remains with us in close to its original form, it has long been obvious that it serves well neither its master nor its wards. Thoughtful men are now wondering if the central concept of institutionalizing the individual is not basically flawed."[2]

The "flaws" in that concept and the manner in which it has been put into practice have been amply documented. Attica may make it impossible for the prisons of this country ever again to return to what they were before. Increased awareness of the possibility of placing more adult convicted offenders in the community—80 percent of those presently confined—by scaling down both sentences and our estimates of "dangerousness" and maximum-security needs is matched by the move in some places to abolish institutions for juvenile delinquents entirely, as Massachusetts has already done.

No social observer in modern times has more trenchantly condemned the contemporary correctional scene nor so amply documented that condemnation than Jessica Mitford, who concludes: "There have always been those who looked beyond palliative reform proposals to the essential character of prison, found it intrinsically evil and not susceptible to reform, hence have advocated abolishing prisons altogether."[3]

What is the future of the institution, then, in the custody—or rehabilitation or re-socialization of the offender? Does it still have a place as a reliable instrument of social control? While some states are reported to be planning new institutions—as in Texas for 4,000 more men, in addition to the 17,000 reported in custody in June 1972—there are signs of a trend in the opposite direction, as well. According to a recent survey, "the influential Institute of Corrections of the American Foundation is now advising the Justice Department to invest in alternatives to incarceration, not in new prisons. The National Council on Crime and Delinquency, which has spent decades trying to upgrade penal institutions, recently called for a nationwide halt to the building of jails and detention centers."[4]

One of the reasons why the institution must go—as a total solution to the problem of dealing with sentenced offenders—is the fact of its very structure, which blocks the road to penal progress: "The solidity of our prison buildings too often obliges us to apply as well as we can, in nineteenth-century surroundings, a regime that is entirely different from that conceived by the builders of these fortresses. In many respects our old prisons, even though they have been modernized, make one think of a turtle shell into which some other animal is being pushed."[5]

The main obstacle presented by the fixed institution is precisely that: it is fixed in place in the setting of an outmoded time. Just as new schools are being built to implement new ways of teaching, so if there is any need for new institutions it is in order for them to incorporate the ideas of today. In doing so, some foresight should be applied to assure that the penology of the future will not be enslaved by the architecture of the past, as today's prisons are, in frozen form, the penology of centuries gone by.

The state of Vermont projected several years ago the construction of a new training school for juveniles. Its architects were instructed to project far enough into the future to a time when juvenile training schools might no longer be needed so that the institution could then, with only slight modifications, be converted to such purposes as a nursing home, a hospital, technical training school, or the like. This is an example of the constructive application of the concept of obsolescence. Similarly, the federal government and the state of California have each had on the drafting board at one time plans for an institution which would serve more than one function. In addition to modern facilities for detaining persons awaiting trial and material witnesses, the multipurpose center would also provide the following: clinical and observation services, a halfway house for detainees, and a residential center for short-term offenders in lieu of imprisonment. Most significant of all, the center would have accommodations for persons on parole who felt themselves in need of supportive services when the going got rough for them on the outside.

There are obvious parallels between this last service and that of the community mental health center which accepts voluntary admissions and readmissions by persons who feel themselves in need of care but who neither require nor desire a more drastic form of commitment. Such an approach opens to people in difficulty the kinds of services which are supposed to be available to them after conviction. They provide another example of the enlightened procedures which can be instituted as the "heat" is taken out of the criminal justice system at every possible, and plausible, point.

Institutions for female offenders have, in many ways and places, led the way to more effective and humane dealing with other offenders. There are few states which house a number of female prisoners under long sentences large enough to justify a separate facility. While the state of Texas confines upwards of 700, Maine averages 60, as do some of the Rocky Mountain states. One institution in the East and one in the West adequately accommodates all the women who are sentenced in federal courts. County jails, as we have seen, detain women for trial as well as those under short sentences of imprisonment, under conditions which can only be described as grossly inadequate. The suggestion has therefore been made that the federal government take the lead in setting up small institutions at strategic locations throughout the country to serve federal needs, and also to permit the states to board their few females there.[6] This is not a substitute for increased community-based facilities for women, at a time when such facilities are being urged for all but a small proportion of convicted males.

With a given reality which will not see all existing penitentiaries leveled within the foreseeable future, and a hopeful expectation that no additional prisons of classical structure and function will be erected, it may be

fairly stated that the institutions of tomorrow will house only a very small proportion of sentenced offenders—only those who represent a truly serious threat
to society.

The prospect of success for any program of open or community-
based facilities may well be determined by what is done with and for this category of truly difficult prisoners, the so-called "hard core," whose numbers may
seldom exceed 15 or 20 percent of any prison population. It will be recalled that
when Massachusetts abolished its training schools, care was taken to make
special provision for the forty or so boys who could not be allowed full freedom
in the community. In the past, it is persons of this sort who have made it necessary to invoke maximum control over the far larger proportion of inmates who
did not actually require it.

At the same time, the successful introduction of therapy into the
closed and punitive settings, which characterize the great majority of institutions
for convicted offenders, raises some serious questions. The first is a basic right of
the individual offender to be left alone with whatever mind-set or attitudes he
may have brought with him into the institution. By what right, it may be asked,
does an administration intrude into his emotional life, his psychic processes, in
order to alter them in favor of what is to the administrator a more desirable outlook or a "superior" set of values for the guidance of conduct? So long as a man
"does his time," follows orders and does not interfere with staff or other inmates,
he has the right, from this point of view, to be left alone.

A common word in prisons for the psychiatrist is "nut doctor"—the
equivalent of "shrink" in the outside world. This term groups together all those
professionals who are in any way seen as involved in therapy—psychologists,
counselors, and the lot.

The second question relates to the reality of any expectation that
intervention into the dynamics of behavior or attitudes of prisoners can expect
to be in any degree effective, when its purpose is to better equip a man to deal
ultimately with a world from which he is, for the time being, completely cut off.
This beneficient process must take place, after all, in an environment which is
the complete opposite—namely, an unfree setting, in which individual will or
choice is all but completely ruled out. There is a final obstacle to success of any
therapeutic approach: sentences of imprisonment are clearly for punishment,
prisons are arch-examples of compulsory conformity. The constructive reorder-
ing of personal values and resulting behavior requires cooperation and not
authority in order to be successfully accepted by those who are to be the
beneficiaries of it.

These are perhaps the most cogent arguments for the open institution—or for no institution at all. Because only in such settings is the element of
raw punishment abated to the point where an inmate can expect to be able to
manifest some degree of individuality, even of acting out, when that is a
necessary part of the therapeutic process. Certainly it gives reason for under-

standing why so many vaunted theories and programs do not succeed with the inmates of institutions which do not allow freedom. There are, of course, rare instances, few of them recorded, where a prisoner has come under the influence of a significant adult—a Malcolm X, a psychiatrist, a social worker, another prisoner, or the warden himself.

The basic living conditions of any institution can therefore either support and reinforce—or contradict and nullify—the positive personality changes sought by any therapeutic program introduced within it. Coldness, rigidity, or punitiveness can cancel out the effectiveness of any program. In this sense, the milieu of the institution, and consistency between it and the therapeutic approach, is more important than any formal program which may be introduced within it.

"Every institution," said Emerson, "is the lengthened shadow of an individual." Nowhere is this truer than in places which assume the responsibility for caring for delinquents and criminals. The history of corrections is replete with examples of individuals who have stamped the institutions under their control with the ideology which guides their entire administration. If the influence of such men as these is felt by every prisoner at the bottom of their chain of command, it is obvious that the philosophy of the institution, whether it is therapeutically oriented or not (and if so, in what direction) will have a decisive influence on the atmosphere in which custody—or, hopefully—treatment of the truly serious offender will take place.

For all others, deinstitutionalization would appear to be very much the order of the day. As a result of the interest generated by the Massachusetts experience of ridding itself—almost surgically—of its juvenile delinquent population, a need is being voiced for a center which would assist other states which may feel ready to plan for returning some of their inmates back to the community.[7] If this experience, and now that of other places, is to develop into a national movement, certain key needs present themselves. The first of these is the need for information—ideas and the progression of steps to be taken in the restructuring of correctional services. The sources and types of likely opposition—financial aspects, timing, public information, legislative support—all these need to be documented and analyzed for the benefit of others who may now be willing to embark on the new course. Existing information from theoretical and applied research and the vast range of available alternatives should now be made available to correctional authorities, juvenile institutions and agencies, universities, and other research bodies.

Such a center could also fill a serious void in the areas of training and technical assistance for the role of youth advocates and correctional personnel. Administrators and superintendents will need to add to their present responsibilities a new function—that of agents for change in seeking support from the community and from other sources. Special courses and reorientation sessions, conferences, in-service training of workers from old-line institutions to some of the newer community modes, can well be decisive in the eventual success or failure of these new ventures.

Research and planning in this rapidly developing field would appear invaluable in a very wide range of challenging problems such as decentralization of authority in the elimination of institutions; regionalization of services; purchase of services from private groups as against state operation of facilities; court liaison programs and prediversion procedures; cooperation with police and probation services; community support and public security; parole; and provision of a milieu for the small proportion of inmates requiring intensive care and therapy.

A national research, planning and information center could also help to recruit, direct and train the large numbers of young people interested in the helping professions, who offer such a rich manpower resource for working with offenders, especially the young, in open settings.

Even granting that the rate of recidivism for persons placed in such community settings may prove to be no lower than for those released from the traditional institution, the former may be viewed as preferable because persons confined to prisons and reform schools are dehumanized and rendered worthless in their own eyes. Treatment in the community cannot possibly degrade them to a like degree. There is the additional advantage that community dealing with the troublemaker from their midst helps to bring home the responsibility which the neighborhood has for both local criminogenic conditions as well as for the individual offender.

The most recent of the seeming unending federal studies on crime gives national prominence to this emphasis on community control, in contrast to the "developed ponderous bureaucracy to deal with symptoms, rather than the problem itself. . . . Much of the alienation in America may result from the lack of power many citizens feel in relation to the institutions they have set up to run their lives. . . . One area where responsible citizen participation is critical is law enforcement. Rather than relying solely on their institutions, citizens must share the responsibility."[8]

If there was a time 200 years ago when imprisonment was not meted out as punishment; if there could be in the early 1800s a revulsion against the application of the death penalty to petty offenders; if public demand could in 1840 segregate children from adults in confinement; if probation could be accepted in lieu of imprisonment at about that same time; then it is not unlikely that the public can be persuaded to accept a change in perspective which permits an even larger number of convicted offenders to be dealt with in the community under supervision.

The poorhouse, the orphanage, and the workhouse, have faded from the social scene, long since. The debates which raged a century ago between advocates of "indoor relief" and "outdoor relief"—between the partisans and opponents of institutions for the poor—have died away. Today the responsibility of government to grant aid to the poor in their own homes is universally accepted, despite the low level at which such aid is pegged. The message of the village of Gel may have taken hundreds of years to be heard, but the day when all retarded and all psychotics were exiled is not likely ever to return. Once we have closed the institution for juvenile delinquents, for school offenders, runaways and "wayward" juveniles, we shall not be able to afford the money or expend the will to rear them, ever again. In this sense, every move in the direction of community placement and treatment of offenders hastens the day when the community becomes—as once it was—responsible for *all* its members.

"Crime," it has been said, "is the ransom of the technical and social progress of our times." This is as valid as the growing realization that what constitutes progress is being severely questioned in many quarters. The biggest, the most numerous, and the latest no longer bespeaks the best. At a time of shortages in what have come to be regarded as the necessities of life, older ways of dealing with the results of our living together on a shrinking planet are being revived.

All this takes place against a national backdrop of charges of breaking and entering, larceny, fraud, invasions of privacy, perjury, and plain mendacity on the part of our elected and appointed national leaders. Because of these alleged crimes, the power of the presidency itself is being called into question, jeopardizing the relationships between the United States and the rest of the world. The power of government to negotiate in matters of trade, disarmament, and peace is seriously undermined.

If these are the effects of crimes at the highest levels, it is at least equally true of ordinary crime committed by less lofty citizens. If we can contrive to deal with crime more successfully than we do today, we shall reduce the tensions within the fabric of our own society and, as a result, among the societies which compose the world, holding out to mankind the hope of a surer opportunity to live together in harmony and in peace.

NOTES

1. "Crime Prevention and Control, Note by the Secretary General, New York, United Nations," 19 October 1972. Document No. A/8844, para. 10, p. 6.
2. Introduction to *Reports of the Prison Discipline Society of Boston, 1826–1854* (Montclair, N.J.: Patterson Smith, 1972).
3. *Kind and Usual Punishment* (New York: Knopf, 1973), p. 272.
4. David J. Rothman, "You Can't Reform the Bastille," *The Nation* (March 19, 1973), p. 366.
5. Paul Cornil, "Postface," in *Three Aspects of Penal Treatment* (Berne: International Penal and Penitentiary Commission, 1969), p. 87.

6. "The Criminal Offender—What Should Be Done?" A *Report of the President's Task Force on Prisoner Rehabilitation* (Washington: Government Printing Office, 1970) p. 20.
7. Yitzhak Bakal and Howard Polsky, "Proposal for a Center for De-Institutionalization," Boston, March 1973 (dup.).
8. "Report on Crime Prevention," issued as Vol. 6 by the National Advisory Commission on Criminal Justice Standards and Goals, AP dispatch, November 26, 1973.

Index

About the Author

Benedict S. Alper, Visiting Professor of Criminology at Boston College, Chestnut Hill, Massachusetts has taught at the Law School of the Victoria University in Wellington, New Zealand, the United Nations Asia and Far East Institute on Crime, Tokyo, Rutgers Law School in Newark and the New School for Social Research in New York City. His initial apprenticeship in the field was as probation officer in the Boston Juvenile Court and as correctional officer in the Massachusetts State Prison. Professional experience includes posts at the state, national, and international levels: as research director of a New York Legislative Committee, Field Secretary of the American Parole Association, chief statistician and special assistant to the Director, Federal Bureau of Prisons, and first Chief of the Section of Social Defense at the United Nations. In the United States Army, at the end of World War II, he administered five prisons in Trieste. He has served as consultant to the American Foundation of Philadelphia and as Research Associate to the Center of Studies in Criminal Justice, University of Chicago Law School. He participated in the Third United Nations Crime Congress in Stockholm in 1965, and was Consultant to the United Nations Consultative Group on Crime in Geneva in 1968 and to the Fourth United Crime Congress in Kyoto in 1970. Recent books include *Halfway Houses* (with Oliver J. Keller, Jr.) and *Crime: International Agenda* (with Jerry F. Boren), both published by Heath LEXINGTON Books, Lexington, Mass.

Photo by Yasuo Ohba

Benedict S. Alper is Visiting Professor of Criminology at Boston College. He has taught at the Law School of Victoria University, Wellington, New Zealand, the United Nations Asia and Far East Institute on Crime, Rutgers University Law School, and the New School for Social Research. His initial apprenticeship in the field was as probation officer in the Boston Juvenile Court and as correctional officer in the Massachusetts State Prison system. In addition, his experience includes research director of a New York State Legislative Committee, Field Secretary of the American Parole Association, chief statistician and special assistant to the Director of the Federal Bureau of Prisons, and the first Chief of the Section of Social Defense at the United Nations. As a member of the U.S. Army he administered five prisons in Trieste at the end of World War II. He participated in the Third United Nations Crime Congress in Stockholm and was consultant to the United Nations Consultative Group on Crime in Geneva and to the Fourth United Crime Congress in Kyoto. His recent books include *Halfway Houses* (with Oliver J. Keller, Jr.) and *Crime: International Agenda* (with Jerry F. Boren).